Choosing an Open Source CMS

Beginner's Guide

Find the best CMS and start working with it to create web sites, blogs, communities, e-commerce sites, and intranets

Nirav Mehta

BIRMINGHAM - MUMBAI

Choosing an Open Source CMS

Beginner's Guide

First published: April 2009

Production Reference: 1070409

Published by Packt Publishing Ltd.
32 Lincoln Road
Olton
Birmingham, B27 6PA, UK.

ISBN 978-1-847196-22-4

www.packtpub.com

Cover Image by Parag Kadam (paragvkadam@gmail.com)

Credits

Author

Nirav Mehta

Reviewers

Chanh Ong

Daniel Chapman

Jeff Potts

Mark Bowen

Sujit Pal

Acquisition Editor

David Barnes

Development Editor

Swapna V. Verlekar

Technical Editor

John Antony

Copy Editor

Sneha Kulkarni

Indexer

Hemangini Bari

Editorial Team Leader

Abhijeet Deobhakta

Project Coordinator

Lata Basantani

Proofreader

Chris Smith

Production Coordinator

Shantanu Zagade

Cover Work

Shantanu Zagade

About the author

Nirav Mehta is well known for his entrepreneurial ventures, his breakthrough ideas, and his contribution to open source. Nirav leads a software development company—Magnet Technologies—in India that specializes in Rich Internet Applications, Web, and Mobile. He wrote a content management system eight years ago and has worked on numerous systems after that. Nirav has led more than 100 CMS projects in his company.

Nirav simplifies the most complicated ideas and presents them in lucid language. Over the last 10 years, Nirav has written and spoken on a variety of topics. His Mobile Web Development book tops its category and has received high-satisfaction ratings.

Nirav loves yoga and programming. In his spare time he builds innovative products, and trains people on leadership and effective programming.

Visit his blog at: `http://www.mehtanirav.com/`

Visit this book's special website at: `http://www.cmsbook.info/`

My love and thanks to family—my parents, wife, and sisters. It's your support and freedom that lets me do all the things I love! Thanks for your constant love, encouragement, and reminders!

Special thanks to all open source CMS developers. Keep up the good job!

I would like to thank the team at Packt—David, Lata, Swapna, John, my reviewers—Jeff, Sujit, Chanh—and everyone else. Thank you for your dedication, suggestions, and follow-ups. You made it possible!

I also appreciate the readers of this book. I believe you are up to something big, and hope my work helps you achieve it.

About the reviewers

Chanh Ong is a Computer Specialist and has many years of experience in various computer platforms and operating systems; programming languages such as PHP, JavaScript (AJAX), C, VB, Perl, Microsoft Access, dBase, and FoxPro; system administration on Unix, Linux, Vax and Microsoft Windows; and DBA of various databases such as Oracle, MySQL, Postgres, Informix, MSSQL, and so on. He utilizes web servers such as Apache and IIS to help build web applications. He also does custom templates for clients.

He has an open source project called COAddOns, which develops several add-ons for Mambo, Joomla!, MiaCMS, and MoseCMS—which is an easy and extensible CMS. He is also a former Mambo CMS core developer.

He researches on CMSs and their tools. He has lot of experience in installing various CMS, including Wiki, and he also sets up sites using Microsoft SharePoint services.

He runs a web site where he blogs about his findings that help him in his research. His web site also provides support for his open source project, COAddOns.

His main web site is `http://support.ongetc.com` and his Wiki is `http://wiki.ongetc.com` and his blog is: `http://blog.ongetc.com`.

He wrote an article for Packt Publishing titled

How to Choose an Open Source Content Management System. You can find it at `http://www.packtpub.com/article/how_to_choose_an_open_source_content_management_system`.

I would like to thank Scott Goodwin for letting me help out at OpenSourceCMS and open my eyes to the world of CMS. He asked me to take on an open source project. I enjoyed working on it so much that it become the COAddOns project, which has grown into various add-ons. It also helped me start my own web site at `http://ongetc.com`.

I want to thank Damian Carvill for exposing me to the world of books by asking me to write an article for Packt Publishing, and involving me as a judge for the Packt Annual CMS Award event.

I want to thank Swapna Verlekar for inviting me to be a book reviewer for this book. I also want to thank Lata Basantani for working closely with me and ensuring that the reviewing of each chapter was on schedule.

I would like to thank the author of this book, who has done a very nice job in researching on the subject. He has written very easy-to-understand material for beginners to have a head start.

I want to thank my family who let me have the time to do this book review.

Daniel Chapman started his career as an Oracle database consultant and trainer, working for various Australian universities, telecommunication companies, and also Oracle Australia. He developed a keen sense of the value of development standards and analysis processes. After 10 years in this arena, he wanted a change and moved into web development in 2004. He quickly picked up PHP, JavaScript, HTML, and CSS while experimenting with various CMSs.

Finally deciding on Joomla! as his CMS of choice, Daniel initially began working as a consultant developing sites and producing a few small extensions before starting one of the first Open Source Extension Clubs: `www.ninjoomla.com`. Eventually, he changed the club's name to `www.NinjaForge.com`, and has become quite well known in the Joomla! sphere.

I would like to thank my wife Kyoko, for her seemingly endless support of my work, even when it takes away time from us being together. I can't thank her enough for being there for me.

Jeff Potts is the Director of the Enterprise Content Management Practice at Optaros, a global consulting firm focused on assembling Next Generation Internet solutions featuring open source components. Jeff brings over 10 years of ECM practice leadership and over 17 years of IT and technology implementation experience in IT departments and professional services organizations.

Jeff has a deep technical experience in content management with custom and packaged solutions (commercial and open source). For the last several years, he has focused on Alfresco. But he has also worked with other open source content management technologies including Drupal, WordPress, Zope/Plone, and Apache Cocoon.

Jeff's areas of business expertise include document management, content management, workflow, collaboration, portals, and search. Throughout his consulting career he has worked on a number of projects for Fortune 500 clients across the media & entertainment, airline, consumer packaged goods, and retail sectors.

Jeff is a frequent speaker at Alfresco and Content Management industry events and has written articles for technical journals. Last year he published his first book, the *Alfresco Developer Guide* (`http://www.packtpub.com/alfresco-developer-guide/book`).

Jeff blogs on all of these topics at `ecmarchitect.com`.

Mark Bowen is a web developer, musician, graphic designer, electronics engineer, and helicopter pilot amongst many other talents. He is currently living in Birmingham, United Kingdom. He is an avid Apple Macintosh user and has been so for well over 15 years now.

Mark studied Performing Arts in college and ended up getting a job at the college as a Music Technician. It was during this time that he gained his City & Guilds 224 in Electronics Servicing. So he is qualified to take a TV apart, put it back together again, leave bits out, and still charge for it!

Now working as a Senior Producer for the second largest independent commercial production house in the UK, Mark has made well over 30,000 adverts-jingles-music-based projects in his almost eight years of work there.

Mark has been developing with Adobe Flash, and was asked to review the *Advanced PHP for Flash* book by Friends Of Ed due to the work he did on a Flash-based chat application.

After Flash, Mark took up learning HTML/CSS, and now codes sites entirely by hand without the use of any WYSIWYG editors. These days, Mark's preferred tool of choice for creating Internet sites is the ExpressionEngine CMS platform. About this platform he states, "It is a designer's dream come true" due to its very nature of keeping code and content completely separate from each other. Mark is an avid reader of the ExpressionEngine forums, and can usually be found there each day answering questions wherever and whenever he can.

He is currently in the process of setting up an aviation-based photography web site with his wife Sarah (who is also a helicopter pilot—Flight Instructor). It will host and sell the most professional images in the world relating to aviation. This came about due to Mark being the sole designer for the largest military helicopter magazine in the world. Through his links with the magazine, he now has access to the best aviation photographers in the business. Keep an eye out on the ExpressionEngine forums for the site's launch!

I want to thank Packt Publishing for giving me the opportunity to take part in helping out with the book.

Sujit Pal started programming some 20 years ago, and never looked back. He currently works at Healthline Networks, Inc., a search vertical focused on health, as a part of its Research and Development team. Apart from his work, his favorite pastime is to explore new software technologies, techniques, and languages. He writes about his experiments at `sujitpal.blogspot.com`.

Table of Contents

Section II – Thinking your choices through

Section III – CMSs by breed

Section IV – Open source CMS tips

Preface

There are many powerful Open Source **Content Management Systems** (**CMSs**) available to take the pain away from managing a web site. These systems are feature-rich, often easy to use, and free. Unfortunately, there are so many choices that it's tough to be sure which CMS is the right one for your needs. How can you be sure that you are selecting and working with the right tool?

This book will guide you through choosing the right CMS for your needs. You can be confident in your choice of CMS for the needs of your project. It will also help you make a start using the CMS, and give you a feel for what it's like to use it—even before you install it yourself.

Are you bewildered by the many open source CMSs available online? Open source CMSs are the best way to create and manage sophisticated web sites. You can create a site that precisely meets your business goals, and keep the site up-to-date easily because these systems give you full control over every aspect of your site. Because open source CMSs are free to download, you have a vast choice between the various systems.

There are many open source CMSs to choose from, each with unique strengths—and occasionally limitations too. Choosing between the bewildering numbers of options can be tough.

Making the wrong choice early on may lead to a lot of wasted work because you'll have a half-finished site that doesn't meet your initial requirements, and you may have to restart from scratch.

This book will show you how to avoid choosing the wrong CMS. It will guide you through assessing your site requirements, and then using that assessment to identify the CMS that will best fit your needs. It contains discussions of the major CMSs and the issues that you should consider when choosing: their complexity to use, their features, and the power they offer. It discusses technical considerations such as programming languages and compliance with best practice standards in a clear and friendly way that non-technical readers can understand.

The book also contains quick-start guideslines and examples for the most popular CMSs such as WordPress, Joomla!, and Drupal. You can experiment with these CMSs, get a feel of how they work, and start using them to build your site.

After reading this book, you can be confident that your CMS choice will support your web site's needs because you have carefully assessed your requirements and explored the available options.

The author has created a special website for this book—`http://www.cmsbook.info/`. You can communicate with other readers and get additional insights and support from there.

What this book covers

Section I: Opening up to Open Source CMSs

Chapter 1 Do I even want an Open Source CMS?—When and how a content management system is useful. Why open source? Readymade or custom-built?

Chapter 2 Evaluating your Options—Different CMS types, their purposes, and different CMS technologies

Section II: Thinking your choices through

Chapter 3 Understanding your Requirements—brainstorm and clarify your requirements, standard compliance, scale of the site, and key features

Chapter 4 Building the Site—trying out CMSs, technical requirements, downloading and installation, configuration, and creating navigation

Chapter 5 Content Editing and Management—using WYSIWYG editors, adding pictures, publishing content, and creating links

Chapter 6 Templates and Plug-ins—adding a photo gallery and customizing design via templates

Chapter 7 Extending and Customizing—understand a CMS's code quality, and make code-level changes to understand their complexity

Section III: CMSs by breed

Chapter 8 Blog CMSs—perform typical tasks with the top three blog choices and evaluate features

Chapter 9 Web CMSs—using top Web CMSs, customizing them, and gaining key CMS skills

Chapter 10 CMSs for E-Commerce—managing product/service-based e-commerce sites with CMSs, and knowing which would be best for you

Chapter 11 Team Collaboration CMSs—internal sites for collaboration and communication, workflow, access privileges, and version tracking; Alfresco

Chapter 12 Specialized CMSs—CMSs that serve niches—e-learning, wiki, photo galleries, discussion forums, and so on

Section IV: Open source CMS tips

Chapter 13 Hosting your CMS-Powered Site—selecting and working with a web host

Chapter 14 Getting Involved in the Community—asking questions, learning from documentation, and getting help

Chapter 15 Working with a Specialist—finding experts, evaluating them, tips for project management, and outsourced teams

Chapter 16 Packt Open Source CMS Awards—Best CMSs voted by the community and experts

What you need for this book

The reader should be an intermediate computer user with a reasonable understanding of what a web site can do, the different kinds of web sites that are out there, and how to work with interactive web sites (as a user—joining discussion forums, for example).

Who this book is for

This book is written for anyone who wants to start a web site and is looking for a good CMS. It is best suited for people who are selecting a CMS for their site and people who want to manage a CMS. Knowledge of web basics is certainly helpful, but not needed.

Conventions

In this book, you will find a number of styles of text that distinguish between different kinds of information. Here are some examples of these styles, and an explanation of their meaning.

New terms and **important words** are shown in bold. Words that you see on the screen, in menus or dialog boxes for example, appear in our text like this: "clicking the **Next** button moves you to the next screen".

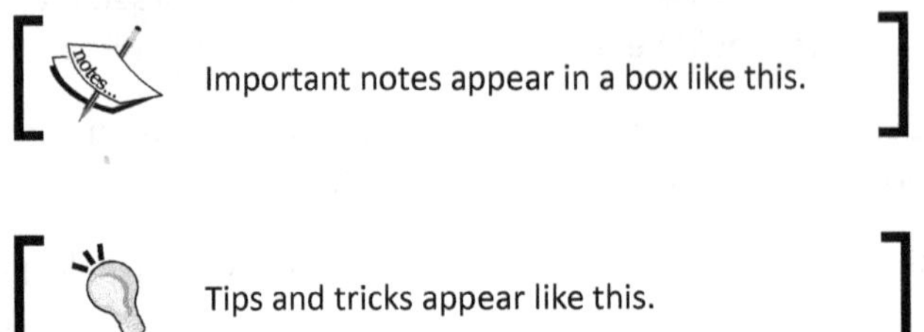

Important notes appear in a box like this.

Tips and tricks appear like this.

Reader feedback

Feedback from our readers is always welcome. Let us know what you think about this book—what you liked or may have disliked. Reader feedback is important for us to develop titles that you really get the most out of.

To send us general feedback, simply drop an email to `feedback@packtpub.com`, and mention the book title in the subject of your message.

If there is a book that you need and would like to see us publish, please send us a note in the **SUGGEST A TITLE** form on `www.packtpub.com` or email `suggest@packtpub.com`.

If there is a topic that you have expertise in and you are interested in either writing or contributing to a book, see our author guide on `www.packtpub.com/authors`.

Customer support

Now that you are the proud owner of a Packt book, we have a number of things to help you to get the most from your purchase.

Downloading the example code for the book

Visit `http://www.packtpub.com/files/code/6224_Code.zip` to directly download the example code.

The downloadable files contain instructions on how to use them.

Errata

Although we have taken every care to ensure the accuracy of our contents, mistakes do happen. If you find a mistake in one of our books—maybe a mistake in text or code—we would be grateful if you would report this to us. By doing so, you can save other readers from frustration, and help us to improve subsequent versions of this book. If you find any errata, please report them by visiting `http://www.packtpub.com/support`, selecting your book, clicking on the **let us know** link, and entering the details of your errata. Once your errata are verified, your submission will be accepted and the errata added to any list of existing errata. Any existing errata can be viewed by selecting your title from `http://www.packtpub.com/support`.

Piracy

Piracy of copyright material on the Internet is an ongoing problem across all media. At Packt, we take the protection of our copyright and licenses very seriously. If you come across any illegal copies of our works in any form on the Internet, please provide us with the location address or website name immediately so that we can pursue a remedy.

Please contact us at `copyright@packtpub.com` with a link to the suspected pirated material.

We appreciate your help in protecting our authors, and our ability to bring you valuable content.

Questions

You can contact us at `questions@packtpub.com` if you are having a problem with any aspect of the book, and we will do our best to address it.

Section I

Opening up to Open Source CMSs

Do I even want an Open Source CMS?

Evaluating your Options

1

Do I Even Want an Open Source CMS?

It's a sunny Sunday morning in Miami. Oprah picks up her coffee and settles in her favorite patio chair. She is in a quiet trance-like state. Gazing at kids playing on her left, her expression turns from deep thoughts to confusion to puzzlement.

Oprah Casey is an established Yoga expert. She is just back from her class. She starts thinking about her web site. She has a four-page web site that Mario, a friend, created a decade ago.

Her current web site consists of an introduction on Yoga, her own biography, a testimonial page, and a page with her Yoga center's address and phone numbers. Last time she wanted to add driving directions to the address page, it took her two weeks to get that done. Here's what happened:

- Day 1: Oprah calls Mario and explains what she wants.
- Day 3: She calls again to check if the work is done. Mario had completely forgotten about it. He asked her to email him the driving directions.
- Day 4: Mario tells her he is finding source files of Oprah's web site and the server login/password.
- Day 7: Mario shows a page with the driving directions updated. Oprah suggests a couple of changes.
- Day 9: Oprah is happy with what's on the contact page now. She gives a go-ahead.
- Day 10: Weekend!
- Day 12: Mario says he is uploading on the server.
- Day 14: After another call, Oprah gets confirmation that it's live. She checks and finds it alright.

Oprah is happy that now she will get less calls asking for directions. At the same time, she is annoyed with this whole process of change. She does not want to go through another such ritual for a new change. What if her phone number changed? What if she wanted to update her bio? Or what if she wanted to add another page to her site? She can't afford to wait too long. She does not even want to take favors from her friend anymore!

She grabs a pen and paper and starts scribbling.

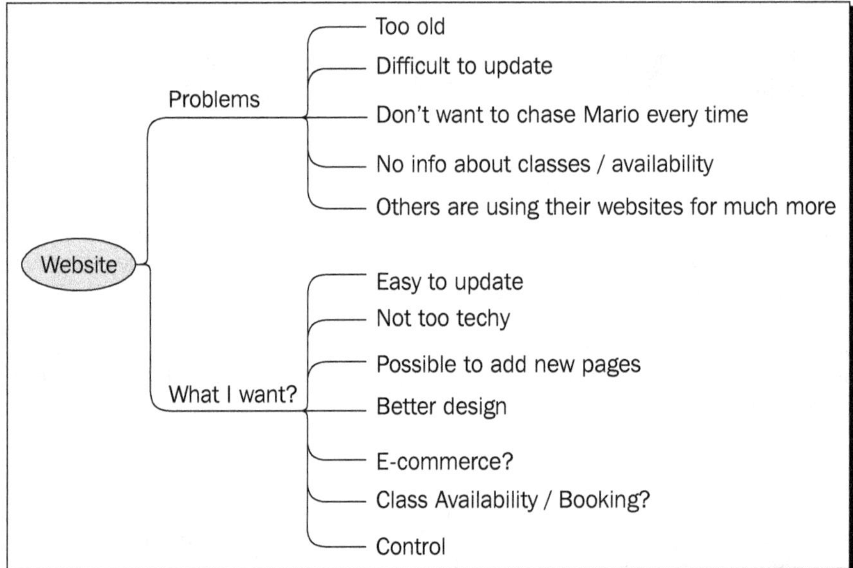

Oprah is clear that she can't continue with her current web site and the way it's managed. She needs a complete reorganization of her web site. Oprah wants her web site to have the following features:

- **Web site must be easy to manage**

  Oprah wants her web site to be easily manageable. She can understand technology, but is not a programmer. She wants to manage the web site content on her own. Whether it's adding a paragraph on a page or removing some old information, she wants to do it on her own.

- **Web site should be dynamic**

  She wants the changes that she makes to be reflected immediately. It should be possible to add a new section or link easily. Oprah wants to add photos and Yoga class information. And this should be updated on the web site immediately.

- **Other features**

  There are many other things that Oprah wants such as e-commerce, class booking, better design, and so on. The new web site should allow addition of all these features. If not right now, she wants them in the near future.

Finally, Oprah calls Mario. She politely explains to him the problems and what she wants. She then pauses to hear Mario's reply.

You need a CMS!

Mario is quick. He asserts that Oprah needs a **Content Management System** (**CMS**). It's a software that will give her all the required features, and he can set it up on her web site. Apart from managing site content and navigation, a CMS may also allow interactive content such as discussions, newsletters, blogs, photo galleries, and so on.

Mario explains a variety of benefits from using a CMS. They are:

- Dynamic content—changes reflect immediately
- Easily make changes—using just a browser and familiar editing tool (similar to Word)
- Manage site navigation and sections—ability to add or order pages and other content
- Control over design—tweak the entire site the way you wish from a single place
- Add interactive content such as discussions, class schedules, shopping cart, and so on.
- Add photos, links, and other rich media easily
- Get full control over the web site
- Allow multiple people to manage the site

Oprah interrupts Mario and says she appreciates these benefits, but wants to know if there are any other alternatives.

CMS alternatives

"What you need IS a content management system. We can go ahead with a readily available system, or hire someone to build one from scratch. I could write a CMS for you, but your needs are not so specific. I would rather use an open source CMS and customize it to your needs. Who wants to reinvent the wheel, you see!", Mario says.

"This makes sense." Oprah is thinking. "If I want things to be dynamic, I will need some kind of software to do that. I know that people use some web-based software to manage their sites. I can easily pick that up..."

Mario continues, "If you simply wanted to publish photos, you can use some photo management software on your machine and publish the site on a server. If you want to write regular updates on Yoga, you could start a blog. And you could use a 'hosted' blog where you don't have to do any server setup, or the like. You just write content. If you want static content, we can use some other online tools that help design web sites. What you want is manage content and site frequently, and on your own. We also want full control and our own site to be the host. That certainly is what CMSs are designed for."

Oprah is now convinced that she needs a CMS.

Which CMS?

The next question that comes to her mind is, "OK, so which CMS should I use?"

Mario explains that there are many options. Content Management Systems have been around for quite some time and have evolved. There are general-purpose systems and some serving niches. There are many commercial and enterprise-class CMSs. But Mario emphasized on going ahead with an open source CMS. He listed many advantages such as:

- Open source usually means **free of cost**. Almost all open source CMSs can be downloaded and used free of cost. That keeps our overall costs down. It's important to control costs—especially in the current economic situation!
- Open source means you can **customize**. We can review and look around the programming code of an open source software. This allows us to customize it as per our wish. We get a strong base ready, and can add whatever we like.
- Open source is generally **better quality**. Most popular open source CMSs are very high quality. Thousands of people may have reviewed and improved them. This results in an overall good quality and security.
- Open source means **community**. Many people use open source software. And when it comes to CMS, most prefer open source CMSs. This means there is a huge community and we can get its support if we get stuck anywhere.

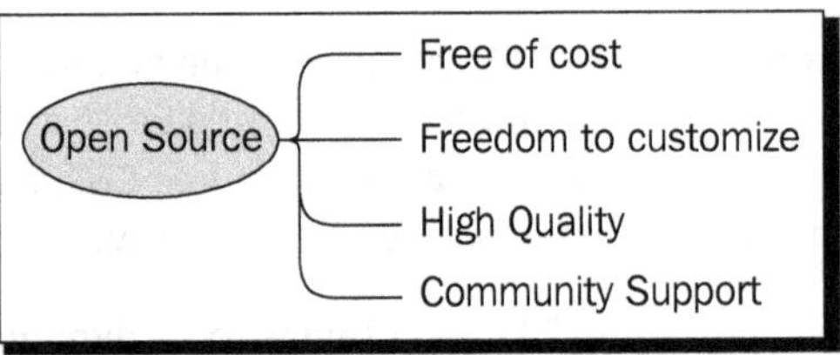

"Apart from telling you to use an open source CMS, I can't suggest much further now. There are hundreds of options you have, and which one you choose depends on your exact requirements and comfort level." Mario suggested. "But don't worry; I am always available if you need any help."

That ended the conversation. Oprah relaxed in her chair and gathered her thoughts.

- A CMS allows managing dynamic content easily.
- I can control and manage my web site through a web browser.
- This is how most people manage large web sites.
- Open source CMS is perfect for my needs because I can obtain the software for free and can rest assured that there are many people who have used it before me, and can help me if I need.
- I now need to find out which CMS serves my requirements, and learn how to use it.

That actually gave her a lot of peace. She felt free and ready to take on a new journey. Oprah is ready to choose a CMS and build her site to her desire. She is thrilled!

What about you?

Your situation may be similar to Oprah's—or at least to some extent. As she concluded that an open source CMS is appropriate for her, you may have too. Or, you may be looking at open source CMSs as an option to manage your web site—public or internal.

When you are starting up a web site, you would like a system that makes it easy for you to manage the site. Open source Content Management Systems help manage different types of content—from blog posts and photo albums to events and e-commerce. There are some really powerful CMSs out there and they can take the pain away from managing a web site.

Unfortunately, there are plenty of choices available and it's tough to make a decision. How do you select the best CMS for your needs? It is daunting to find a good content management system. There is no comprehensive guide that understands users' needs and suggests suitable CMSs for them.

Even after making a choice, installing, customizing, and managing a CMS is generally too technical for new users. We need something that will quickly make us productive with the CMS we select.

Then there are important subjects that are neglected such as hosting, and working with developers and communities.

About this book

This book walks you through understanding your requirements by elaborating on the different options available for your CMS, and thus helps you make a choice. It then covers common tasks—installation, design customization, plug-ins, content editing and management, and so on—in detail, for specific CMS types. The book even covers specialized CMSs, hosting, working with developers, and getting help from the CMS community.

This book helps you understand your requirements first. It walks you through a simple yet effective method of listing down what you want your web site to do. You are then introduced to different types of CMSs such as blogs, forums, general purpose CMS, e-commerce tools, collaboration, and more. This helps you narrow down your search.

This is followed by practical guides on doing some common tasks with any CMS. These tasks include installation, setting up a design, creating navigation structure, entering and editing content, adding pictures, enhancing functionality with extensions and plug-ins, and publishing the site. Here you learn skills that can be applied to any CMS you choose.

It then covers different types of CMSs in detail. The book is full of how-tos for popular CMSs, and listings of other choices that you have. No matter what your need is, you will certainly develop useful skills with this book.

At the end, the book covers important subtopics that usually go uncovered: how to select a web host for your site; how to select and work with a software developer/vendor for customizations; how to get help from community resources and winners of Packt's CMS awards.

Overall, this book helps you throughout the process of building and launching your CMS-powered web site.

Approach

The book takes a task-centered approach. Each task is taken through steps with detailed instructions. The book is complete with screenshots and resources. It even has supplementary tasks that readers can carry out to further build their skills in each task. Everything is oriented towards day-to-day tasks of managing content with a CMS.

We will be working with Oprah on her Yoga Site. In the process we will learn what we need to do for our own sites.

Let's get started!

Just like Oprah, we are excited to start a new journey—a journey in which the path and the destination are equally important. Let's start by looking at what options we have for building our site.

2
Evaluating Your Options

Now that we have seen the benefits of open source CMSs, we are ready to explore further. Let us look at different types of open source CMSs. In this chapter we will:

- *Learn about the different types of CMSs*
- *Understand the different purposes that they fulfill*
- *Learn about the technologies these systems use*

A Google search for **open source content management system** yields more than 18 million results. If you browse through the CMS category of Open Source Scripts (`http://www.opensourcescripts.com/`), it too gives more than 300 options. How do you find a suitable CMS?

Let's begin by looking at different types of content management systems.

Genres of Content Management Systems

CMSs come in all shapes and sizes. They can also be classified by their purpose. Some are made to publish blogs, some for image galleries. General-purpose CMSs allow the dynamic publishing and management of site content. The following is a screenshot of the CMS classification tree on **OpenSource CMS** (`http://www.opensourcecms.com/`), which is a service with live demos of major CMSs:

- ASP.NET Demos
- All PHP Demos (195)
- CMS / Portals (93)
- Forums (19)
- Blogs (15)
- Image Galleries (13)
- Lite (13)
- Groupware (12)
- Learning Management (10)
- Miscellaneous (8)
- eCommerce (7)
- Wiki (5)

The top three categories—**Portals**, **Blogs**, and **Forums**—cover most of the CMSs. The others are more specific—**Groupware**, **e-Commerce**, **Learning Management**, **Image Galleries**, **Wiki**, **Light weight CMSs**, and **Miscellaneous**. Now, you may be asking: "OK, but what is the difference between them?" Let me explain.

Portals or general-purpose CMSs

General-purpose CMSs are used in a variety of places. They are the most common for building dynamic corporate web sites. They eliminate the need for a technical person to update a web site's content. With a CMS, non-technical end users can publish their own content. Wikipedia's definition of web content management systems applies very well to the general-purpose CMSs. The definition is as follows:

> *A* **Web Content Management System** *(***WCMS** *or* **Web CMS***) is content management system software, usually implemented as a Web application, for creating and managing HTML content. It is used to manage and control a large, dynamic collection of Web material (HTML documents and their associated images). A WCMS facilitates content creation, content control, editing, and many essential Web maintenance functions.*
>
> *Usually the software provides authoring (and other) tools designed to allow users with little or no knowledge of programming languages or markup languages to create and manage content with relative ease of use.*

Core features

Let's now review the core features of a general-purpose CMS.

- Create and manage content sections or hierarchy
- Create pages and easily add text or image content
- Rearrange or edit published content at any time
- Automatic linking and content publishing
- Allow multiple users to administer or manage content

Most web CMSs also allow you a good level of control over how your site looks. The question is: How can we use a system that gives us such features? We have plenty of options actually!

Possible uses

Here are some possible uses of a portal or a general-purpose CMS.

- Newspaper or magazine web sites
- Corporate or community web sites
- Sports, recreation, or other topical sites
- A personal or bio site
- To provide any other information

As such, you can use a general-purpose CMS for almost anything. Many such systems even support plug-in architecture. You can add new features by installing readily available plug-ins or develop one on your own.

Here are some example sites.

Example sites

Thousands of web sites use CMSs. Here are a few examples covering a wide variety of purposes:

- `http://www.fastcompany.com/`
- `http://corp.aol.com/`
- `http://www.gsas.harvard.edu/`
- `http://www.quizilla.com/`
- `http://hasselblad.com/`
- `http://discovermagazine.com/`
- `http://www.fsf.org/`

Top general-purpose CMSs

If you are wondering what CMSs were used to build the sites listed above, here is a list of some top general-purpose CMSs.

- Joomla!: `http://www.joomla.org/`
- Drupal: `http://www.drupal.org/`
- CMS Made Simple: `http://www.cmsmadesimple.org/`
- SilverStripe: `http://www.silverstripe.com/`
- Plone: `http://plone.org/`

Let us now review more specific CMSs—tools that serve particular needs.

Blog CMSs

Web logs (better known as blogs) are diary like web sites. Blogs are very popular and also one of the easiest CMSs. Here's how Wikipedia defines blogs:

> *A* **blog** *is a website, usually maintained by an individual with regular entries of commentary, descriptions of events, or other material such as graphics or video. Entries are commonly displayed in reverse-chronological order.* **Blog** *can also be used as a verb, meaning to maintain or add content to a blog.*

Essentially, a blog is a one-to-many communication medium. Blogs are easy to set up and maintain. People blog on particular subjects or use their blog as an online diary. The popularity of blogs has led to different types of blogs such as photo blogs, video blogs, audio blogs or podcasts, mobile blogs, and such others.

Core features

Blogs are web sites, but have certain unique features. Let's see what they are. Using blogs we can:

- Create posts
- Categorize posts and tag them with keywords
- Allow commenting on each post, make it interactive (and subsequently, manage spam comments)
- Create permanent links to each blog post
- Create an automatic notification to another blog when it's referred to in your blog (pingback/trackback)
- Add images, videos, or other content
- Chronologically display posts, with a calendar-like navigation structure
- Create blog rolls—lists of blogs the author reads (promotes cross-linking)
- Manage the design of the blog and install easily available themes
- Export content as RSS, removing the need to visit a blog to read it

Possible uses

Blogs are **social media**. More than 100 million people blog these days, and they also use blog CMSs. Here is how you can use a blog:

- Online diary: Posts about personal experiences and opinions
- Commentary on specific topics: For example politics, technology, business, and so on
- News posting: It could even be subject-specific such as a blog on the latest gadgets
- Multimedia: Photo blog, video blog, blogging from a mobile device
- Corporate blog: To share updates and create buzz
- Aggregator blog: To pull together valuable content from other blogs
- Self publishing: Writing about anything you like

You can use a blog however you like. After all, it's all about your self-expression.

Example sites

Here are some of the popular blogs that use open source blog CMSs:

- `http://www.perezhilton.com/`
- `http://boingboing.net/`
- `http://www.smashingmagazine.com/`
- `http://www.techcrunch.com/`
- `http://offtherack.people.com/`
- `http://nelsonmandela.org/`

Of course, there are millions of other blogs.

Top blog CMSs

Most of the top blogging sites mentioned above run on open source blogging software. The following are some top blog CMSs:

- WordPress: `http://www.wordpress.org/`
- Movable Type: `http://www.movabletype.org/`
- Expression Engine: `http://expressionengine.com/`

Blogs are great for running personal sites and can be extended for many other purposes with plug-ins. We will cover using blog CMSs in detail later. So, let's look at another type of CMSs.

e-Commerce CMSs

An e-Commerce CMS is aimed at running an online store. It allows managing products, categories, product options, and may have other sophisticated features. You may be familiar with online shopping sites. There are many e-Commerce software applications that can be used to create online stores. Such software has been around for many years now. As a matter of fact, e-Commerce software is not even regarded as pure CMS.

Core features

There are some e-Commerce software applications that have solid CMS features. For our purposes, we will consider the following as the main features:

- **Product Management**—categories, attributes, options, photos, pricing
- **Shopping Cart**—compare, wish list, checking out, payment gateways
- **Customer Management**—users, newsletter, order tracking
- **Marketing Tools**—reports, promotions, special pricing, cross selling

- **Site Management**—pages, sections, menus
- **Search Engine Optimization**—friendly URL, keywords, and so on

Possible uses

Online commerce has matured now. There are many commercial and open source e-Commerce CMSs. How would you use them? The following are some of the possible uses:

- Sell books, gifts, toys, or any other products
- Book event tickets, subscriptions, and appointments
- Publish informative content and promote relevant products
- Compare products and sell them
- Use a general-purpose CMS for content, and e-Commerce for revenue generation
- Send marketing newsletters and increase repeat business
- Run affiliate program to sell even more

Example sites

The uses of an e-Commerce CMS are obvious. The purpose is to sell, and a CMS should make it easy to sell. Here are some example sites:

- `http://www.4-pieds.com/`
- `http://www.smallable.com/`
- `http://www.mobileedge.com/`
- `http://www.copperpebble.com/`
- `http://www.geekgears.com/`
- `http://www.jazzwise.com/`

Top e-Commerce CMSs

Again, there are millions of other e-Commerce sites and you can learn a lot from them. Here are some top CMSs you can use to build an online store.

- Magento: `http://www.magentocommerce.com/`
- Freeway: `http://www.openfreeway.org/`
- osCommerce: `http://www.oscommerce.com/`
- PrestaShop: `http://www.prestashop.com/`
- DashCommerce: `http://dashcommerce.org/`

We have covered the main types of CMSs so far. Let's look at some of the more specialized CMSs now.

Wiki CMSs

We have referred to the definitions of some terms from Wikipedia. Wikipedia is a collaborative encyclopedia—and well, it's a Wiki! Here's how Wikipedia defines a Wiki:

> *A* **wiki** *is a page or collection of Web pages designed to enable anyone who accesses it to contribute or modify content (excluding blocked users), using a simplified markup language. Wikis are often used to create collaborative web sites and to power community web sites.*

In a Wiki, anyone can edit site pages. This means your site can correct and grow based on user contributions. Small contributions of site visitors can lead to a pool of collective knowledge. This is how Wikipedia has grown.

Core features

Wikis are used both in private and public networks, and can be customized to suit your needs. Here are some core features:

- Easily create and edit pages just with a browser
- Simple formatting markup syntax
- Automatic/simple link creation, even if the target page does not exist (yet)
- Invites visitors to contribute
- Complete revision history—roll back at any time
- Can restrict editing by logged in user or group of users

Wikis are collaborative by nature. The quality of content improves as people contribute.

Possible uses

Wikis are great for research web sites, or any site that wants its users to freely contribute. Here are some of the possible uses of Wikis:

- Create a holiday or travel site—let visitors write reviews and recommendations
- Create an internal knowledge-base system—allow employees and partners to store useful information
- Create an events calendar or an experts' directory—let people add their own entries
- Write a book collaboratively—let anyone edit anything!
- Create documentation—visitors can add and correct as they see fit

As you use Wikis more, you get bigger benefits. Wikis can be used inside an organization to promote a culture of collaboration and contribution. It's easy to correct a piece of information, but difficult to capture it.

Example sites

Wikis allow the capturing of knowledge, and also refining it. Take a look at what people have created with Wikis in the following list of sites:

- `http://www.wikipedia.org/`
- `http://wikitravel.org/`
- `http://c2.com/cgi/wiki`
- `http://lyricwiki.org/`
- `http://www.wikibooks.org/`

Top Wiki CMSs

There are many other sites using Wikis, or similar styles. If you want to build a Wiki, the following are some CMSs that you can use:

- MediaWiki: `http://www.mediawiki.org/`
- DokuWiki: `http://www.dokuwiki.org/`
- PmWiki: `http://www.pmwiki.org/`
- TWiki: `http://twiki.org/`

That was quite exciting! Let's look at another CMS type that breeds on collaboration.

Forum CMSs

A discussion forum is generally a place to ask and answer questions. It's also a place to hang around and make friends. Wikipedia defines **Internet forums** as:

> *An Internet forum, or message board, is an online discussion site. It is the modern equivalent of a traditional bulletin board, and a technological evolution of the dialup bulletin board system. From a technological standpoint, forums or boards are web applications managing user-generated content.*
>
> *People participating in an Internet forum can build bonds with each other and interest groups will easily form around a topic's discussion, subjects dealt with in or around sections in the forum.*

Core features

Forums are one of the oldest web-based collaboration tools, and have evolved over time. Here are the core features that you can expect in a forum CMS:

- Hierarchical or threaded discussions
- Public or private messages
- Extensive access control—visitors, users, moderators, administrators
- User features—subscribe to topics, profile page, ignore lists
- Simple formatting—and yes, emoticons—those smiley faces ;-)
- Allowing attachments with posts
- Search—simple and advanced
- Pin important topics at the top of the list
- RSS feeds
- Polls and surveys

Since forums have been around for years, you will find a number of them online. People have started using Wikis, blogs, and other systems instead of forums in some places.

Possible uses

Nothing can beat a forum when it comes to discussions!

- Support forum for your product or services
- Photo reviews—post a photo and others can comment on it
- Technology solutions—solutions to problems
- School discussion board system—discussion among students, and also with teachers

Example sites

Forums are used mainly for support sites these days. But innovative uses are possible. Here are some examples.

- `http://forum.kde.org/`
- `http://www.pianostreet.com/smf/`
- `http://forums.mozillazine.org/`
- `http://www.flashdevelop.org/community/`
- `http://forums.cocoaforge.com/`
- `http://www.englishclub.com/esl-forums/`
- `http://www.veganfitness.net/forum/`

Top forum CMSs

You can use a forum to support users or to encourage collaboration. Here are some CMSs you can use to build your own forum.

- phpBB: `http://www.phpbb.com/`
- Simple Machines Forum—`http://www.simplemachines.org`
- myBB: `http://www.mybboard.net/`
- JForum: `http://www.jforum.net/`

If you are looking for commercial alternatives, vBulletin (`http://www.vbulletin.com/`) and InvisionBoard (`http://www.invisionpower.com/`) are the most popular.

Now that we have looked at discussion forums, let's check out online learning.

eLearning CMSs

Online learning tools can streamline a lot of processes for a school. **Electronic Learning** is a vast subject, and an eLearning CMS can cover portions of it. Here's Wikipedia's definition of eLearning:

> **Electronic learning** *(or* **e-Learning** *or* **eLearning***) is a type of Technology supported education/learning (TSL) where the medium of instruction is through computer technology, particularly involving digital technologies. E-learning has been defined as ""pedagogy" empowered by digital technology" [1]. In some instances, no face-to- face interaction takes place. E-learning is used interchangeably in a wide variety of contexts. In companies, it refers to the strategies that use the company network to deliver training courses to employees.*

As you can see, the definition is broad.

Core Features

Here are some features you will see in top open source eLearning CMSs (often called as Learning Management Systems).

- Manage courses, students, teachers
- Create a course, add learning paths
- Add documents, tests, discussions, and announcements
- Manage course agenda or schedule
- SCORM import/standard compliance
- Additional interaction tools—videos, chat, blogs, and so on

You can use an eLearning system to run a simple course on cooking, or manage the operations of a university.

Possible uses

Open source eLearning solutions have grown over years. The following are some of the possible uses:

- Offer a course that you teach online about cooking, yoga, or anything!
- Take your institute online, and let students learn from their home
- Manage student assignments and discussions online, continue offline training
- Publish a tutorial on a subject you are passionate about

Although eLearning is not a common need, a CMS can ease a lot of pain involved in offering online education.

Example sites

Most open source eLearning solutions were developed at universities, and may require some reworking to suit a corporate environment. But they help you effectively manage and deliver your course content. Here are some of them:

- `http://campus.dokeos.com/`
- `http://www.ugent.be/`
- `http://moodle.org/sites/`

Most eLearning deployments are for internal users, so we don't have a lot of example sites here.

Top eLearning CMSs

Here are top eLearning CMSs. You can find a lot more information from their web sites.

- Dokeos: `http://www.dokeos.com`
- Moodle: `http://moodle.com/`
- .LRN: `http://www.dotlrn.org/`
- LAMS: `http://lamsfoundation.org/`
- Sakai: `http://www.sakaiproject.org/`

A few of the CMS types that we covered—Wiki, eLearning, and so on—are popularly used within organizations, too. You may even want some additional features if you are doing an internal deployment. Let's quickly look at CMSs made specially for Intranets.

Collaboration CMSs

A collaboration CMS is generally designed for internal users of an organization. Users could be all employees, partners, or customers. The needs of every organization may be different, and an Intranet may have variety of systems—from HR to groupware to ERP.

Core features

The following are the core features you can expect from a collaboration CMS:

- User management
- Document/Records Management—assets, revisions, comments
- Workflow and approval processes
- Groups/Spaces to organize work
- Blog, forum, Wiki, and so on for collaboration
- Desktop access, APIs, and standard compliance for integration with other systems
- System-specific features—contact management, knowledge base, project management, and so on

A wise choice would be to take an open source Intranet CMS and customize it to your needs.

Possible uses

Intranets can significantly reduce email, or communication, overload and speed up processes. They also help to keep most of the information in a single place. Here are some possible uses of Intranets. They:

- Keep all your policies, forms, and documents in one place
- Use workflows to manage design or documentation approvals
- Manage changes to documents through revision control
- Build third-party integration and hook up to a payroll or project management system
- Manage marketing campaigns by centralizing all information, documents, media assets, and reports
- Set up a knowledge base using a Wiki or document management

Top intranet CMSs

You can come up with innovative uses of a collaborative CMS as you start exploring options. Most of them (shown below) are very powerful and can easily be extended.

- Alfresco—`http://www.alfresco.com/`
- Nuxeo—`http://www.nuxeo.com/`
- Jahia—`http://www.jahia.com/`

From work-centric Intranet CMSs, let's now move to something more fun—photo galleries.

Photo gallery CMSs

You may be already publishing your photos on Flickr, or Picasa, or some other service. What if you wanted to have your own photo gallery? A photo gallery CMS can serve that need. As a matter of fact, you can even publish audio and video with top photo gallery CMSs.

Core features

Let's look at the core features of photo gallery CMSs. They:

- Create galleries or albums
- Add photos, create thumbnails, and add titles or captions
- Elegantly display album images and slideshows
- Allow rating and comments
- Have a popular or new photos list
- Batch import, integration with Flickr and so on
- Share with all or a limited audience, using password-protected albums

Possible uses

You can publish photos of your bachelor parties using a photo gallery, or keep it limited to corporate-event photos! Here are some uses of a photo gallery CMS. Using it, you can:

- Publish family or organization photographs online
- Sell high-resolution versions of images you have taken
- Invite feedback on your photography skills.
- Create a network of photography enthusiasts and share/publish/earn together
- Publish videos or podcasts
- Manage screenshots of your products using gallery software
- Link up a photo gallery with your realty/event site/blog

Managing your photo gallery on your own gives you full control. It allows you to customize the design—and this itself is worth the effort!

Example sites

The following are some nice photo galleries:

- `http://www.misspoloniacanada.ca/gallery/`
- `http://www.3dvalley.com/gallery/`
- `http://www.mehtanirav.com/gallery/` (Yes, that's my gallery!)

Top photo gallery CMSs

If you want to set a gallery for yourself, you can easily do that with one of the top gallery CMSs.

- Gallery: `http://gallery.menalto.com/`
- Coppermine: `http://coppermine-gallery.net/`

Have fun with your galleries.

That completes our overview of the major CMS types. We have gained an insight into what's special about each CMS, and how they serve different purposes. But there is a lot of overlap in major CMSs because a lot of things they do are common.

Different types, but strong overlap

We looked at the different types of CMSs, from general-purpose to photo galleries. Each had its own core feature set, but all the CMSs have a strong overlap of functionality. They all essentially allow you to add and manage some type of content—text, images, and files. The way content displays to the end user may be different, but a lot of internals are the same. Here are some of the features you will see in many CMSs:

- **WYSIWYG Editor**: A **What You See Is What You Get** editor allows you to enter text and format it. Most such editors even allow you to add images and other media.
- **Categories and content hierarchy**: Sections, categories or nested levels to organize content are very common.
- **Search Engine Optimization**: Search engine friendly URLs, meta tags are supported.
- **Tagging**: Tag content with keywords, then display a "tag cloud" or list.

- **Different User Levels**: Most CMSs allow multiple users to manage content. Many even have roles and access levels to control what each user can do.
- **Plug-in Support**: Extend core features by adding plug-ins and extensions.
- **Themes/Skins**: Customize the look and feel with themes.
- **Comments, and so on**: Comments and other social media, or Web 2.0 features, are widely available.

As we evaluate each type of CMS later in the book, you will experience the striking similarity in the way content is managed. This is good news actually—you can easily apply lessons you have learned from one CMS to another.

One more striking similarity you may notice is that most open source CMSs are written in PHP. Let's quickly review CMS technologies to understand this phenomenon.

Understanding CMS technologies

We haven't discussed the technical aspects of CMSs so far. Let's quickly review them here.

Web-based CMSs have a simple three-tier architecture, just like any other web application: **Browser → Web Server → Database Server**. Internally, different CMSs may have different system designs. However, the overall components and flow still remain the same. Take a look at Joomla!'s architecture in the following figure:

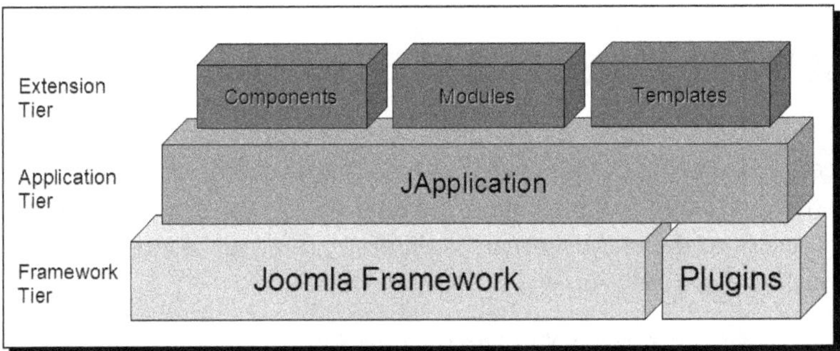

And here's Drupal's execution system flow:

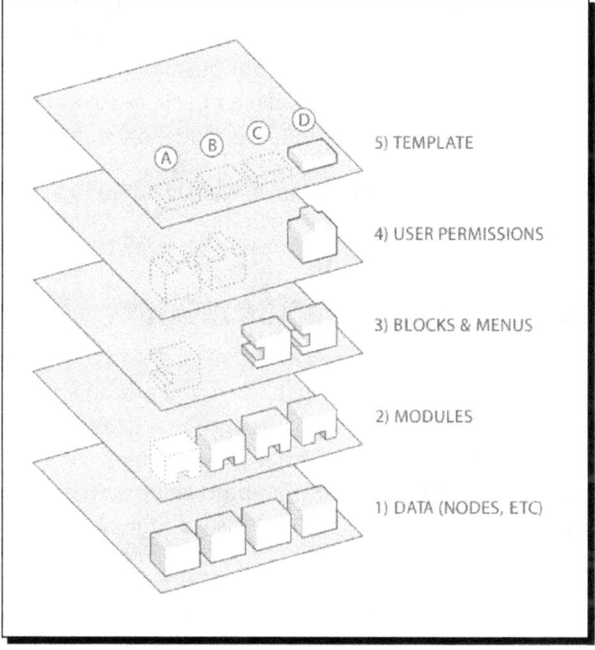

Most CMSs will have similar design, which consists of a few core components, plug-in systems, and template handlers. The flow will be similar too—process templates, permissions, content blocks, and actual content.

> You can learn more about Joomla! architecture at `http://dev.joomla.org/content/view/1137/80/`.
>
> Find how Drupal's flow works at `http://drupal.org/getting-started/before/overview`.

Apart from the system architecture similarities, you may have noticed another similarity in top CMSs—the backend technologies that they use. Most are written in PHP with MySQL as the database.

PHP is most popular for CMSs

PHP (`http://www.php.net`) was designed "to solve the Web problem", and it is no surprise that most CMSs are written in PHP. PHP is easy to learn and is very powerful. It allows building solid frameworks and writing elegant business logic. On the other hand, PHP also forgives badly written code. So when you select a CMS, make sure to go for one that has good code. Popular CMSs typically have high-quality code, so you can rest assured.

If PHP is not your preference, you can find CMSs in .Net, Java, Ruby, Perl, and Python too. All of them have their own strengths.

But why does the technology choice matter?

A technology choice matters because you will host your CMS on a web server, and it needs to support the technology your CMS is using. Especially if you are on shared hosting, you must check if your host supports the programming language (that is, PHP, or Perl, and so on) and database (that is, MySQL, MS SQL, and so on) that you are going to use. There may be other system requirements such as the GD library for a photo gallery. Ensure that your existing infrastructure supports those requirements. Otherwise, you may need to change the server configuration, service provider, or the CMS.

That's enough of technical background for us. In the next few chapters we will learn how to select a CMS for which we will revisit the technology. For now, let's summarize what we covered in this chapter.

Summary

We learned about different types of CMSs. We reviewed their core features, looked at example sites, and got to know the top choices in each category.

Specifically, we looked at:

- General-Purpose CMSs: Joomla, Drupal, and so on
- Blogs for diaries and commentary: Wordpress, MovableType, and so on
- Online Commerce CMSs: Magento, Freeway, and so on
- Wikis for easy collaboration: MediaWiki, DokuWiki, and so on

- Discussion forums for support and community: phpBB, JForum, and so on
- Intranet and Enterprise CMSs: Alfresco, Nuxeo, and so on
- eLearning tools: Dokeos, Moodle, and so on
- Photo gallery and media managers: Gallery, Coppermine, and so on
- An overview of the technologies and architecture of CMSs

That's a lot of homework done! We are progressing well in building a great site with an open source CMS. But, a crucial factor in achieving success is to understand our requirements before we go further. Let's get into action and figure out our requirements in the next chapter.

Section II

Thinking your choices through

Understanding your Requirements

Building the Site

Content Editing and Management

Templates and Plug-ins

Extending and Customizing

3

Understanding your Requirements

We have reviewed different types of open source CMSs. However, before selecting a software, we must understand what are the requirements for our site. Once the requirements are clear, selecting and deploying the software is much easier.

In this chapter we will:

- *Clarify and set our expectations for Oprah's Yoga site*
- *Measure the scale—how big is the site and how big is the audience?*
- *Determine the standards to comply with and the need to work with other systems*
- *List the features we want to add to the site*

So let's get on with it.

Setting our expectations right

If you want to be successful, the first thing you need to do is define what success means. While selecting the best open source CMS for our site, we must be clear about our requirements. Being clear about our needs and setting expectations improve our chances of success.

Oprah wants her web site to help a lot of people and, thus, make it a success. What does it really mean? Let's work out our expectations one step at a time.

Time for action-setting your expectations for "The Yoga Site"

1. Pick up a pen and a blank paper. Put a title at the top—**The Yoga Site**.
2. On the extreme left, write down **Intended Outcomes**.

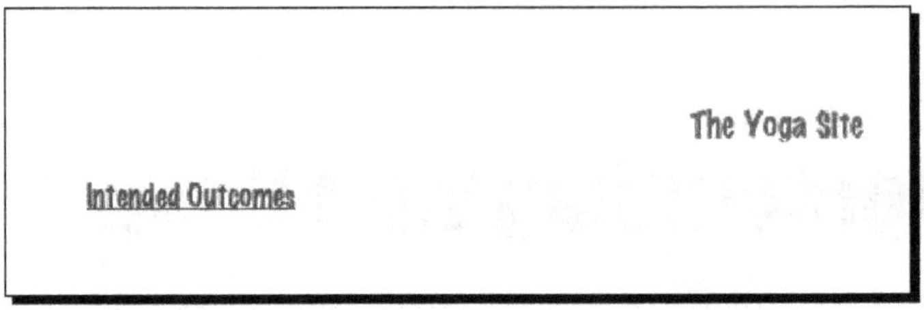

The Yoga Site

Intended Outcomes

3. Below this, write down top three results we want from our site. In this case, we want to provide yoga-related information to visitors, make money by selling yoga products from our partners, and create a community of yoga followers. Write these points in a bullet form and keep three blank lines between each point.

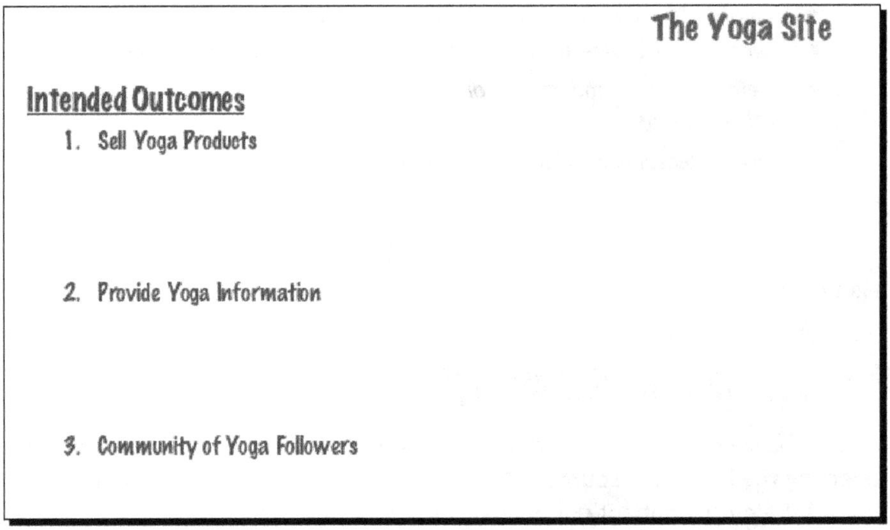

The Yoga Site

Intended Outcomes

1. Sell Yoga Products
2. Provide Yoga Information
3. Community of Yoga Followers

4. Now is a good time to look at each outcome individually and think through what exactly we want. Look at those three lines we left after each outcome. Write **What** in the first line, **Why** in the second, and **How** in the third.

The Yoga Site

Intended Outcomes

1. Sell Yoga Products
    1. What:
    2. Why:
    3. How:
2. Provide Yoga Information
    1. What:
    2. Why:
    3. How:
3. Community of Yoga Followers
    1. What:
    2. Why:
    3. How:

5. Think about answers to these three questions: What do we want to do in selling yoga products? Why do we want to sell them? How will we sell them? Repeat these questions for all outcomes. Once you are through, write down some key words from your answers next to what, why, and how.
6. Read through the list now and revise it as you see fit.
7. The final **Intended Outcomes** list may look like this.

Intended Outcomes

1. Sell Yoga Products
    1. What: Books, Videos, Equipments, Genuine Products only
    2. Why: Cover costs, Hosting bills, Secondary income
    3. How: Partners, Content linked with relevant products, Testimonials
2. Provide Yoga Information
    1. What: Postures, Methods, Ideal sequences, Background
    2. Why: Correct learning
    3. How: Text, Pictures, Videos, Links to resources, Articles, News
3. Community of Yoga Followers
    1. What: Experiences, Testimonials, Regular contact, Product reviews
    2. Why: Learning from others, Contribution, Richer content
    3. How: Newsletters, Interviews, Content feed, Offers

What just happened?

We just set clear outcomes for the Yoga site.

First, we wrote down the top three results we want from our site. We limited ourselves to only three results because we wanted to be clear about our most important targets.

Then we brainstormed the **What** part, which helped us clarify the kind of information we want to provide. We used key words to keep our list short yet meaningful. We did similar brainstorming to answer the **Why** and **How** questions. Answering the **Why** question allows us to understand the real purpose of our site. The answers to the **Why** questions should be real focus of our efforts.

We forced ourselves to think about our implementation strategy to achieve the desired outcome via **How** questions. This is important because the key words in the **How** section represent real content that should be available on our site.

This list will now serve as a guide. Whenever we are in doubt about adding some content or feature, we can consult this list to determine whether we should do it or not. Of course, we can update this list as and when we want. Focusing on the most important targets help us achieve them.

Note that we used pen and paper for this exercise because they are flexible and powerful tools for brainstorming. If you prefer some other tool, you can use that too.

Here's a wrap up on the process.

Creating intended outcomes

1. Limit yourself to the top three results.
2. Think about the needs of your target audience.
3. Ask:
    - **What**—What will it do? What will be there? What will not be there? What will the site stand for? and so on.
    - **Why**—Why will it do that? Why do you want it? Why will people come to the site? and so on.
    - **How**—How will it be done? How will the goals be accomplished? and so on.
4. Show your list to someone who's interested in the subject. Get feedback.
5. Review and revise the list as needed.

Selecting a CMS before defining clear requirements is the foremost reason for project failures. Do not get into product evaluation until you know exactly what you want from your site/CMS.

Pop quiz

1. What CMS should we use for Oprah's site?
   - Joomla is good and will satisfy the goals we listed.
   - We need to evaluate our requirements further, before selecting a solution.
   - A blog—Wordpress—is best for Oprah. It will even allow her to post yoga lessons.
   - We will have to build one from scratch.
2. Why are **What** questions important?
   - Human minds can think of ends better than means. So, it is easier to start with **What**.
   - Well, **Why** and **How** are more important than **What**.
   - They clarify the requirements of a site. We are forced to think exactly what we want.
   - They are the first questions that come to one's mind.
3. What is the foremost reason for CMS project failures?
   - Weak management support
   - Unrealistic schedules
   - Integration with existing systems
   - Getting into technical details before defining requirements

Have a go hero-different goals for different sites

We looked at a yoga information site and listed down its goals. Different sites may have different goals, even if they are related to yoga. A yoga personal trainer may want visitors to inquire for his or her services or host podcasts. A yoga school may need a calendar of events, contributed content, and a way to take appointments. A larger yoga center may want to provide ways for trainers to talk to each other, send out a newsletter to subscribers, and show information in multiple languages.

It is important to think about what you want for your site. So go ahead and create **Intended Outcomes** for the site of a yoga school with three branches.

Identify market niche and target audience

Identify market niche for your site and position your site correctly. If your site provides information about some products and services, think about a market niche of those products and services.

Similarly, be clear about the demographics of your target audience. That will ease content development, site design, and marketing efforts.

Measuring your site

Imagine a bicycle carrying a truckload. It'll be difficult for a poor bicycle rider to handle that load for long. The scale and size of a web site affect technical decisions—server capacity, bandwidth requirements, and so on. Now, let's measure how big our site will be.

Time for action-measuring the scale of your site

1. Pull out the paper we used to create **Intended Outcomes**.
2. Below the heading, write **Scale & Size**.

The Yoga Site

Scale & Size

3. An important factor determining efforts on a site is its content. Write **Content** below **Scale & Size**.
4. List down the different aspects of our site content.

Scale & Size

1. Content
    1. Sections:
    2. # of Pages:
    3. # of Images/Page:
    4. # & size of Audio/Video:
    5. Archives?
    6. Frequency of Updates:

5. Think about each aspect and put in your answers next to it. For our Yoga site, we will have about 300 pages in five sections. At least one video with each yoga posture (Aasana). We won't need to update this content frequently. Mostly, we won't have to do any editing after our site is launched. Similarly, our content is not time sensitive and archives won't be applicable to us.

1. Content
    1. Sections: ~5 (Basics, Aasanas, Products, Resources, About)
    2. # of Pages: ~300 (10 + 80 + 150 (Db) + 10 + 5 + more...)
    3. # of Images/Page: ~3
    4. # & size of Audio/Video: ~100 videos
    5. Archives? -NA-
    6. Frequency of Updates: Monthly

6. Another important factor that will determine the scale of operations is the number of users and what they will do on our site. Write down **Users** and the key factors related to site users below it.

2. Users
    1. # of Users:
    2. Content Languages:
    3. # of Visits/User/Month:
    4. # of Pageviews

7. Now speculate about the number of users. We may have fewer users in the first few months, but we can expect approximately 10,000 users eventually.

8. Our site is going to be only in one language—English—for now. Write down **English** against **Content Languages**.

9. How many times do we expect a user to visit our site in a month? Maybe once or twice. Most of our visitors will be first-time visitors coming via search engines. Write this down.

10. Similarly, we may have about five million total page views or visits in a month. Once you have written that, our list may look like the following image.

2. Users
    1. # of Users: 1st month - 500, 3rd - 3000, 5th - 10000
    2. Content Languages: English
    3. # of Visits/User/Month: 2, mostly via search engines
    4. # of Pageviews: 5mn per month

Alexa (`www.alexa.com`) is a useful tool to understand hits and site popularity. Review your competitors' statistics and you can get a fair idea of where you need to reach.

11. Make a new main item called **Overall** at the same level as **Users**. Under that, write down **Disk Space**, **Bandwidth**, and **Team**.

3. Overall
    1. Disk Space:
    2. Bandwidth:
    3. Team:

12. Now look at the list and the numbers we have written. Look at the number of pages and the amount of media content. For the Yoga site, our estimate is that we will need about 1GB space for all files and database combined.

13. As we have video content, we will need more bandwidth. For a start, a monthly usage of 300GB bandwidth is sufficient. Bandwidth is typically calculated by multiplying the average page size (including images and video), number of pages, and number of hits. A typical CMS site may need a 5GB bandwidth every month. Let's write that down.

14. Reviewing all information so far, we can also say that we will need a content writer, a graphic designer, a person for online marketing, and a general administrator. Who else will we need to create and manage our site? Well, we will need to involve our existing staff in the entire process. One of our team members can take care of general administration after the site goes live. We will also need to get professionally created videos. Let's put all this down in **Team**.

Finally, our **Overall** section may look like this:

3. Overall
   1. Disk Space: ~1GB
   2. Bandwidth: ~300GB/month
   3. Team: Editor, Designer, Marketing

What just happened?

We evaluated the size and scale of our web site. Size and scale are mainly driven by the amount of content and the number of visitors. These numbers are interdependent. If we increase the number of pages or users, the disk space and bandwidth will be affected as well.

You may not come up with exact figures here. If you don't know the number of visitors or page impressions you should expect, compare with competitors and then take a guess.

Our purpose in calculating these numbers is to determine server, team, and management requirements. If we expect to scale quickly, we should even consider scalability options now.

Are you expecting a lot of visitors?

If you expect a lot of visitors and traffic on your web site, you should give weight to the performance optimization features of a CMS. Let us first review some features needed for better performance.

- **Well-written code**: If code is messy, other performance enhancements will yield limited results. Messy code may have too many database queries, inefficient use of disk or network resources, and too many loops or operations that may take a long time to complete. This will slow down any web application. Look out for what people say about the code quality of a particular CMS before you make your selection.
- **Caching**: Typical CMSs generate all pages dynamically, querying the database on every page request. This would be an overhead if you don't have a lot of dynamic content, or even if your frequency of updates is low. Caching stores dynamically generated pages for a while, eliminating the need to query the database for that time. Just enabling caching on your CMS can give you a huge performance boost. A variation of caching would be exporting your site as static HTML pages. Every time you change something, all affected pages can be published again.
- **Load balancing and database replication**: You may want to distribute server load across multiple servers via load balancing. You can also add multiple database servers and keep them in sync via database replication. In most cases, you will need to take the help of specialists, but you want to make sure that your CMS can work in such environments.

If these points sounded too technical to you, you can consult an expert. Server management and scaling up may be new to many development teams. So, if you really need high performance, get someone who's done it before.

Pop quiz

1. If your average page size is large, let's say 300Kb per page, what will be the impact?
    - It will take lot of time for me to generate that content.
    - It will take lot of time for the server to process that page.
    - It will take lot of time for a page to load and user may get irritated.
    - It will take time to load for user, and also a higher bandwidth.
2. If your server is slow, what will be its impact?
    - All dynamic pages will be processed slowly, increasing page load time.
    - Video files will take longer to load.
    - We can't have thousands of users on it.
    - No visible impact.
3. What could be an easy performance optimization for a CMS?
    - Add an additional server and load balance.
    - Remove unnecessary plug-ins from CMS.
    - Keep the database on a separate server.
    - Publish the site as static HTML pages.

Have a go hero-take some measurements!

We talked about reviewing competitors' statistics to understand what we can expect. It's a good time now to do that. Go ahead and find out about the scale and size of three competitors' web sites. Use Alexa, Google Analytics, or any other service.

Working with others

One goal for our Yoga site is to sell related products and services. As a matter of fact, that's going to be our primary source of income. How will we get product and service information? We can either go to individual vendor sites to pick information from there, or we can give a tool to vendors to upload their product information on our site.

We also want our customers to be updated with the latest news, articles, and products we post on the site. Our users could visit our site frequently to check for updates, but frankly, we want something easier than that. Updating users regularly makes it effortless for our users to find the latest about us.

In both these cases, we will need to work out some methods that are standards-based, making it easier for us and the vendors, or users, to interoperate. An *upload inventory using Excel CSV file* feature for vendors and a *subscribe to news using RSS feed* feature for users will do the trick.

What are standards?

Standards are commonly agreed practices and methods of doing things. Using a commonly known and accepted technology or tool makes it easier for both developers and end users. For example, HTML is a standard language to create web sites. Whenever you think about integrating your CMS with someone else's system, ensure that you follow common standards.

Now is a good time to look at such requirements and list down how we will implement them.

Time for action-determining compliance and interoperability needs

1. By now, you are familiar with our **Brainstorming Sheet**—the paper sheet we used so far to list down intended outcomes and scale measurements. Pull that sheet or pick up a fresh one.
2. Give a heading: **Standards / Interoperability**.
3. Give a subheading: **Overall**.
4. What are the web development standards we want to follow? Surely, we want the site to be done in strict XHTML. We also want it to follow **WAI** (**Web Accessibility Initiative**) guidelines for accessibility—making it usable for users with lower vision, hearing deficits, or other accessibility limitations. It's good to design the site using CSS layouts, so we want to comply with CSS3 standard as well. Start listing these below the **Overall** heading.

If you don't understand these technical words, don't worry. You can look them up on Google, but you can also just dish them out while speaking to developers!

5. We know that creating a Google Sitemap can get us better search engine rankings. As such, we also want to optimize our site for search engines. Let's put SEO (Search Engine Optimization), SEF (Search Engine Friendly URLs), and Google Sitemap too in our standards requirements.

6. How about accessing the site from mobile devices? We don't want to work on developing phone-specific applications yet, so a mobile web site would do. As a matter of fact, ours could be the first Yoga site viewable even from mobiles! This would be a very good feature, so let's add XHTML **MP** (**Mobile Profile**) to our list.

7. We are going to launch our site only in English for now, but we certainly want the ability to add content in other languages. This means we will need UTF-8 support too. UTF-8 text encoding is supported in all modern browsers and allows showing multilingual content. Our list may now look something like this:

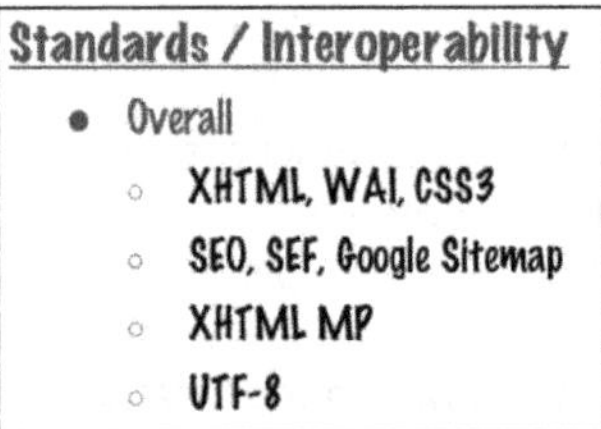

8. Give another subheading: **Users**.

9. We want users to get the latest updates to our site via RSS feeds. This could be the main content feed or a feed of comments on some topic we have. Write down **Subscription – RSS** under **Users**.

10. A similar feature will be letting people get yoga-related event information via the iCal standard. This will allow them to use calendaring systems to remember events. Let's add **iCal for events** to our list too.

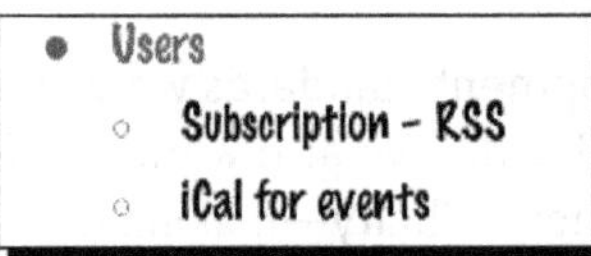

11. What are the ways in which we want to integrate with our vendors? We saw that a **CSV product upload** feature will make it easier for them to maintain their product or service listings. If we think about other partners, we may want to syndicate content from other partner sites on our site. So let's add a **Syndication – RSS** feature to the list as well.

12. That covers most of the features we want. But there could be some other standards you want to comply with, or some other group of partners you need to interact with. Let's add another heading—**Others**—and add such requirements there. For example, we want to support FTP protocol for file uploads and HTTPS for secure logins and transactions. We may also want PCI Compliance for protecting credit card information. Think of anything else that you need on your site and add it to the list. Our additions may look like the following when done:

- Vendors / Partners
  - Syndication - RSS
  - CSV product uploads
- Others
  - FTP, HTTPS

What just happened

We brainstormed and listed down our interaction points with our vendors, partners, and users. We also listed other standards we want to follow for our site. Listing standards like this makes site requirements clearer and forces us to think about the integration points before we begin working on the CMS.

Have a go hero-learn the terms

If you don't know them already, Google and learn about these terms:

- XHTML
- CSS
- RSS
- FTP
- HTTPS
- CSV
- SEO

Determining additional feature requirements

A content management system is a system that allows us to manage site content. The definition is very broad and can include a variety of elements. You may want to write a blog or run a discussion forum. You may even want some surveys done. Such features may or may not be part of standard CMS software. It is important to determine your needs for such additional features at the beginning. The good thing is that many CMS systems support plug-ins, allowing you to add features of your choice later on.

Time for action-choosing additional features

1. Make a new heading on our **Brainstorming Sheet**. Call it **Other Features Needed**.
2. Review the following list and write down all the features you want to have on your site below the heading.
    - **Blog**: Date-wise diary-like entries on topics of your liking
    - **Chat**: Live chat between users, or between you and the users
    - **Classifieds Advertisements**: To buy or sell things, list jobs, and so on
    - **Discussion Forum**: Here users can discuss their ideas, opinions, and ask for help
    - **Document Management**: Upload, download, annotate, and manage different documents
    - **Events Management**: List, browse, and find out events
    - **File Repository**: To create a downloads area or something similar
    - **Help Desk or Bug Reporting**: Make it easier for users to ask for help
    - **Invoicing or Billing System**: Manage orders or subscriptions
    - **Knowledge Base or FAQ**: Articles explaining features of your site or product, and a Frequently Asked Questions list
    - **Mail Form**: Allow users to send you an email using a contact form
    - **My Home or Dashboard**: Custom page after logging in for users, should customizations or personalization be allowed?
    - **Newsletter**: Updates via email
    - **Outgoing Link Management**: Track what links people are clicking
    - **Photo Gallery**: Upload photos, manage albums, ratings, and comments
    - **Plug-in Support**: Extend functionality by adding plug-ins
    - **Polls / Surveys / Quizzes**: Analyze your users' opinions
    - **Rating System**: Rate each article

- **Site Search Engine**: Internal search engine for your site
- **Social Networking**: Friends, network, scraps, and so on
- **User Contributions**: Allow users to contribute content
- **Video**: User-contributed or admin-published
- **Web Services**: Provide others easy access to your site features
- **Widgets**: Embed content from your CMS on others' sites
- **Wiki**: Allow free and easy content updates via a wiki

3. Go through your Intended Outcomes list. If you feel you need to add any other modules or features, go ahead and do that.

4. For our Yoga site, we need some of these features. Here's how your list may look once you complete it.

Other Features Needed

- Blog
- Events Management
- Mail Form
- My Home / Dashboard
- Newsletter
- Outgoing Link Management
- Photo Gallery
- Plugin Support
- Polls / Surveys
- Site Search Engine
- Subscription Management

What just happened

We evaluated what add-on features our site needs apart from basic content management components. We reviewed a list of popular additional features and picked the ones that we need on our Yoga site.

Reviewing a checklist simplifies the selection process. When you look at an item in a checklist, you can evaluate how useful it will be, and then choose it if it's worth it. Making this feature list also strengthens our understanding of site requirements. We can then identify whether a plug-in to the CMS of our choice will fulfil our needs.

We are now at a very good stage. We have a very good understanding of what we want for our Yoga site. We have not only listed our functional requirements, but also a lot of technical needs. Let's review what we covered in this chapter.

Summary

We learned a lot in this chapter about understanding our requirements. We started with intended outcomes and went on to list additional requirements.

Specifically, we covered how to:

- Discover intended outcomes for a site—top three, what, why, how questions
- Measure scale and size—number of users, content items, hits
- Determine interoperability and standards—RSS, HTTPS, and so on.

We discussed many other points in between—reviewing competitors, being clear about requirements, and listing things down. We have now created a solid base to move ahead. We are now ready to build our site!

4
Building the Site

We got insights into the requirements and the possibilities with Oprah's Yoga site in the last chapter. We are now ready to build our site using a CMS. However, you may have many questions such as: How can you evaluate different CMSs? What technical factors should be considered? How can you get hands-on experience of the CMSs you are evaluating? How easy will they be to use? Will you require programming knowledge to get them to work?

Let's learn all that in this chapter. Here we shall:

- *Get hands-on experience of some CMSs*
- *Create site a navigation structure using a CMS*
- *Understand the technical requirements of CMSs*
- *Set up a blog and learn what it takes to install a CMS*

Let's dive!

Get hands-on experience with a CMS

Would you ever buy a car without taking a test drive? Taking a test drive allows you to get a first-hand experience of the car and determine if it's the right car for you. No matter how many specifications and reviews you read, you won't get the real feel without a test drive!

We always research, review, and compare products before buying. Unfortunately, for many, selecting a CMS is just a "checking boxes" exercise. They would compare their requirements with the CMS's feature list, tally totals, and go with one that scores higher. The good thing about open source is that you can actually take a test drive of the CMS, just like a car. You can even build your site using multiple CMSs and keep only what works best.

So let's take a test drive of some content management systems. That should give us a good idea if they are right for the Yoga site.

Time for action-taking a test drive

1. Open your web browser and go to `http://www.opensourcecms.com/`. opensourceCMS allows you to try content management systems before you install them.
2. Locate **Open Source Demos** on the left bar. Click on **Portal/CMS** option.

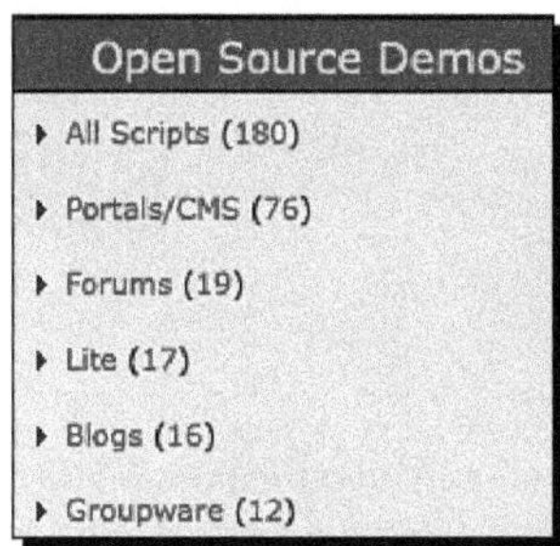

3. This shows a page full of different Portal CMSs. Locate **Joomla** in the list and click on it. That will bring you to following page:

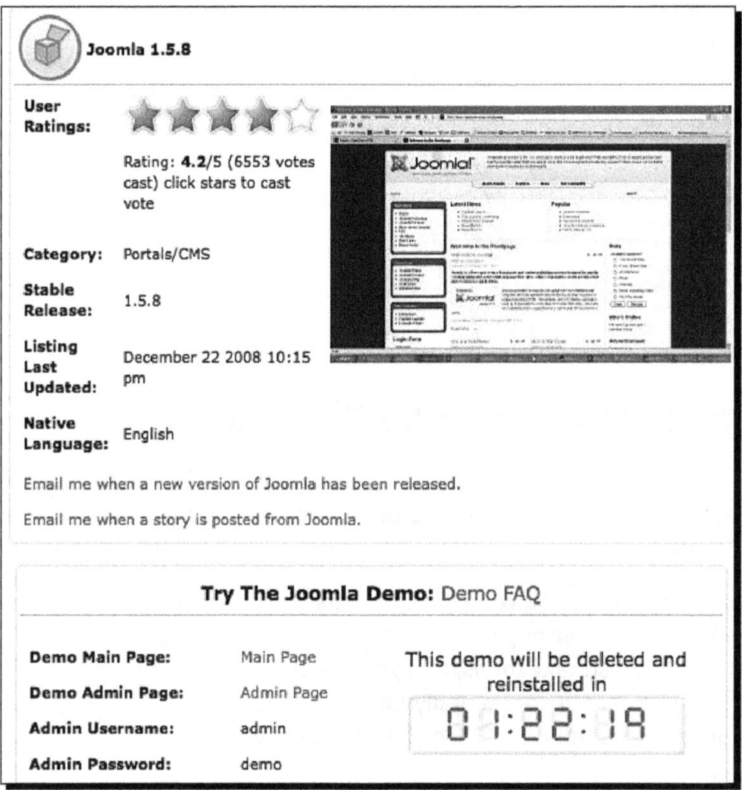

4. The page offers live demos for **Main Page** and **Admin Page**. The **Main Page** shows the end user view of a CMS. It includes some default modules and sample content. Here's what the Joomla! front page looks like.

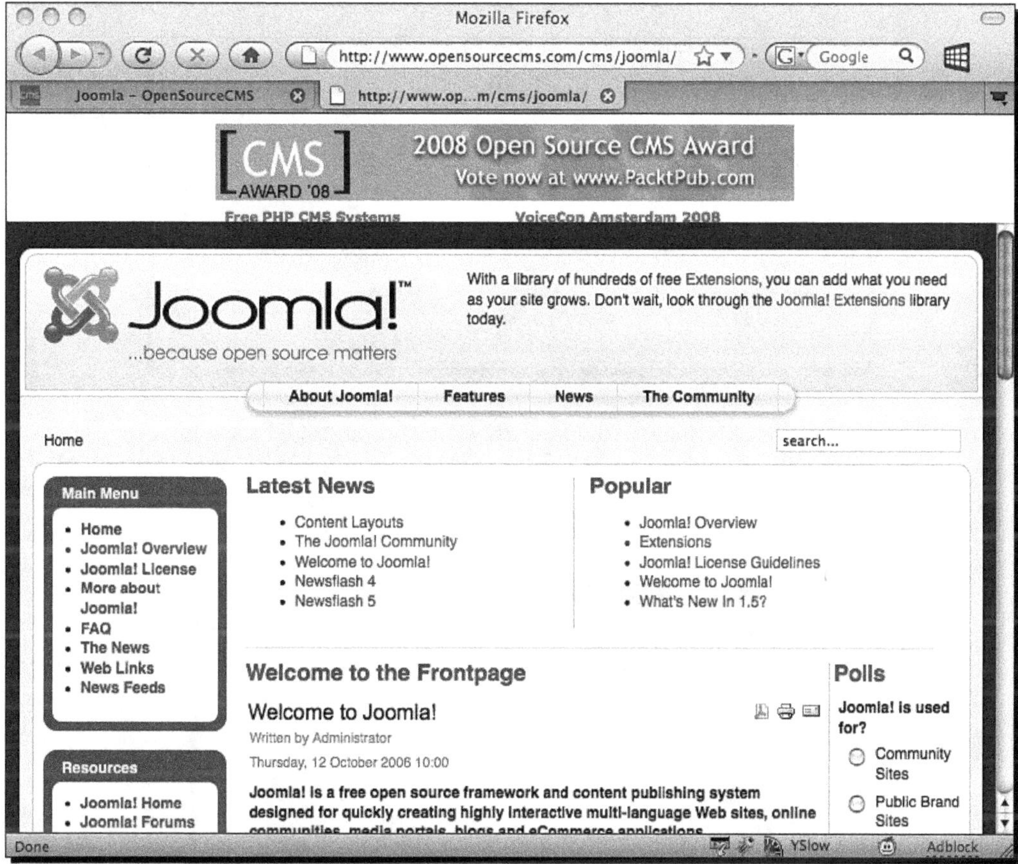

5. We can see that Joomla! provides multiple navigation systems—tabbed links at top, menu bar on the left, and content links in the middle section. It even has a provision to show the latest news and popular items on the front page. This page also has a poll, user login form, multicolumn content layout, and a few ads. We can organize content on our Yoga site in a similar way, but we prefer a cleaner look with some photographs.

6. Click on the **About Joomla!** link in top navigation to see what a content page looks like.

7. Review a few links on the left to see how different types of content can be displayed. The following image shows the **FAQs → General** page. A lot of this can be useful for our Yoga site—the way FAQs show up, multipage articles, and so on. Go ahead and look at other links as well.

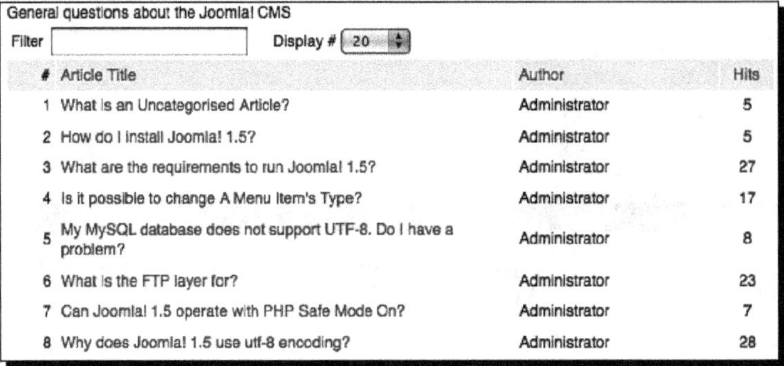

General questions about the Joomla! CMS

Filter Display # 20

#	Article Title	Author	Hits
1	What is an Uncategorised Article?	Administrator	5
2	How do I install Joomla! 1.5?	Administrator	5
3	What are the requirements to run Joomla! 1.5?	Administrator	27
4	Is it possible to change A Menu Item's Type?	Administrator	17
5	My MySQL database does not support UTF-8. Do I have a problem?	Administrator	8
6	What is the FTP layer for?	Administrator	23
7	Can Joomla! 1.5 operate with PHP Safe Mode On?	Administrator	7
8	Why does Joomla! 1.5 use utf-8 encoding?	Administrator	28

8. Now that we have familiarized ourselves with user pages, let's see how the administration interface looks. Go back to the Joomla! page on opensourceCMS and click on the **Admin Page** link. **Username** and **Password** are given right below the link; use them to log in. You may see a page like this:

9. Review the top menus, other administration options, and help and stats on the right side. Looking around at different menus is a great way to understand how Joomla! works.

10. Look around to find out how we can organize our content. What are the ways to create a navigation structure? Can you understand the names of different links?

11. We saw the web site's front page and different articles a while ago. Let's see how they are managed. Click on **Article Manager** from main screen (Control Panel) and study the page that comes up. Here's a screenshot:

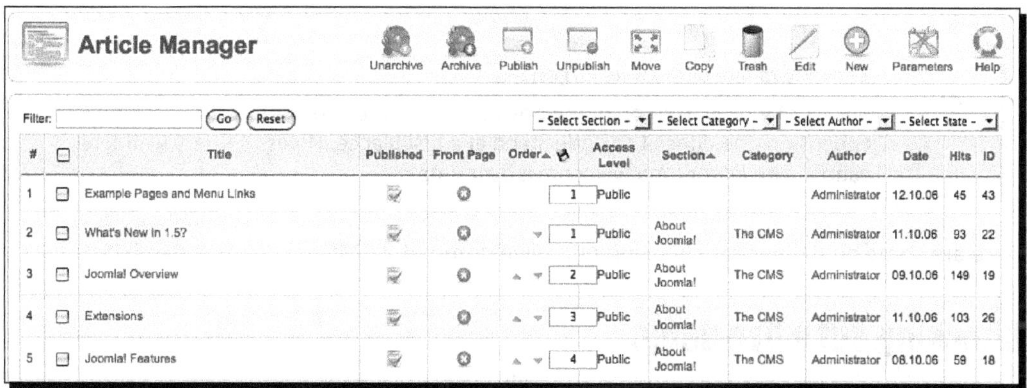

12. As you see, you can easily mark articles to be published on the front page, change their order, set their access level, and also filter and sort the list. Top icons provide further actions. Seems understandable!

What just happened?

We dived in and tried out Joomla!—a leading open source content management system.

We could go to the Joomla! site at `www.joomla.org` and take a demo from there, But that requires us to create an account, verify our email, and then be granted access to live demo. That is a long process. Similarly, we can go to each different CMS we want to evaluate and try their live demos. We wanted something faster and simpler. Thankfully, opensourceCMS web site solves this problem. It hosts live demos of the most popular PHP/MySQL-based content management systems. To review both the user and administrator side of Joomla! we used their service.

We first saw the main page of a Joomla! demo site. We reviewed different components, the navigation system, and how articles appear. The default installation of a CMS typically showcases its best features, so we went to each link and reviewed how it looks. Our purpose is to evaluate whether this CMS will fit our needs. Reviewing different pages and options tells us whether or not this CMS is understandable and has all the features we need.

We then logged in to the administration interface. We saw different menus and options. We figured out how content is organized in different menus, sections, categories, and articles. We also reviewed the **Article Manager** screen to understand how easy it is to publish and re-order articles.

We looked at different administration options to familiarize ourselves. Again, the intention is to understand how easy the system is and whether it suits our needs.

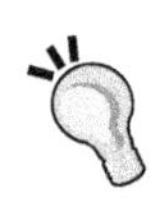

Be ready to live with some jargon

Many CMSs have a jargon of their own. The way they organize content and menu options may be difficult to understand at a first glance. Unless it's very weird, be patient with jargon. You will learn it over time.

Here are some guidelines for checking out a live demo of a CMS.

Checking out a live demo

Here is a checklist you can follow while going through a live demo:

- Review overall layout and design.
- Understand navigation structure and how you can create it.
- Look at how a single article or a content page is displayed.
- Is it easy to understand? Is the interface cryptic? Does it use jargon that you can't understand?
- Go through the administration interface very carefully. That's what you (and whoever else is going to manage your site) will have to work through. Well-organized menus and options are good. Well-named links are a definitive plus point!

Pop quiz

1. Why would you take live demo of a CMS?
    - To understand how it works and evaluate whether it's suitable to your needs
    - To compare its features with other CMSs
    - To mess around with sample content and advertise your site
    - To learn the CMS jargon

2. What Joomla! features can we use on our Yoga site?

    - Hierarchical content organization
    - Frequently Asked Questions
    - Important content on homepage
    - Polls
    - All of the above and more

Have a go hero-test drive some more CMSs

We just looked at one CMS. How about test-driving a few more?

1. Try out **Wordpress** from opensourceCMS for both main page and administration login page. Wordpress is the most popular blogging content management system.
2. Also, try **Magento** from opensourceCMS. Magento is a leading e-commerce platform. It's especially useful if the main intention of your site is to sell things.

3. Go to `Alfresco.com` and review product screenshots. Alfresco is an enterprise-grade open source CMS.

4. Review the list of different CMS types on opensourceCMS—Portals, Blogs, e-Commerce, Groupware, Forums, e-Learning, Image Galleries, Wiki, Lite and Miscellaneous.

Create navigation structure

All content needs organization. For our Yoga site, we must work out a navigation structure. A good structure will make it easier for the users to find information. We can also continue our CMS trial and see how easily a skeleton site can be created. Let's get into action and create a navigation structure.

Time for action-creating navigation structure

1. Take out the papers we used to create intended outcomes and determine the size and scale of our site in Chapter 2. Review them.
2. Take a fresh page and start creating possible navigation structure. We can follow a top-down hierarchical structure for our site by listing down sections, subsections, and pages from the site home page. List the main sections we need in our Yoga site.

3. Now go through each section and span out subsections. For example, our Postures section may group yoga postures by age, problems, or sequences. We may also want to list them alphabetically. Similarly, our **About Us** section can have the company vision and team information.

4. Expand further and rearrange until you are satisfied with the structure. It may look like the following.

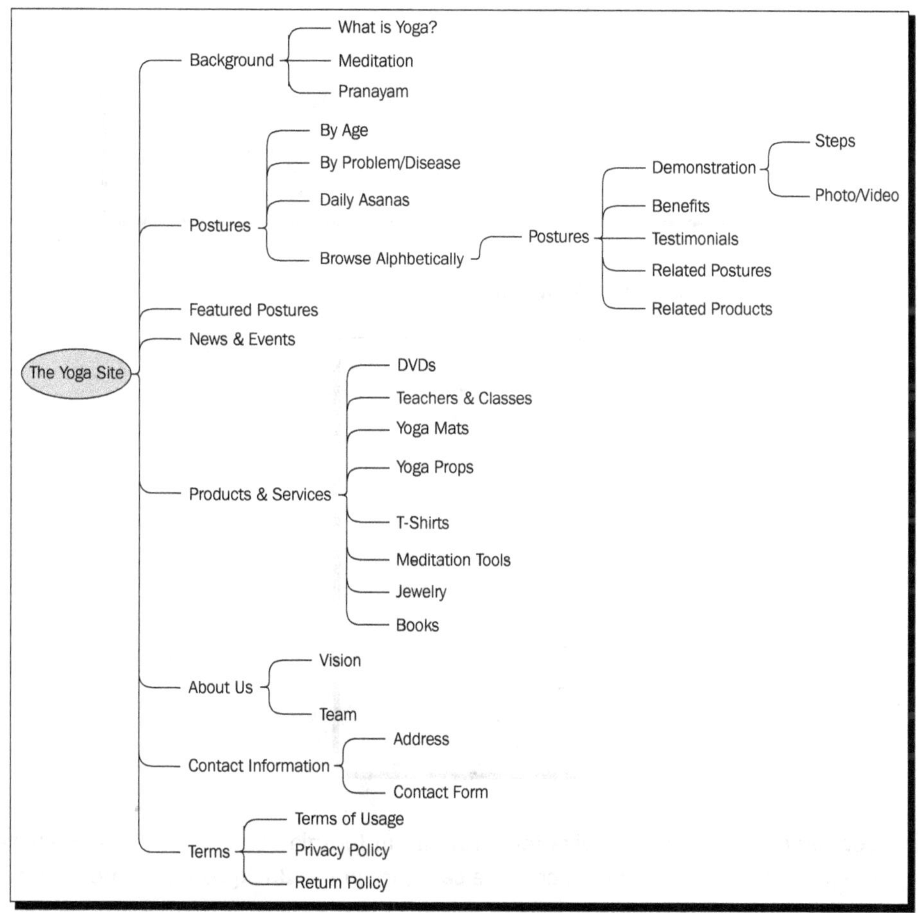

5. At this stage, we have our navigation structure ready. Now is a good time to see how a CMS can accommodate this navigation. Let's try it out with Joomla!

6. Go back to `www.opensourcecms.com` and take the Joomla! demo. Make sure you have sufficient time before the demo is re-installed. A countdown timer on the Joomla! page will tell you the remaining time.

7. Log in to the admin panel and create a few sections. The following image shows the section creation screen:

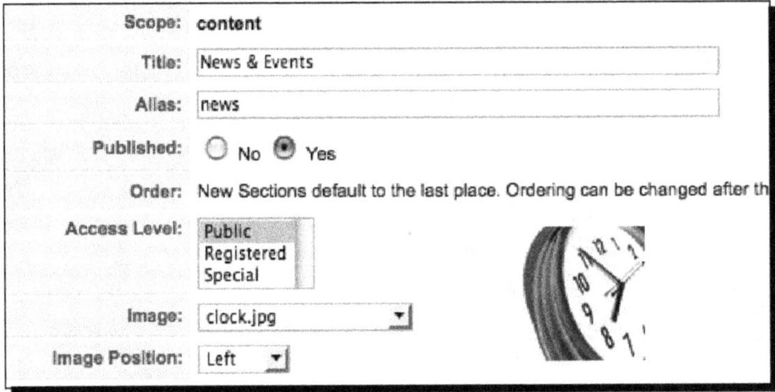

8. After we add our section, the list of sections may look like this:

9. **Section** is the top-level navigation structure in Joomla!. For subsections, we have to create categories. Go ahead, create a category in the **Background** section for now.

10. For a section to be linked from home page, we need to add a link to it in the **Main Menu**. Go to **Menu Manager**, click on the **Menu Item(s)** icon next to **Main Menu**, and add a new menu item. Have it point to the **Background** section. You can remove other menu entries if you wish. Your **Menu Item Manager** screen will look like this once you are done.

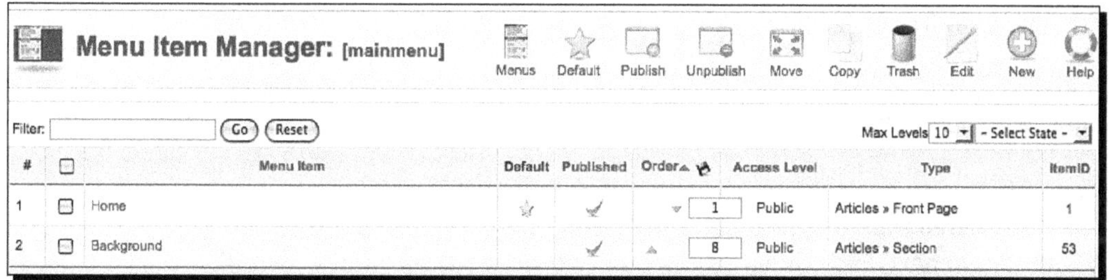

11. That should be enough for us to get started. Let's see how this shows up for end users. Click on the **Preview** link near the top of the administration page and you should see how the main page will look. Voilà! The link we added to main menu is right there. Click on it.

12. It shows a blank page for Background. Congratulations! We have successfully set up a basic navigation structure with Joomla!.

What just happened?

We structured the content of our site and created a navigation flow. Users can easily find content they are looking for, if the navigation flow of our site is simple. We followed a hierarchical structure—general sections at the top, then the more specific subsections, and then the actual content pages.

We sketched the navigation structure like a tree. While creating it, we thought about how the actual content can be accessed. We also listed down content elements that each "Posture" will have. We put ourselves in a user's shoes and came up with posture-browsing options—by age, disease, or sequence.

Sketching the navigation structure allowed us to map it to the Joomla! navigation scheme. We first created top-level sections. Subsections are called categories in Joomla! and so we created them next. Each category has a parent section associated with it. We did not create any content pages for now. We modified the site's **Main Menu** to remove unnecessary links and added a link for the **Background** section. This showed the link on the site preview and clicking on it showed us a blank page. The page is blank because we do not have any content pages yet.

We learned a lot about Joomla! administration in this exercise. We learned how to add, modify, and delete sections, categories, and menu items. These operations were similar and you can expect other options to follow a similar style.

Do you need a different navigation structure?

Will a hierarchical structure suit your site? Do you need to organize content chronologically? Or does it need to be free flowing?

- A Photo Tour site may need sequential (back—next) navigation
- A personal diary or a blog may need chronological navigation
- An encyclopedia may need great number of internal links, resulting in a free-flow navigation (for example `Wikipedia.org`)

Now is a good time to review your requirements and think about the best way in which you can organize your content. Accordingly, you can determine a navigation structure.

> Check `TED.com`—the 2008 Webby Award winner for best navigation. Also, while you are there, look at `http://www.schematic.com` and `http://www.apple.com`.

Pop quiz

Why is navigation structure important?

- ❑ Improper navigation is like a maze. Most users will get lost in it.
- ❑ It gives direction to users about what they can do on the site.
- ❑ Because it is the way of organizing site content.
- ❑ All of the above.

We have a good grip on navigation now. What else will we need while building our web site? We surely need to set up a CMS. And for that, we need to know its technical requirements. Let's quickly review some technical factors you should be aware of in selecting and setting up a CMS.

Understanding technical requirements

Let us say that you bought the car you took for a test drive last time. You have a superb audio system in your current car and you want to get that set up in the new car. You tell the mechanic to do that. But he grins at you and says, "If you wanted to fit that audio system, you should have bought the DX version, not the EX."

Ouch! That hurt!

Going ahead with a CMS purely by its demo can hurt even more. If you already have a web site or other systems, you must understand technical requirements of the CMS you are shortlisting. You should then compare those requirements with your existing setup and see if they fit.

Most open source CMSs use PHP as the server-side programming language and MySQL as the database. Typically, they are hosted on Linux servers with Apache as the web server. If your hosting company provides these (most probably they do), you are fine.

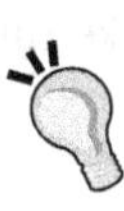

Of course, there are powerful open source CMSs in Java, Python, Ruby, and other languages too. Some also use PostgreSQL or flat file databases. The combination of Linux, Apache, MySQL, and PHP is commonly referred to as LAMP stack. Apache, MySQL, and PHP also work very well on Windows and Mac OS.

Wordpress, a popular blog engine, is also a feature-rich content management system. It's easy to use and famous for its quick five-minute installation. Let's use Wordpress for the next few exercises. We will also get familiar with one more CMS.

So are you ready? Let's get techy!

Time for action-understanding technical requirements

1. Go to `www.cmsmatrix.org`.
2. From the list in the left column, select **DotNetNuke**, **Joomla!**, **Movable Type**, and **WordPress**. WordPress is our preferred CMS for now, but we are also interested in others.
3. Click on **Compare**.

4. This gives you an extensive feature comparison. For now, we are interested in the **System Requirements** section at the top. It will look like the following image.

Product	DotNetNuke 4.8.1	Joomla! 1.5.4	Movable Type 3.0	WordPress 2.2.1
Last Updated	3/4/2008	7/8/2008	6/25/2008	7/25/2007
System Requirements	DotNetNuke	Joomla!	Movable Type	WordPress
Application Server	IIS	Any that supports PHP (Apache recommended)	Any that supports Perl	Apache recommended, any server that supports PHP and MySQL
Approximate Cost	Free	Free	Free version available	Free
Database	MSSQL 2005/2000, MSSQL Express 2005, MSDE	MySQL	MySQL, mSQL, PostgreSQL, BerkeleyDB, Flat File, sqlite	MySQL version 4.0 or greater
License	BSD (Modified)	GNU/GPL v2	Commercial, includes full source code	GNU GPL
Operating System	Windows	Any	Unix, Linux, FreeBSD & All BSD's, HP-UX, Windows 2000, 2003, XP, Solaris, AIX	OS Independent
Programming Language	ASP.NET 2.0, VB.NET, C#	PHP	Perl 5.8+	PHP version 4.2 or greater
Root Access	No	No	Yes	No
Shell Access	No	No	Yes	No
Web Server	IIS 5.0 & IIS 6.0 & IIS 7.0	Apache	Apache, IIS	Apache, mod_rewrite

5. The most important aspects are the **Application Server**, **Database**, **Programming Language**, and **Operating System**. Notice that **WordPress** and **Joomla!** use **PHP**, **DotNetNuke** is on **ASP.NET**, while **Movable Type** uses **Perl**.

6. For detailed technical requirements, you may want to visit the CMS's web site. For example, WordPress's minimum requirements can be found at `http://wordpress.org/about/requirements/`.

7. If you already have a web hosting account, go to your host's site and check out the plan details. See the technical features and find out if your host supports the technical requirements of your preferred CMSs. Our host shows features like this:

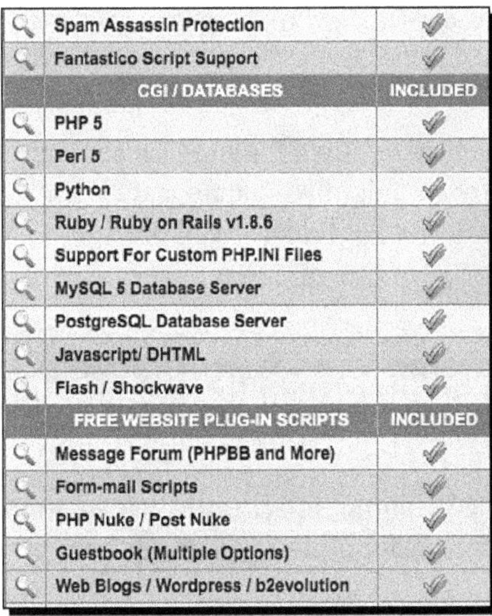

Spam Assassin Protection	✓
Fantastico Script Support	✓
CGI / DATABASES	**INCLUDED**
PHP 5	✓
Perl 5	✓
Python	✓
Ruby / Ruby on Rails v1.8.6	✓
Support For Custom PHP.INI Files	✓
MySQL 5 Database Server	✓
PostgreSQL Database Server	✓
Javascript/ DHTML	✓
Flash / Shockwave	✓
FREE WEBSITE PLUG-IN SCRIPTS	**INCLUDED**
Message Forum (PHPBB and More)	✓
Form-mail Scripts	✓
PHP Nuke / Post Nuke	✓
Guestbook (Multiple Options)	✓
Web Blogs / Wordpress / b2evolution	✓

8. At this time, you may also want to review any other technical requirements your site has. For example, if you are hosting videos, you may need a large disk space and bandwidth. You may also need SSL support to improve security of the site.

9. At this stage, we know that our web host can support WordPress easily. But will also support Joomla!, Movable Type, and a whole lot of other CMSs.

What just happened

We confirmed that our web host can support our preferred CMS. We first went to CMS Matrix to find out the system requirements of a few CMSs. The best part of CMS Matrix is that it shows a side-by-side feature comparison of your shortlisted CMSs. This makes it very easy for us to determine which CMS will fit our needs.

We then looked at the specific requirements of WordPress. Checking out detailed technical requirements helps us understand them better and confirm them with our host.

Equipped with this information, we went to our host's site to check if our host supports those requirements. Thankfully, it does support PHP and MySQL. As a matter of fact, it has WordPress among its included plug-ins. This means, it should be really easy to set up WordPress on this host. We also saw that the host can support any PHP/MySQL or Perl-based system.

If you can't understand whether your host supports your preferred CMS or not, you should contact them and find out. If they have specific restrictions on what features are available, you should find a CMS that can work with that restriction. If that fails, change your host!

We have now confirmed that our host supports WordPress, so let's go ahead and install WordPress! Let's see if it's really as easy as it claims to be.

Installing a CMS

Before we can add content to our site, we must set up the CMS. Installing a CMS can be too technical; especially if this is the first time you are setting up a web site. Most CMSs try their best to make the installation process easy and as automated as possible. Many hosting companies have CMS systems available from their control panels for easy installation. If your host allows this, you can go ahead and install a CMS using its control panel.

Before the installation

Setting up a CMS typically involves these steps:

- Downloading and unzipping CMS files
- Creating a new database on your web site and creating database username and password
- Updating database name, username, and password in configuration file(s)
- Uploading CMS files to your server via FTP
- Going to the CMS's installation page and following on-screen instructions

If you are new to installing things on your web site, you should review the following tutorials before the installation.

Creating a database

Plesk and **cPanel** are popular web-based control panels. Here are some tutorials that explain how you can create a new MySQL database using cPanel or Plesk:

- `http://www.cpanel.net/support/docs/11/cpanel/databases_create_sql.html`
- `http://www.revver.com/video/654055/how-to-create-a-database-using-cpanel/`
- `http://www.metacafe.com/watch/1431561/cari_net_creating_a_database_in_plesk/`

Uploading files using FTP

FTP stands for **File Transfer Protocol**, and is a way to upload files from your computer to your host's server. Refer to these tutorials for some very good background information and instructions on using FTP tools.

- `http://essentialkeystrokes.com/tutorial-ftp-its-easy-as-1-2-3`
- `http://www.interspire.com/content/articles/12/1/FTP-and-Understanding-File-Permissions/`

Using phpMyAdmin

phpMyAdmin is a popular tool to manage a MySQL database over the Web. You should get familiar with phpMyAdmin for installing your CMS and troubleshooting any small issues.

- `http://www.truveo.com/tag/phpmyadmin`
- `http://www.killerphp.com/mysql/videos/`

Managing file permissions

Uploading images and other media via CMS may require permissions to write to a folder on the web server. This will require that you understand some basics of file permissions on Linux/Unix servers. Here are two great resources to learn this:

- `http://www.linuxcommand.org/lts0070.php`
- `http://www.veoh.com/videos/v2061669XeXtWJd5`

Alright, we are now ready to install WordPress.

Time for action-install WordPress

Now that we are ready to install WordPress, let's go ahead!

1. Go to `www.wordpress.org` and download the latest version of WordPress.
2. Unzip the source code.
3. Create a new database on your host—call it **wordpress**. Create a new user **oscms** with the password **oscmsPass** and give it access to the database. You can do this using your web host's control panel. Otherwise, you can run the following SQL queries as MySQL root (administrator) user:

   ```
   create database wordpress;
   grant all privileges on wordpress.* to oscms@localhost identified
    by 'oscmsPass';
   flush privileges;
   ```

4. Locate a `wp-config-sample.php` file in the WordPress source code you unzipped. Copy that file as `wp-config.php`.
5. Open `wp-config.php` and edit the first few lines to add database connection information. The file may look like the following:

   ```
   <?php
   // ** MySQL settings ** //
   define('DB_NAME', 'wordpress');
   define('DB_USER', 'oscms');     //
   define('DB_PASSWORD', 'oscmsPass');
   define('DB_HOST', 'localhost');
   define('DB_CHARSET', 'utf8');
   define('DB_COLLATE', '');
   ```

6. Using FTP, upload all contents of the **wordpress** folder to your web server's web root folder. The web root folder may be called **public_html**, **htdocs**, **www**, or something similar.

SSH/Control Panel will be faster than FTP

You can also use SSH/SCP to copy files to your server. You can SCP a compressed file (for example `.tar.gz`) to your server. SSH to it and unzip it on the server. Similarly, your web host may allow uploading a compressed file using its control panel and unzipping it online. Both these approaches are much faster than FTP.

7. Now open your web site's URL in your browser. You should see the WordPress installation page. The URL may look like `http://www.yourdomain.com/wordpress/wp-admin/install.php`.

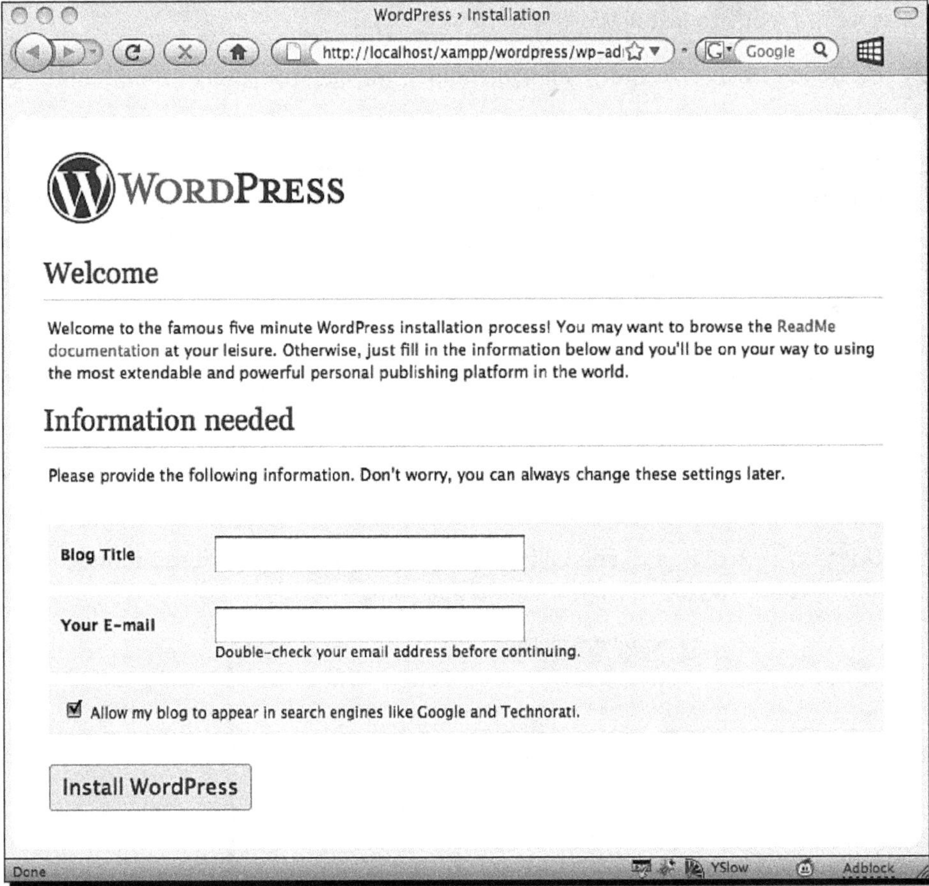

8. Enter your blog title and your email address. Click on **Install WordPress**.

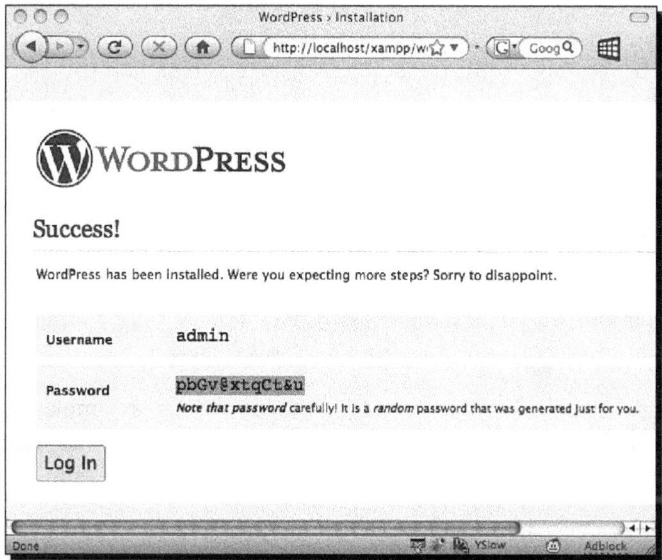

9. Ah, it's done! Just one step! Copy the administrator password. **Log In** to the admin panel.

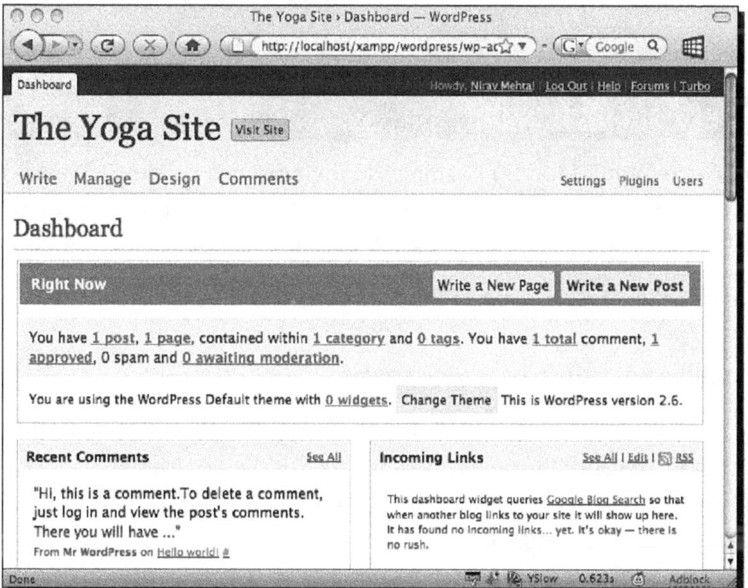

10. Click on the **Visit Site** link to view how the default site is set up.

11. Celebrate! Your WordPress installation is done in five minutes as they promised!

What just happened

We downloaded, configured, and set up WordPress—the most popular blogging CMS. In this process we created a new MySQL database, entered database connection information in the WordPress configuration file, uploaded all files to server, and experienced the famous five-minute install of WordPress. The actual install took less than a minute though!

Understanding these steps is crucial to setting up any content management system. You may have a technical team that can set up your CMS. But if you have done it yourself, you are always better prepared!

The most complicated part in setting up WordPress can be creating the database and a database user. If you need help during the process, you can refer to the WordPress installation guide at `http://codex.wordpress.org/Installing_WordPress`.

We chose WordPress as we wanted to keep the installation process simple, and yet learn all the basics of installing a CMS. As we mentioned, most CMSs are installed in a similar manner. You may just have to tweak some additional files or change permissions of some folders you need.

Have a go hero-set up your navigation structure with WordPress

Earlier in this chapter we set up a navigation structure for our Yoga site using Joomla!. WordPress is a blog where content is organized on the basis of the date of an entry. Yet it has a provision to create pages. Go ahead and figure out what is the best way to use WordPress for our Yoga site!

Have a go hero-set up Joomla!

We are going to use Joomla! for our examples in the next few chapters. Now is a good time to set it up. The following are some steps to set up Joomla!. For more information on getting it started, visit `http://www.joomla.org/about-joomla/getting-started.html`.

1. Download the latest version of Joomla! from `http://www.joomla.org/download.html`.
2. Unzip and upload the files to your server.
3. Create a MySQL database. Set up a MySQL user for it.
4. Navigate to your Joomla folder, for example `http://localhost/joomla/`.
5. Follow the instructions displayed on the screen. If Joomla! detects any problems during the pre-installation check, fix them before going further.
6. You can choose to install sample data during installation. This will help you to understand the system better.
7. Once the installation is complete, remove/rename your `installation` directory.

We now have enough background on preparing for and setting up a CMS. Let's summarize what we covered.

Summary

We learned a lot in this chapter about building a CMS.

Specifically, we covered how to:

- Evaluate CMSs via live demos
- Develop site navigation structure and create it in Joomla!
- Review and confirm technical requirements in setting up a CMS
- Install a CMS—WordPress

We also discussed some common steps in setting up a CMS and learned about a few sites that will help you in evaluating the best CMS for your needs.

Now that we've learned about building our site, we are ready to learn about maintaining and editing the content. That's the topic of our next chapter.

5
Content Editing and Management

We set up a content management system and also created the site's navigation structure in the last chapter. We are ready to start adding content now. We also want to learn how easy a CMS will be for our authors, so let's discover that in this chapter.

In this chapter we will:

- *Add content to our site—pages, images, and more*
- *Add additional information—metadata, tags, and links—with content*
- *Get a sense of how easy is it to maintain content with a CMS*
- *Learn what we need to support multiple authors*

There are exciting things ahead in this chapter, so let's get started.

Adding content to our site

Adding, updating, and deleting page content is at the heart of a CMS. We will use the Joomla! content management system for our examples in this chapter. Joomla! is a very popular and powerful CMS. Let's see how we can manage content with Joomla!.

Time for action-adding a page

1. Log in to the administration section of Joomla!. It is generally at `http://yoursite.com/joomla/administrator/`.
2. Click on the large icon that says **Add New Article**.

3. We want to create a page about Surya Namaskara, or Sun Salutation, one of the most popular yoga postures. Enter **Surya Namaskara** in the **Title** field, and **Sun Salutation** in the **Alias** field.

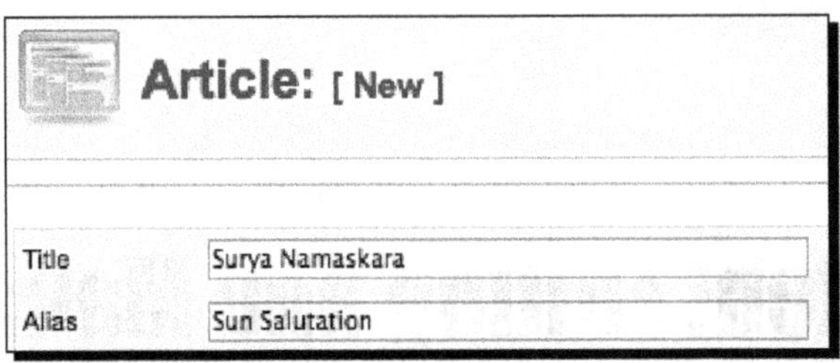

4. We have already created a few sections and categories in Joomla!. Select **Postures** as **Section**, and **Featured** as **Category** from the drop downs.

5. The Word-like area below is a content editor. It is also known as the WYSIWYG (What You See Is What You Get) editor. Type in the following text in the area that looks like a white page. We took this text from Wikipedia, but you can type a statement of your choice.

Surya Namaskara or Sun Salutation (lit. "salute to the sun"), is a common sequence of Hatha yoga asanas. Its origins lie in a worship of Surya, the Hindu solar deity.

Don't see a Word-like editor?

If you don't see a Word-like text editor, you may be missing some browser plug-ins. Your browser may warn you of missing plug-ins. In such a case, go ahead and install the missing plug-ins. If it still does not work, go to **Site | Global Configuration | Site | Site Settings | Default WYSIWYG Editor** and select **TinyMCE** or **XStandard**. You can also configure the editor per user from **User Manager**.

6. Press *Enter* after the first paragraph. Add two more sentences like this:

Surya Namaskara is an excellent exercise for the whole body. Mastering this asana will help you stay fit forever.

"Asana" is the Sanskrit word for posture. Yoga postures are called Asanas.

7. We want to highlight that **Surya Namaskara is an excellent exercise for the whole body**. Select that portion of text and click on the **B** icon to make it bold. You will immediately see the result in the editing window. At this stage, your editing window will look like this.

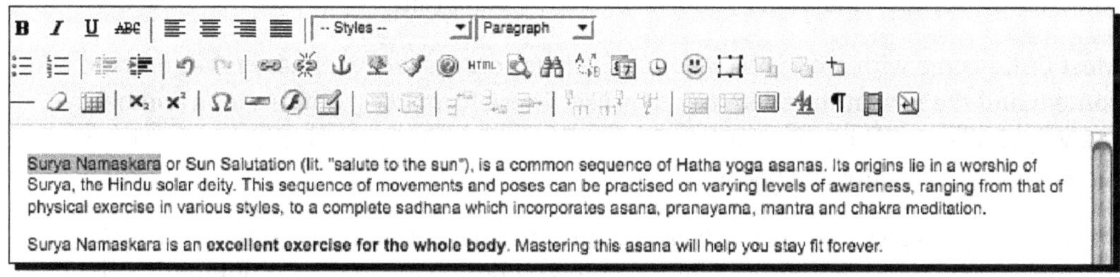

8. If you want to write additional text, go ahead and add it.

9. Click on the large **Save** icon at the top right of the page when you are done.

10. Now our content is saved. Click on the **Preview** link in the Joomla! menu bar and you will see the content on the site's home page. Here's how it will look:

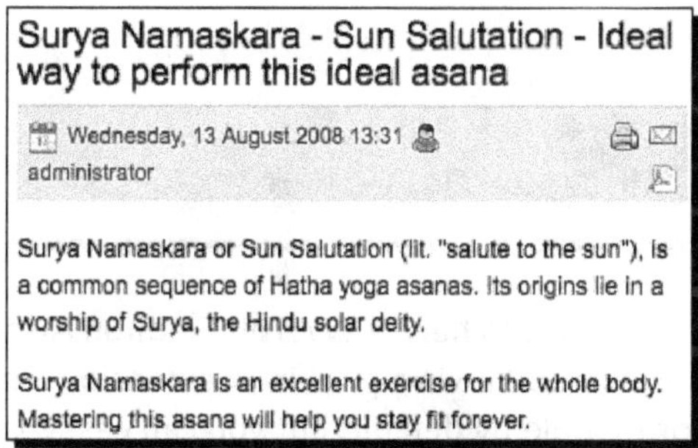

What just happened?

We used Joomla! to create our first content page. We added a page title, an alias, and the section and category this page belongs to. We then used a Word-like editor to enter text for our page.

We emphasized keywords by making them bold. This was done by selecting the keywords, and clicking on the **B** icon button in the toolbar. Notice that we can use this editor to apply a variety of other formatting to selected text. This kind of text editor is called a WYSIWYG editor.

What is WYSIWYG? Why is it important?

WYSIWYG (pronounced 'wizē,wig) is an acronym for **What You See Is What You Get**. The Word-like content editor we saw is WYSIWYG because our page looks the same in the editor as it does on the site. The fonts, formatting, colors, and alignments—all work consistently between the editing interface and the actual site.

Most CMSs come with a WYSIWYG editor. Such editors make it very easy for authors to add content and the formatting style that they like. These formatting options look and behave in a way similar to Microsoft Word or OpenOffice Writer. But the complexity of options provided may vary between CMSs.

The following image shows the WYSIWYG editor toolbars of Joomla! (top) and WordPress (bottom). As you see, WordPress offers a simpler editor, but with lesser options. An amateur user will find it easier to work with an editor with fewer choices. As a matter of fact, WordPress's editor toolbar shows only the first row of options by default. You can enable a second row by clicking on the last button in first row: **Show / Hide Kitchen Sink**. On the other hand, Joomla! comes ready with all options visible. This is useful for a professional who wants better control over content formatting.

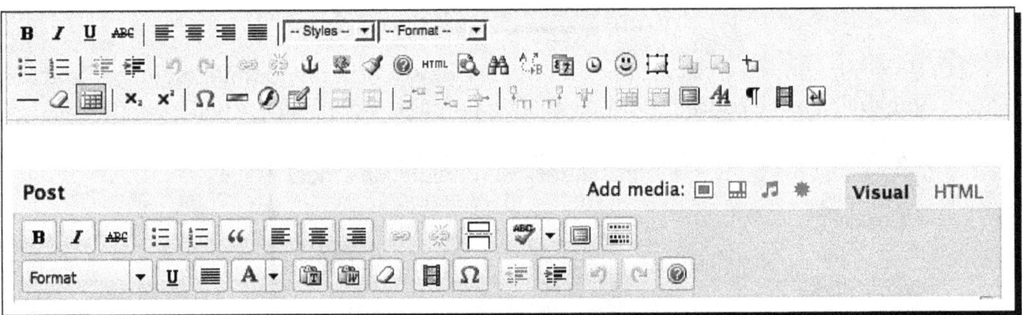

Evaluate how important is it for you to have a WYSIWYG editor. Also, see if the CMS comes with it by default, or you have to add it via a plug-in or extension. For example, Drupal does not have a WYSIWYG editor module by default; but you can easily add it via a module.

This also means some CMSs may not have a WYSIWYG editor. So, if there is no WYSIWYG editor, how do you add content? Well, if your content does not require a fancy format, you can live with simple textual content. Else, you can always use HTML.

Do I need to learn HTML?

HTML is the language to layout and format web site pages. If you know HTML, it will be easier to manage your CMS. If HTML is not an option, a WYSIWYG editor can be really helpful. Here are some links for learning the basics of HTML:

`http://www.html.net/tutorials/html/`

`http://www.w3schools.com/html/DEFAULT.asp`

Adding images

We have added the basic content to our page. Now, we will try to include some pictures in our page. Images add a lot of meaning to the content, apart from adding a decorative value. Let's add an image to our page now.

Time for action-adding images

1. If you are not already logged in to the Joomla! administration, log in now.
2. Click on **Site** in the main menu. That should open a submenu of site management options. Click on **Media Manager**.

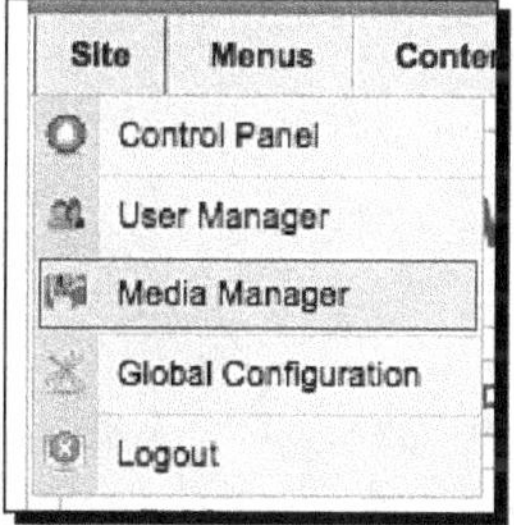

3. You will see previews of current images in Joomla!. Click on the **stories** folder to go into it. You will now see images within this folder.
4. Let's create a new folder here to store images of different asanas/postures. In the **Create Folder** text box near the top right side, type in **asanas** and click on the button.

5. This should create a new folder within **stories**. Click on it to move inside.

6. We can now upload an image here. Click within the text box of the **Upload File** section at the page end. This will bring up a dialog window to select a file you want to upload. We want to upload an image for Surya Namaskara. Select an image of your choice. Now click on the **Start Upload** button.

File uploading requires correct permissions on the server

To upload files to your site, you require correct permissions on your server. In technical terms, this is called making a folder **world-writable** or **changing mode to 777**. You can change folder permissions using an FTP application, or your site's control panel. Technically, it's sufficient to give a 666 permission—read-and-write permission to the owner, group, and others—but normally everyone gives a 777 permission, including execute permission for all three. Here's a screenshot of setting these permissions using FireFTP, an FTP extension for the Firefox browser.

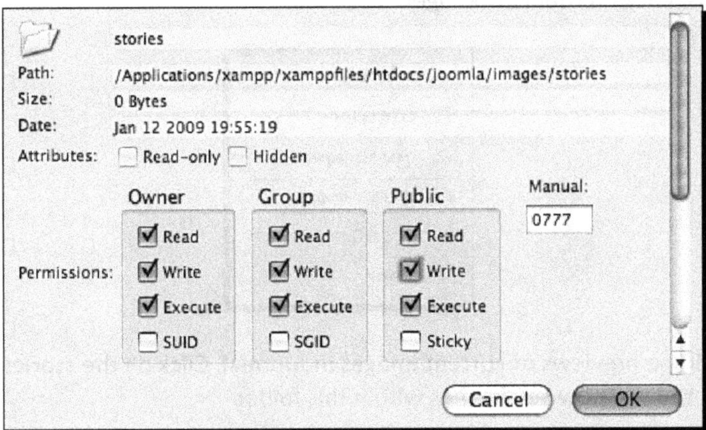

7. The file upload operation may take a few seconds to complete, depending on image size. Once the image is uploaded, you will see its thumbnail in the list. Upload more images if you want to.

8. Finally, your folder may look like this.

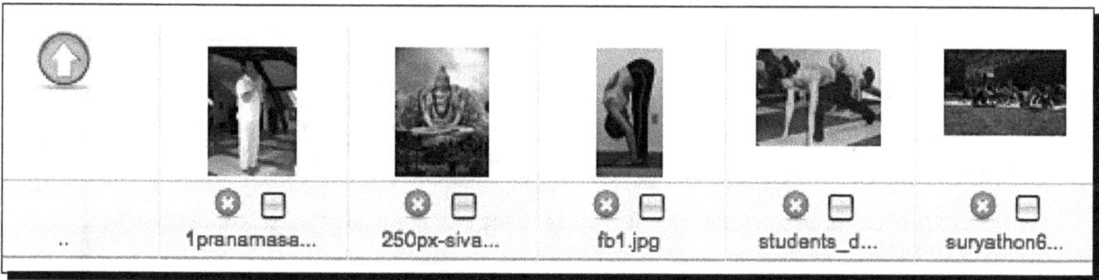

9. We are now ready to insert an image in our page. Select **Content | Article Manager** from the main menu. Click on the **Surya Namaskara** page to edit it. Inside our WYSIWYG editor, keep your cursor where you want to insert the image.

10. Click on the **Image** button below the WYSIWYG editor.

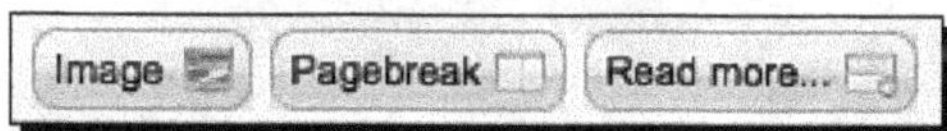

11. A window will open up with a thumbnail list of images available. Click on the **asanas** folder we created earlier.

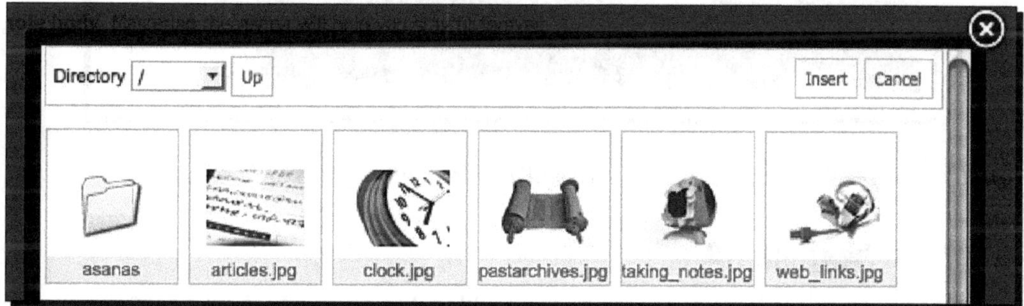

12. Click and select an image you want to insert. Add a description and title.

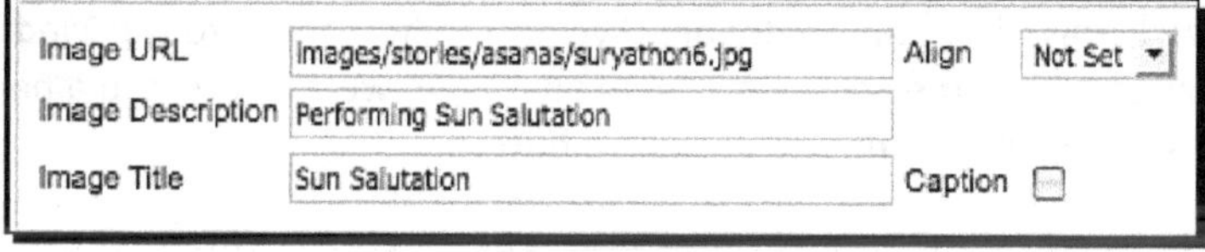

13. Click on the **Insert** button at the top right.

14. That will insert our image into the content area. Re-size it using the handles on the corners if you wish. Here's how it will look:

15. Congratulations! You have successfully added an image to our page.

What just happened?

We uploaded an image from our computer and added it to a page. In the process, we learned about the **Media Manager**, creating folders, and uploading files to Joomla!. We also learned how to select images to use on a page and even saw image insertion options.

Adding an image involved multiple activities. We had to first add it to the **Media Manager**. Because this was the first time we were adding an image, we also created a new folder. It was as simple as typing in a name and clicking a button.

We added images within folders since it will help us manage the images better. Once we add an image to the **Media Manager**, we can use that image on as many pages as we want. The **Image** button on the content editing screen allows us to select images to use on that page. It also helps us to add captions and correctly align inserted images with the text.

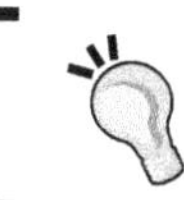

You can also upload images using that image selection window itself. We took the **Media Manager** route to learn more.

Have a go hero-image formatting options

We have learned enough about inserting images to content now. It is time we try out something else. Once you insert an image, click on it, and then click on the small photo icon in the WYSIWYG editor's toolbar. Go ahead and try out different image properties, different alignment options, spacing, caption, and alternative text. See how the result changes in the preview.

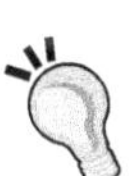

Don't let your images sink your site!

Make sure your images are optimized and sized for web usage. Avoid changing the width and height via image properties. If you want to show a smaller image than the one you uploaded, resize it using photo editing software and use that new version. Large images take longer to load and can make your site slow.

Have a go hero-adding a video

Our Yoga site may also require videos. Look around and find how a video can be added to the page.

Completed? Alright! We have now looked at how to edit a page and insert images/videos into it. Let's see the other options we have in editing and maintaining site content.

Maintaining content

Apart from editing text content and images, there are many other content maintenance activities we may have to do. We may need to assign categories to content, add metadata, and manage contributions. Let's quickly review how we can accomplish each of these tasks, and assess the CMS in that process.

Our Yoga site will have a lot of information about asanas. Apart from that information, we also want to put up yoga-related products. Hence, it is important for us that our site ranks well in search engines. When someone searches for a particular asana, we want our site to show up on the first page of search results. There are numerous techniques to achieve this, and this subject is known as **Search Engine Optimization** (**SEO**).

One of the techniques for SEO is having good page titles, meta tags, and relevant text. Let's start by adding some metadata to our page.

Time for action-adding metadata

1. Log in to Joomla! administration and edit the **Surya Namaskara** page we created earlier.
2. On the right bar, locate the **Metadata Information** tab.
3. Enter a description and some important keywords about this page.

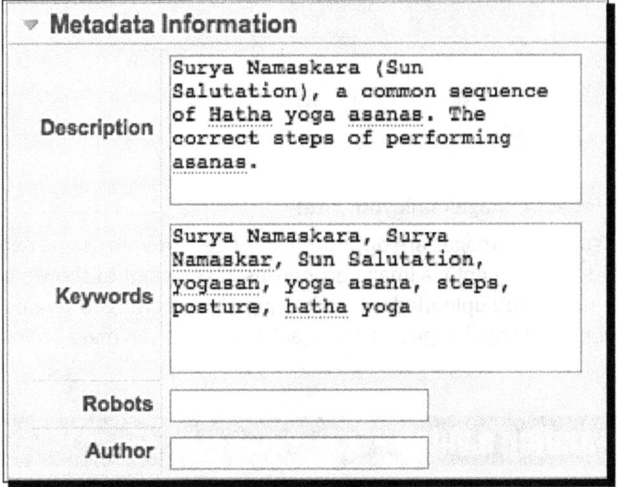

4. Let's also make the page title more descriptive. Instead of just calling it **Surya Namaskara**, change the title to **Surya Namaskara - Sun Salutation - Ideal way to perform this ideal Yogasana**.
5. Click on the **Save** button at the top right to save the page.
6. Joomla! sets some global metadata by default. Let's change that to our requirements. Go to the **Site | Global Configuration | Metadata Settings**.
7. Change the **Global Site Meta Description** and **Global Site Meta Keywords** fields. Values entered here will show on all pages of our site. Save the settings.

Note that the `configuration.php` file in the Joomla! installation root folder, should be writable for these changes to be saved. You will get an error message if it is not.

Metadata Settings

Global Site Meta Description	Yoga Site - the best resource for authentic information on yoga postures, asansa, products, teachers and event listings.
Global Site Meta Keywords	yoga, yogasan, asana, posture, authentic, indian, kerala, peace, relaxation, steps, products, yoga teachers, yoga events

8. Now, go to site **Preview** and navigate to the **Surya Namaskara** page. Right-click on the page and click on **View Source** to view the source code of the page. Near the start of the HTML source code, you may see something like the following image.

```
<head>
  <meta http-equiv="Content-Type" content="text/html; charset=utf-8" />
  <meta name="robots" content="index, follow" />
  <meta name="keywords" content="Surya Namaskara, Surya Namaskar, Sun
Salutation, yogasan, yoga asana, steps, posture, hatha yoga" />
  <meta name="title" content="Surya Namaskara - Sun Salutation - Ideal way to
perform this ideal Yogasana" />
  <meta name="description" content="Surya Namaskara (Sun Salutation), a
common sequence of Batha yoga asanas. The correct steps of performing
asanas." />
  <meta name="generator" content="Joomla! 1.5 - Open Source Content
Management" />
  <title>Surya Namaskara - Sun Salutation - Ideal way to perform this ideal
Yogasana</title>
```

9. It's the description and keywords we entered. If you go to another page where we haven't entered metadata earlier, you will see the global metadata. The search engines—and humans—should be able to understand our pages much better now. Job well done!

What just happened?

We set up site-wide and page-specific description and keywords. We also changed the page title to be more informative—something that could attract visitors to our site if they see it on the Google search results page.

Metadata embedded in a page is not visible to the users, but software can see it. So, you can use metadata to help search engines or other software that is going to read that page.

This metadata can also help in identifying content. **Description metadata** can be used to show a summary of the page in archives. If we have a site search engine, keywords can be searched to find a match for the user. As a matter of fact, some search engines (not Google) rely on metadata from title, keyword, and description tags along with the content body—giving more weight to metadata.

Some CMSs allow adding custom metadata. This is a great way to embed additional information. You can put in the author name, revision date, source of the content, licensing attributes, or anything else that you prefer. In our case, we can possibly use metadata to find products related to a posture.

Tagging is keywords on steroids!

You may have heard about "tagging" your content. Tagging essentially means associating some keywords to content. These keywords are searchable, and can be shown on a page. Clicking on one tag or keyword can show you a list of all other content items that belong to that tag. This concept originated on blogs and is now available in many CMSs. Adding tags even allows you to build beautiful tag clouds using font sizes in proportion to usage of tags in content.

Do you need more SEO?

If you need more Search Engine Optimization, enable Search Engine Friendly URLs on your site. This will include page title, category, or other such information directly in the URL. This is a simple and effective way to improve search engine rankings.

We saw how we can use metadata to help our search engine positions and to organize content. One more thing we will need often is to link one page to another. How do we do that?

Have a go hero-adding links

Linking one page to another is very important. Linking increases hits, and makes it easier to find relevant content on your site. Every CMS will allow adding links to the content. You typically do this by selecting a piece of text and clicking an anchor-like tag in a WYSIWYG editor. Look around and find out how you can do this with your favorite CMS.

Does the CMS allow linking internal content without using full URLs? Is it easy to manage related content? How easy will this be for content authors?

Allowing people to contribute

On our Yoga site, we will have multiple authors. Each will write some content. An editor will review this content, edit it as needed, and publish it to the site. We also want to make sure we have old versions of content. In case something wrong gets published, we can quickly revert to an earlier version. And of course, authors won't have access to site administration features.

Have a go hero-determine multiuser needs

Answer the following questions for your site to determine your needs to support multiple users:

1. Do you want to allow multiple authors to contribute content to your site?
2. Do you want to allow anyone to edit the site content? Wiki-based software will be best in such a case.
3. Do you want to assign different access rights to different users?
4. Do you want to keep different versions of content and compare between revisions?
5. Do you want to be able to revert/rollback to a previous version without actually editing the content?
6. Would you like your site users to add comments? Can any user add comments? Do you want users to register before adding comments?
7. If users can contribute content/comments, what will the approval process be?

Now check the CMSs you shortlisted to support these features. This can get critical because not all CMSs will support these features. A wiki supports ad hoc editing of the content, and is ideal for many-to-many communications. A blog is perfect for one-to-many communication, and to allow reader comments. Strike a balance between the CMS's features and your needs.

Understand tech skills of authors

If you are going to manage content yourself, you have to worry less about the technical skills of others. You can choose a CMS that you find comfortable. But if you have other people writing and editing content, make sure they don't get daunted by the complexity of the software. An author's job is to create and manage content, and not fiddle with nuances of a CMS. So, understand the technical skills of your authors and select a system they can use.

Summary

We went through a lot! From WYSIWYG editors to uploading images and adding meta tags, we have covered a lot of distance.

Specifically, we learned about:

- A WYSIWYG editor and using it to format our content; adding images to content, changing image properties
- Meta tags—how to add them, and how to use them
- Features to look for while working with multiple authors

In this whole process, we understood how easy (or difficult) it can be to use a CMS. A certain CMS may be very easy for you, but may prove complicated for someone else. We learned that we must keep our authors in mind while selecting the CMS.

Now that we've learned about maintaining content on our site, let us look at how to add missing features to our favorite CMS. Our next chapter is dedicated to extending a CMS with plug-ins. Let's extend!

6

Templates and Plug-ins

We have seen how to set up and use a content management system. We now know how to add text and image content, create content categories, and manage multiple authors. As a matter of fact, we have learned most of the basics of a CMS. What remains is to learn how to get a CMS to function to our liking. How can we add features that we need? How can we make our site look the way we want?

Let's discover that now. In this chapter we will:

- *Give a professional look to our site*
- *Add a photo gallery feature*
- *Learn how to add other such features*

To get something to work in the way that you want could be either easy or challenging, but always exciting. Let's start by giving a nice professional look to our Yoga Site.

Giving a professional look to our site

Oprah's Yoga Site does not look bad as it stands, but doesn't meet our expectations. An attractive design will entice visitors to continue reading. It will even establish the credibility of our business. How can we change the site's design? Do we have to hire a professional designing company to do it for us? Are there things that we can do? How do other people do it?

Using templates

Templates are design blueprints. A CMS takes a template and generates site pages from it. This unifies the graphical look of the entire site, since all pages are derived from a common template. Everyone customizes the graphical design of their site with a CMS template. We too can change our site's design just by changing its template.

We can hire a professional designer to create a template for us, but the Web is full of readymade templates—both free and paid—that we can use. Templates (sometimes called themes) are available for all major CMSs. A Google search for **free joomla templates** tells us that there are thousands of templates available for Joomla!.

The problem then is finding a good template. How do we find a good template for our Yoga Site? Let's get cracking!

Time for action-finding a good template

1. Open your favorite web browser and go to Google.
2. Search for **free joomla templates**. You may get results similar to the following image.

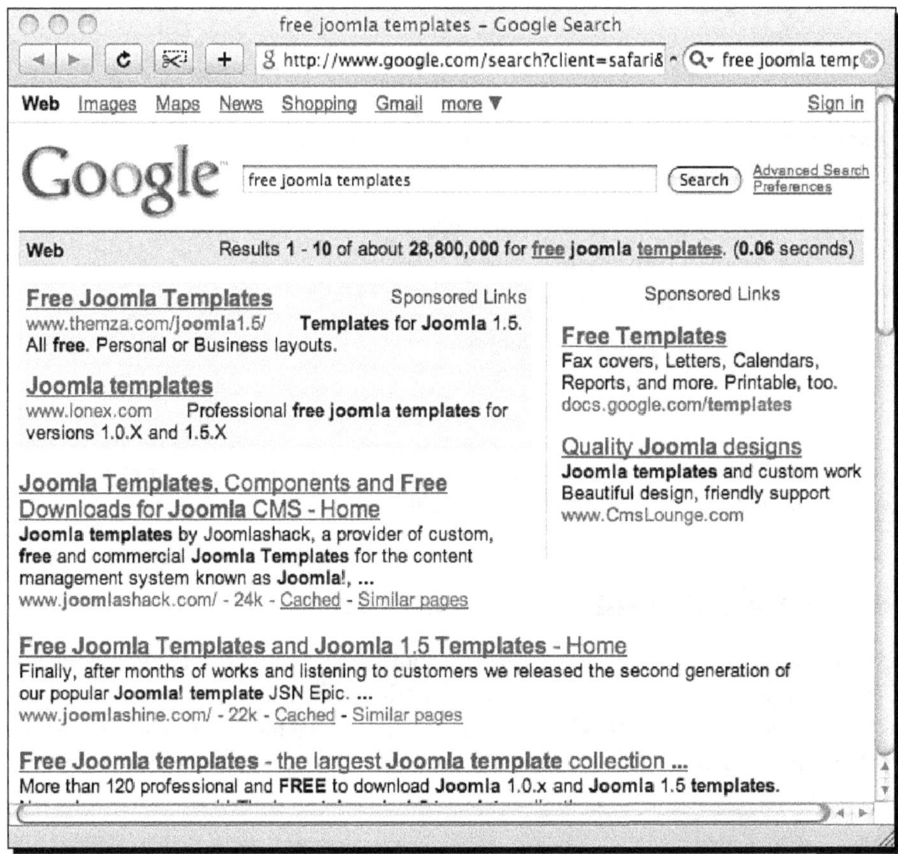

3. There are some sponsored results at the top and on the right-hand side of the page. Scan through the results. It looks like there are many interesting links that we can follow.

4. Let's check the site Joomla! Shack. Click on the result and it will take you to `www.joomlashack.com`. The web site shows that it provides both free and paid designs. The site's own design looks good. Let's click on the **Free Joomla Templates** link under the **Products** menu.

5. I am feeling lucky! The very first template looks interesting. Click on the **Live Demo** link to try it out.

6. Jamba is a good template. Its typography is crisp, the color scheme aligns with our site's purpose, and the overall content organization looks good. View a few other templates as well. Evaluate how they fit our needs.

7. Jamba is certainly a design we can use for our Yoga Site. Come back to the demo. In the righthand column there is a link to **Download the Jamba Template**. Let's go ahead and click on the **DOWNLOAD** button.

8. This brings us to a page with more information about this template. The actual download link is just below the **JambaLive Demo** link on this page. Click on it.

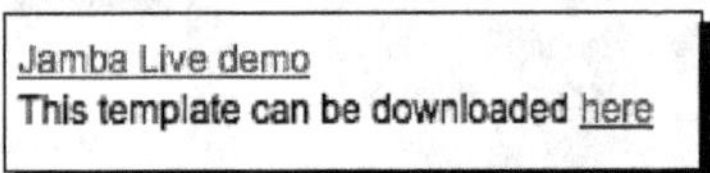

9. We are now on a page with download links for all free templates Joomla! Shack is offering. Click on the Jamba thumbnail to begin the download. If you prefer another template, you may download that as well.

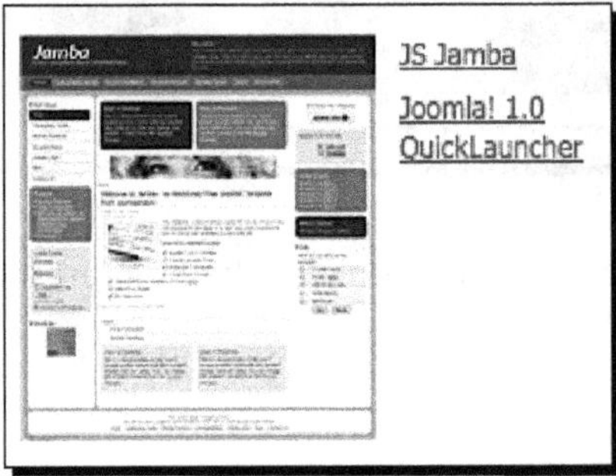

10. This will download a ZIP file package. Congratulations, we got a template we like!

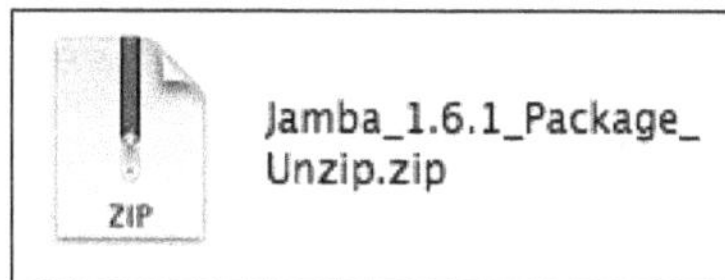

What just happened?

We searched Google for free Joomla! templates, reviewed a few templates, and downloaded the one that we liked the most. It was easy for us since we liked the first template we saw. There are lots of template sites, and not all designs are good. In fact, most templates just have a good header image and the rest of the page is a standard CMS design. Things can get boring if you have to keep looking at mediocre designs over and over.

How do you select a good template? Here are a few tips.

Template selection criteria

- Prefer designs that have readable text. Large headings, distinct colors, and enough whitespace make textual content readable.
- Select templates that follow a consistent design—alignment, matching colors, and an overall coordination between different screen elements.
- Always select standards-compliant templates. Look for templates that follow XHTML and CSS.
- Take a live demo of the template. Don't just go by how good a template's thumbnail looks.
- Go with simple yet attractive designs.

Applying these checks on thousands of templates can be daunting. So, it makes sense to start at a place where you will find good templates.

Where to find templates

Here are some sites to get started.

- Here is a site where you can get 10 free templates and 400+ commercial templates: `http://www.joomladesigns.co.uk`.
- For a complete list of Joomla templates, visit: `http://www.joomla.org/content/blogcategory/19/51/`.
- To access 1500+ templates, go to: `http://www.joomla24.com/`.

- ThemeBase—templates for major CMSs can be found at: `http://www.themesbase.com/`.
- Wordpress Themes Directory—`http://wordpress.org/extend/themes/`.
- For great Wordpress Themes, visit: `http://www.templatesbrowser.com/wordpress-themes/`.

Before using any CMS, do a few searches on Google before you narrow down. Sites that offer thumbnails and live demos are more useful. Some bloggers evaluate and post a list of their favorite templates. Review them first.

Have a go hero-shortlisting some more templates

Go ahead and try some other template sites. Review more templates and evaluate their suitability for your site. Check out paid templates too and see if they are worth their price.

At this stage we have downloaded the templates of our choice. How do we see them working in our site? We will need to install them using Joomla!—our CMS. Let's do that now.

Time for action-setting up a template

1. We have a `.zip` file of the Jamba template. Unzip it.
2. This results in two folders and one HTML file. These two folders show that the ZIP file actually contains two different versions of this template: one for Joomla version 1.0 and another for 1.5.

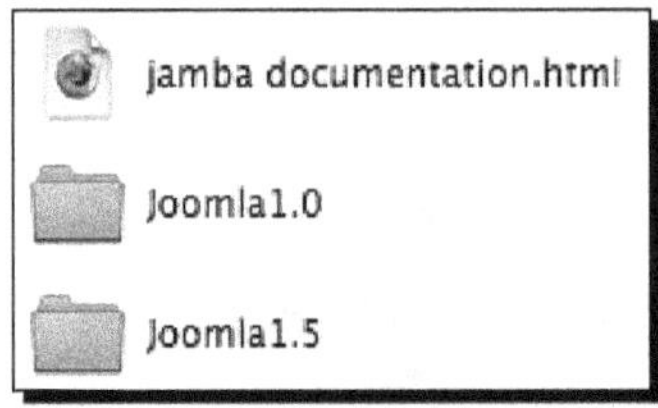

3. Let's find out which version of Joomla! do we have. Go to the Joomla! administration panel and look for the version number. If you have Joomla 1.5, it shows at the top right of the page. If you have version 1.0, it is shown in the page footer. For our installation, it shows like this.

Your version may be different

Joomla! (like other open source CMSs) is upgraded regularly. Your Joomla! version may be higher than 1.5.5. Your Jamba template may also be newer. If you do not find the exact links and options we describe here, look around for something similar. Basic functionalities will stay more or less the same across different versions of a CMS.

4. Select **Extensions | Install/Uninstall** from the main menu. This will show you an interface to upload and install a package.

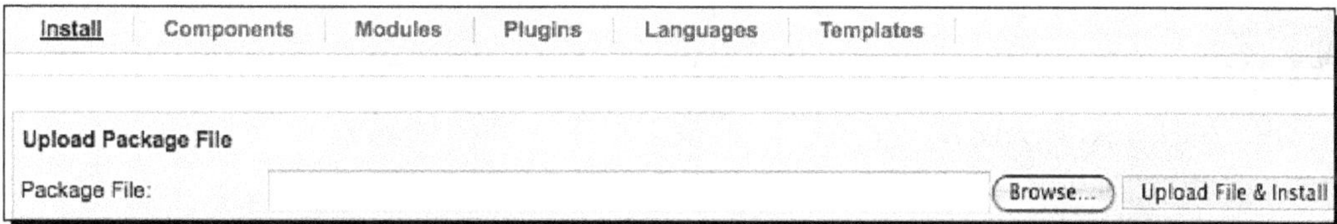

5. Click on the **Package File** field. Navigate to the folder where you unzipped the Jamba template, and pick up the `js_jamba.zip` file from the **Joomla1.5** folder, or a folder that corresponds to your version. Click on **Upload File & Install**.
6. If everything goes well, you will see a success message as shown here.

Do you have permissions?

A security mechanism that most operating systems have is restricting permissions on drives or folders. When you upload something from your browser, your server needs to save that file in a folder. If it cannot do that, you will get a **Permission Denied** error. Please ensure that folders that you want your CMS to save files into (and only those folders), have sufficient permissions. You should be able to manage this by right-clicking on a folder name and checking its properties. On the Mac/Linux command line, this can be done via the `chmod` command.

7. From the main menu, select **Extensions | Template Manager**. This will show you a list of installed templates. Our newly installed **js_jamba** template shows up on the list!

8. You could have another template set as default. We have **rhuk_milkyway** as the current default.

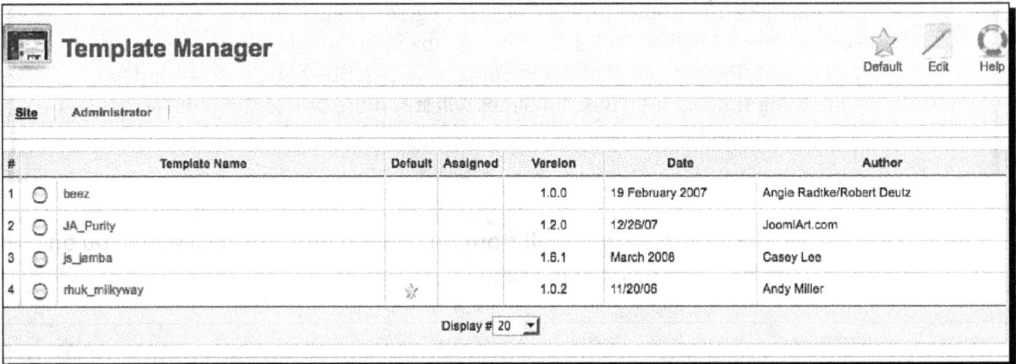

Template Manager

Default Edit Help

Site | Administrator

#		Template Name	Default	Assigned	Version	Date	Author
1	○	beez			1.0.0	19 February 2007	Angie Radtke/Robert Deutz
2	○	JA_Purity			1.2.0	12/26/07	JoomlArt.com
3	○	js_jamba			1.6.1	March 2008	Casey Lee
4	○	rhuk_milkyway	☆		1.0.2	11/20/06	Andy Miller

Display # 20

9. Click on the radio button near **js_jamba**. Click on the **Default** icon, which is at the upper right.

10. This will activate our new template. At this stage, your template listing may look like this.

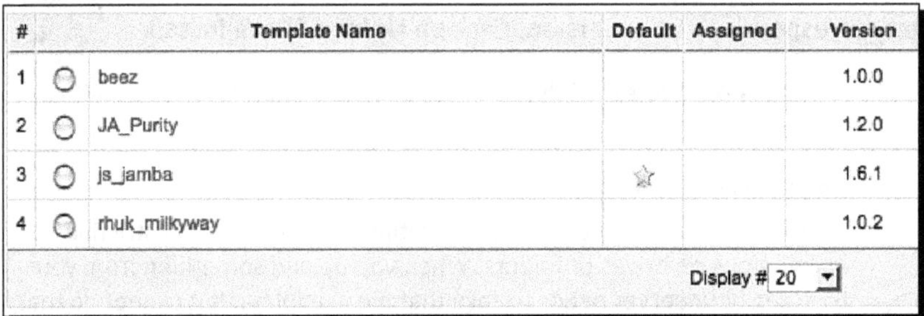

#		Template Name	Default	Assigned	Version
1	○	beez			1.0.0
2	○	JA_Purity			1.2.0
3	○	js_jamba	☆		1.6.1
4	○	rhuk_milkyway			1.0.2

Display # 20

11. We are now ready to see how our site looks with this new template. Click on the **Preview** link in the top right menu.

12. Voilà! The new design is live, and it indeed looks very good.

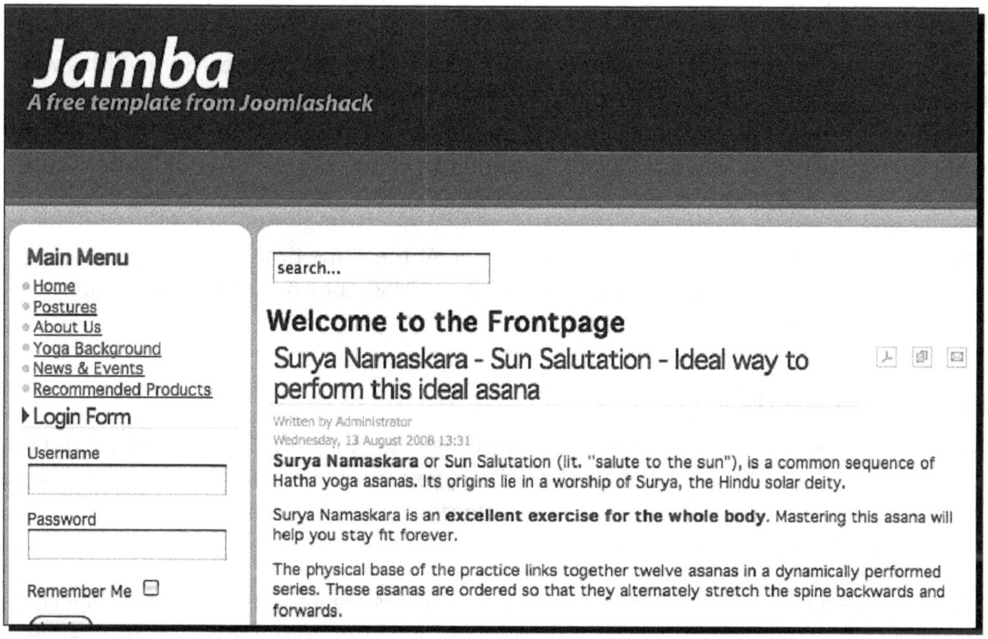

What just happened?

We installed a new template on our Joomla! site. We determined the Joomla! version we had, and used Joomla! package installer to upload the appropriate ZIP file of the Jamba template. Joomla! did the unzipping and installation on the server automatically. We then set the new template as default, which activates it, and we can see it live on our site via preview.

It's very easy to set up a new template with Joomla!. Download a ZIP file from a template site, upload it to Joomla!, and you are done. You can make a template default, and it will be used for the whole site. Or, you can assign specific sections that will use a template.

You can set up as many templates as you like, and can easily switch back and forth to understand which one will work best for your needs.

It's also important to understand that a template may not look exactly like what you saw in the live demo. This is because a live demo has different content. It may also have had different modules configured. You can go to the **Module Manager** menu option and manage active modules. For any customizations to a template, refer to its documentation.

This was all about Joomla templates. How about other CMSs? Do they have a similar system?

Different CMSs have different templates

Some CMSs call these designs **templates**, while others call them **themes**. Some CMSs will allow you to upload a zipped package of a template (like Joomla!). Some will need you to unzip those files and upload them in a particular folder (such as Wordpress). There will also be a system to select an active template, and you can apply your own customizations to a template if you want.

Templates for one CMS will not work with another. At the same time, many popular templates of one system have been ported to other CMSs. Look around template sites and you will find a lot of useful information.

Free, paid, or custom

If you want a unique design for your site, you will have to get it custom-designed. If you are looking for higher quality, less common templates, you can go for paid templates. If you are OK with common yet good designs, and can squeeze in a few customizations of your own, you can be happy with free templates.

Unless you are running a blog (where common templates are a norm), you want a specific look for your site. Dig around the template a bit and modify it to suit your needs. Change colors, positioning, and font styling—and you can create a new design for yourself.

Paid designs come with source files (Photoshop, or Illustrator, or Flash, and so on), so you can do whatever modifications you want with them. There are even subscription-based sites that allow you to download as many paid templates as you want, for a small fee.

Consider your needs and limitations, and go for one of these options. You can always change the template later on.

Have a go hero-setting up a template in your favorite CMS

We saw how to add a template in Joomla!. If Joomla! is not a CMS you are planning to use, go ahead and try setting up a template in your favorite CMS. Search on the CMS's site for a list of available templates and Google them. Download a few templates and try them out with your CMS. See how it goes and keep a note of what you learn along the way.

At this stage, we have learned enough about giving a professional look to our site with templates. Now is the time to add a photo gallery feature. Are you ready?

Enhancing functionality with plug-ins

You can expect a CMS to be good at managing content, but it is not fair to expect it to do e-commerce and run mailing lists. However, these are both valid needs for a web site. If we can easily add or remove features to or from a CMS, it will allow us to build a site to suit our needs. Plug-ins do just this.

Plug-ins, or modules, or extensions

Plug-ins are ready additions to an existing CMS that extend the core CMS functionality. They may be called by different names such as plug-ins, modules, components, extensions, or anything else. They add features to the out-the-box CMS features.

The most popular CMSs have an extensible architecture. Developers can create a new plug-in for a CMS by adhering to a defined guideline. The number of plug-ins available for a CMS is an indicator of its popularity. It also indicates the different uses that CMS may have been put to.

The plug-ins that you need

Recall the **Additional feature requirements** we created in Chapter 3. These additional features are not always a part of the core CMS. So that list shows you the kind of plug-ins you may need for your site.

One of the things that we want for our Yoga Site is to be able to show a collection of photographs. Each Yoga posture has a set of steps. We now want to demonstrate these steps via photographs and videos. A nice photo gallery plug-in will make it easier for us to manage these photographs.

Let's go ahead and find a photo gallery plug-in.

Time for action-finding a photo gallery plug-in

1. Go to the Joomla! Extensions Directory at `http://extensions.joomla.org/`.
2. You will see that there are lots of categories and thousands of extensions.

3. One way to find a good extension is to rely on collective intelligence—if an extension has been downloaded several times and has better ratings, it may suit your needs as well.
4. Locate the **Photo Gallery** category and click on it.

5. This shows you a list of extensions. Read through the descriptions and votes, and learn which extension could be a good choice. We chose **MorfeoShow**—It has a cute little elephant icon! MorfeoShow has a good rating and a number of reviews. It seems like a good choice for our needs.

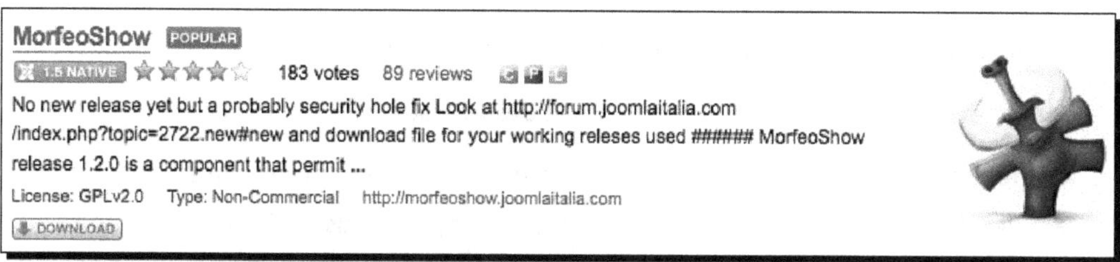

6. Click on the **Download** link.

7. This takes us to the MorefeoShow home page. It has a few demos of its gallery system, and they look good. It has a good collection of display options, which will be handy for us.

8. Look at the lefthand bar. Locate the **Download** button and click on it to download.

9. Save the downloaded ZIP file in a folder of your choice. We have found ourselves a nice photo gallery.

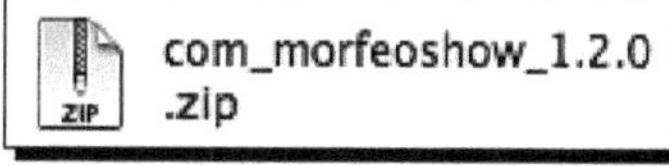

What just happened?

We went to the Joomla! extensions directory and located the **Photo Gallery** category. We got a list of all the extensions that would allow us to show photographs on our site. We liked the MorfeoShow plug-in, reviewed its examples, and downloaded it.

We did this by looking at the reviews and ratings of each extension. The higher the reviews and better the rating, the better the chance of that plug-in being good. It essentially means that a lot of people have tried out that plug-in and found it to be suitable to their needs. The rule of collective intelligence applies here. What works for others will most probably work for us, too.

So, it's not just the cute elephant that made us select the plug-in!

Here are a few things you should consider while evaluating a plug-in:

- Take a demo. Make sure the plug-in demonstrates the features you are looking for.
- Review the number of downloads and ratings by other users. There may also be detailed reviews by other users. Go through them to understand the pros and cons of a plug-in.
- Check the compatibility of a plug-in with the version of your CMS. They may not always match.
- If you can, check out the frequency of updates for a plug-in. One that's updated regularly is better.
- Rather than looking at more features, look at features you really need. Pick the one that solves your problems the best!
- Check the system requirements of a plug-in. Some plug-ins may need specific server settings or libraries to work.

Most CMSs have a list of available plug-ins on their site. Some even have sites dedicated to plug-ins. You should be able to find a plug-in for your need from there. If you don't find it there, check again in some other category. Do a search.

If you still don't find it, Google it.

If you still don't find it, it's time to hire a professional to write it.

That's a lot about finding a plug-in of your choice. But how would we install it to our CMS? Is that going to be easy? What's your guess?

OK, let's try it out.

Time for action-showing a photo gallery on our site

1. Go to the **Extensions | Install/Uninstall** menu. Select the MorfeoShow ZIP file we downloaded, and upload and install it like we installed our template. You will see a success message, as in the following figure.

Once again, you need write permissions on the components folder (and a few others depending on the plug-in). If you don't have proper permissions, you will get error messages about it. Apply the correct permissions and these problems will go away.

2. Click on **Continue**.
3. This brings us to the Morfeo management screen. Click on the **New** icon to create a new gallery.
4. Enter **Surya Namaskara – Steps** in the **Title** field. Select **Polaroid Flash** for the **Gallery Format** option. Enter a **Short Description**. You can also upload a thumbnail image for the gallery from here.

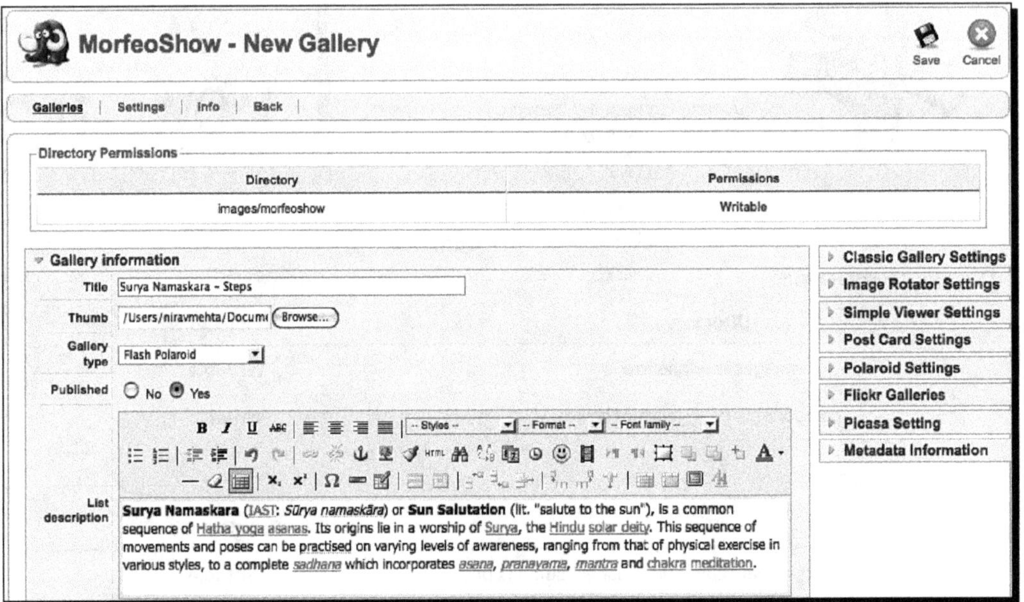

The gallery extension requires GD support in PHP. Similarly other extensions may require certain PHP settings or libraries. Please ensure your server meets the minimum system requirements for these extensions before installing them.

5. Click on **Save**.
6. This creates a new photo gallery. Now we will to add some images to it.
7. Click on the upward-pointing arrow next to our gallery's name in the **Images** column.

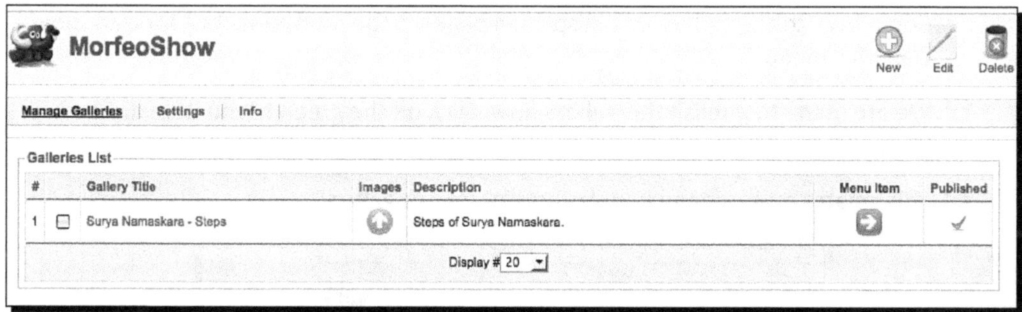

8. This brings us to a screen where we can upload an image. Select the first image. For us, it's a photo of Pranamasana—the first step in Surya Namaskara. Add a short description and title for this image. Click on the large **Save Image** button.

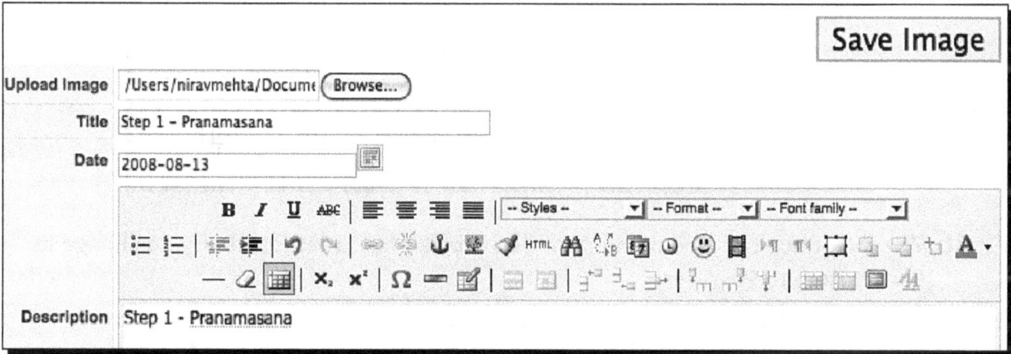

9. Add as many images as you like in a similar fashion.

10. We can see a list of uploaded images near the end of the page. Notice that it orders images by file names. So we must name our files correctly before uploading them. For now, we are OK with the current order.

11. Come back to the gallery administration page via the **Components | MorfeoShow | Galleries** menu.

12. We are ready to publish this gallery now. Click on the green **Menu Item** arrow for this gallery.

13. This creates a new menu item in Joomla! for our gallery.

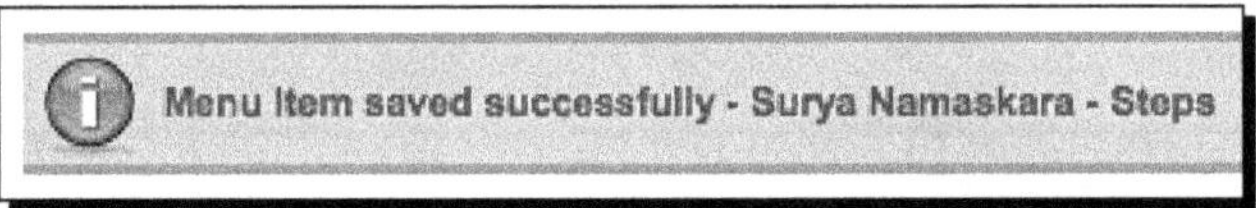

14. We now need to edit the newly created menu item and place it in a menu we want.

15. Go to **Menus | Menu Manager**, and click on the **Menu Items** icon for the **Main Menu**.

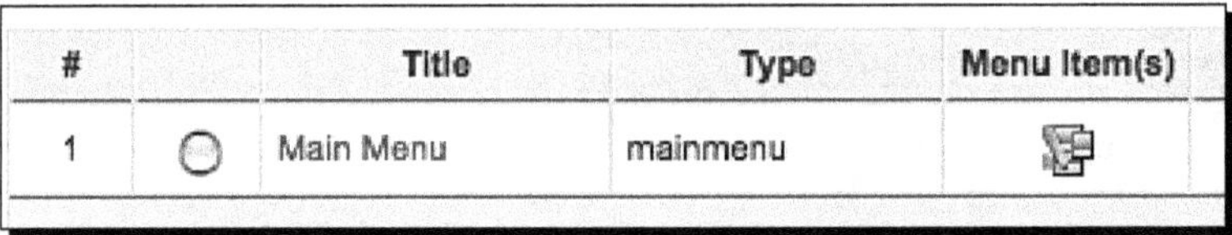

16. You will notice the new menu item that Morfeo has created. Edit it and change its **Parent item** to **Postures**.

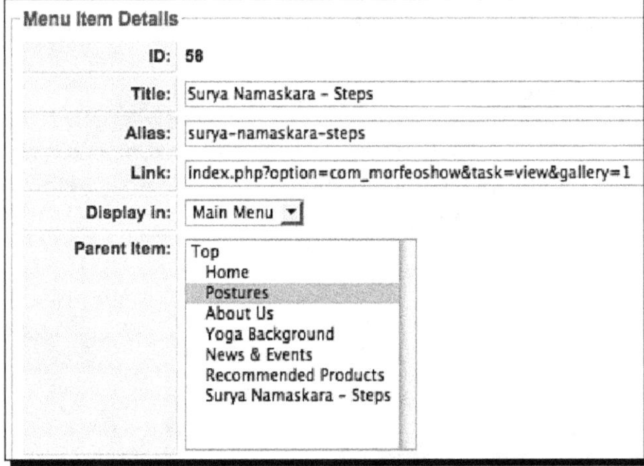

17. We are now ready! Click on the **Preview** link in the top bar. Then, click on the **Postures** link in the **Main Menu**, and then on **Surya Namaskara—Steps**.

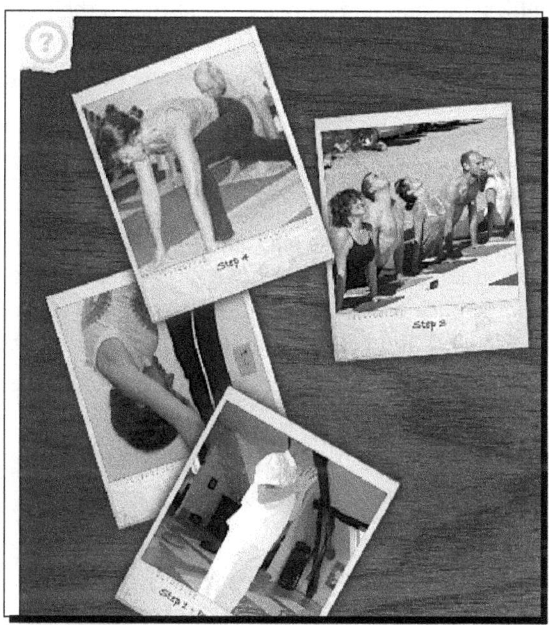

18. Wow! That's a great gallery, isn't it? Congratulations on successfully setting up your first plug-in!

What just happened?

We installed a photo gallery plug-in to Joomla!. We created a new photo gallery and then added images in it. To make this gallery viewable from our site, we created a new menu item for it and placed it at an appropriate place in our site's menu structure. That made our gallery live.

The installation procedure was similar to adding a template. Also, the procedure for adding a new gallery was similar to adding a new content item. The things that we had to do differently were adding images and using a menu item to display the gallery—But that would be something that we would have to do while setting up any kind of a photo gallery.

The plug-in worked with default settings. We could customize these settings if needed. We could also try different gallery formats and see which best suited our need.

One thing to note is that each plug-in will have its limitations. For example: How would we embed a Morfeo gallery into another content page? It's easier to add our content to a Morfeo gallery page than to add a Morfeo gallery to our content page!

No coding required

We didn't have to write any code to get this plug-in to work. Some plug-ins may need you to modify some source files and add a few lines of code to see their effect. This will depend a lot on your CMS. Learn how plug-ins work with your CMS. If you are not comfortable with coding, you should stick to a CMS that does not require any coding to install, remove, and manage plug-ins.

Uninstalling a plug-in

Removing a plug-in is a very simple process in most CMSs. Just go to the plug-in manager page, and click on **Delete**, or **Deactivate**, or **Remove**. In Joomla!, we can go to the **Extensions | Install/Uninstall** menu and click on **Components** to get a list of installed components. We can now select a component and click on **Uninstall** to remove it from the system.

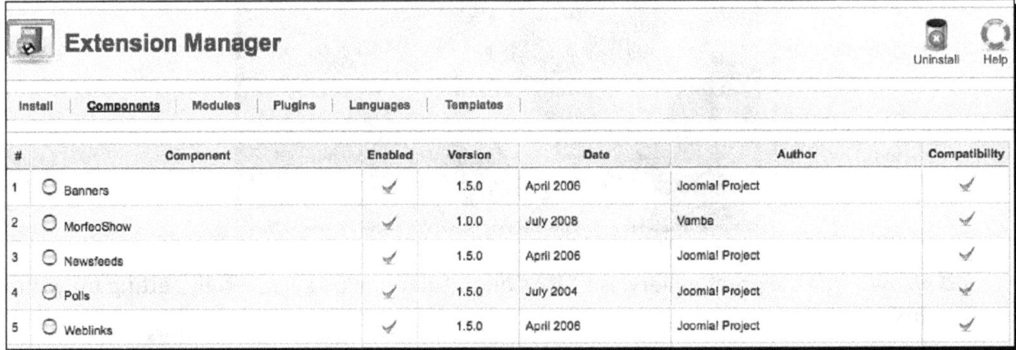

So far, we have learned a lot about plug-ins. How about going ahead and trying out something on your own now?

Have a go hero-set up an e-commerce extension

Find an e-commerce plug-in for your favorite CMS and set it up. Add a few products and configure options, and see how it integrates with the rest of your site!

But if e-commerce is not something you intend to do on your site, go ahead and set up a plug-in of your choice.

Summary

In this chapter we saw our site transform! From a simple and basic look, we gave it a professional and trendy look.

Specifically, we learned about:

- Templates and how they are used to change the look of your site
- Finding and installing a template
- Understanding plug-ins and their needs
- Finding and installing a plug-in
- Using a plug-in to add a feature to our site

We also looked at key factors that we should consider while selecting a template or plug-in. In the process, we learned how a CMS in general, and Joomla! in particular, uses templates and plug-ins to extend its functionality.

We learned a lot about templates and plug-ins, and now it's time to dig deeper into them and see how we can fix some annoyances. Did you notice the Jamba logo in the template? How can we get rid of it and put in our own logo? Time to get down and dirty! Let's get to those details in the next chapter.

7
Extending and Customizing

We installed a new design and a few plug-ins to our CMS in the last chapter. That took us to a new level in using a CMS. Plug-ins and templates open up a plethora of opportunities for enhancing the functionality of the core CMS. But in some cases, we may need to further customize a template or a plug-in to suit our needs. Or we may have to develop one on our own. How do we do this?

Let's understand the basics of extending and customizing our CMS. In this chapter we will:

- *Change the logo in template design*
- *Evaluate documentation and support*
- *Find a specialist to perform additional customizations*

Making enhancements to an existing plug-in will save us a lot of development time. We will also do the same thing for a template. There may be an initial learning curve, but that will save a lot of time while moving forward. Let's get started by customizing our template.

Customize a template

One thing we need to change on the new template that we installed is our logo. It still shows the Jamba template logo. The other thing we want to change is the left menu design. Currently it just shows the menu in bulleted links. We want to make this look better.

Let us try adding a logo of our own and also background colors for the bullet links in the left menu.

Fixing the site logo

The logo is the first thing people notice on a site. And we are still carrying the Jamba logo. It's time we replace that with a new Yoga Site logo. Let's see how we can do that with Joomla!.

Time for action-replacing the default logo in our template

1. Log in to the Joomla! Administration section. Now go to **Template Manager** via the **Extensions** menu.
2. You will see a list of templates on the lefthand side. We want to edit the **js_jamba** template. Click on its name.

3. This brings you to template parameters and the information screen. You will see the **Details** of this template on left side and the **Parameters** on the right side. We can see that it can display the header either as a graphic or as text. We can also change the headline text and slogan text from here. The last parameter is for the **Theme color** style. Jamba comes with multiple color combinations and we can pick a style from here.

4. For now, select **Text** in **Header Style**. Enter **Yoga Site** in **Headline Text**, and **Your wellness resource** in **Slogan Text**. Keep **Style 1** as **Theme Color**. Click on the **Apply** button near the top.

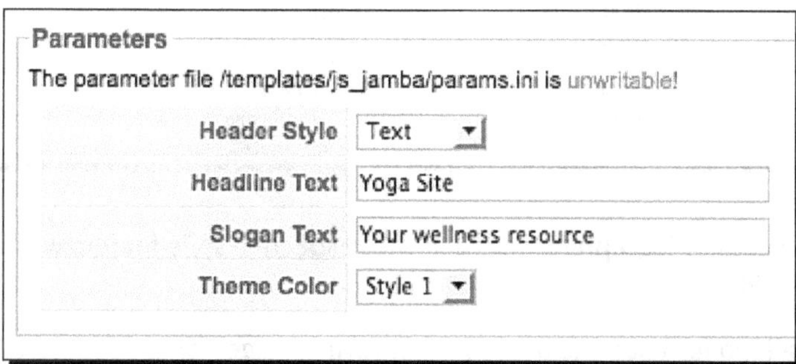

> You need write permissions on the `templates/js_jamba/params.ini` file. You will see a notification about it right above all parameters. Change it to `Chmod 777` to make it writable. You can change it back to `644` once you are done.

5. Our changes are saved.

6. Click on the **Preview** link (either the button in template's action bar or the topmost menu bar). Success! The site now shows our name.

7. We can go ahead and change the logo now. To understand the file structure of the template, extract the original template ZIP file on your hard disk. It has a structure like this.

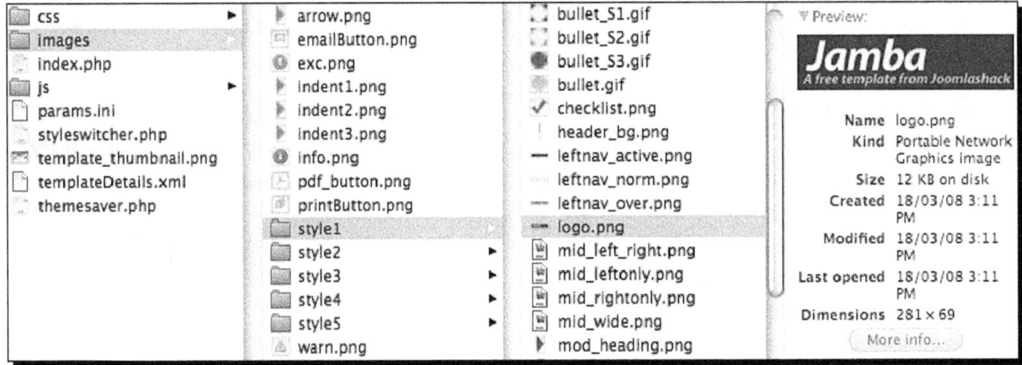

8. We can see that **logo.png** is saved in the respective style folders within the **images** folder.

9. Create a logo for your site using your favorite image editing software. We have created a logo using the Jamba logo itself—keeping same height and width.

10. Replace the default `logo.png` with your logo. If you have set up the installation on your local machine, you can simply replace it using your file browser. Otherwise, you will have to upload it to your server using an FTP program. Make sure you save it in the correct folder, for example `templates/js_jamba/images/style1/`.

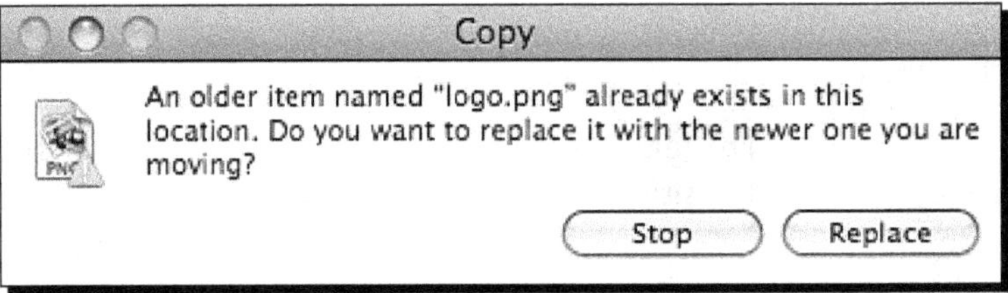

11. Come back to **Template Manager** in Joomla! Administration. Click on **js_jamba** to edit it. Change the **Header Style** to **Graphic**. Click on **Apply**.

12. Preview the site. If all went well, you will see your new logo on the site. Notice that the font style has changed. It's no longer text, but the new image we created.

What just happened?

The Yoga Site now shows up its own logo. We did a lot of things to reach this stage, though. First, we saw the template editing screen. Since Joomla! allows changing important parameters for a template within the administration section, it was easy for us to try out a text header. We could simply edit the headline text and slogan, set the header style to text, and preview how it looks.

This was non-technical. We did not need to fiddle with code for this. The only technical thing in the process was making sure that the `params.ini` file was writable.

With a textual header in place, we went on to add a graphical header. This required that we figure out the location of the logo's image file. We learned that the HTML, CSS, and images for a template are stored in the `templates` folder. Each template has its own folder within `templates`, and may have subfolders as it needs. Jamba had subfolders for different styles. We created a new logo file and replaced the original file with it in the `style1` folder. By flipping back the header style to graphic, we could see our new logo.

Changing the site color

Jamba comes with a couple of color options. We could have picked up a style from a dropdown to change the site color. We did not try this in our practice, but you can try it yourself.

This works because picking up a different style loads another CSS file. This CSS file controls colors and other graphical elements for the site. Style-specific images are also stored in individual image folders. This makes it easy to customize the design in whichever way we like.

Let's see how we can change the left menu now. It currently shows up as a bulleted list. We want to make it look better.

Changing the menu style

Menu styling is done internally in templates. The template editing interface in Joomla! does not provide any parameters to change the menu's look. This means we need to change some code to customize the menu design.

We are not happy with the current bulleted list of menu items. It would look much better if each menu item stands out, without bullets and with more spacing between each item. It will be great if we can highlight an item when the mouse moves cursor over it, thus, letting users know it's an actionable item.

Let's examine what we need to change to get such a look.

Time for action-advancing customization via CSS changes

1. Open the site in a browser. Using your browser menus, view the HTML source for this page. Locate the HTML code for the left menu. You can do this quickly by searching for `Main Menu` in the source code. It looks like this in our case.

```
<h3>Main Menu</h3>

<ul class="menu"><li id="current" class="active item1"><a href="http://localhost
/joomla/"><span>Home</span></a></li><li class="parent item53"><a href="/joomla
/index.php?option=com_content&amp;view=section&amp;id=5&amp;Itemid=53">
<span>Postures</span></a></li><li class="item54"><a href="/joomla
/index.php?option=com_content&amp;view=section&amp;id=6&amp;Itemid=54">
<span>About Us</span></a></li><li class="item55"><a href="/joomla
/index.php?option=com_content&amp;view=section&amp;id=7&amp;Itemid=55"><span>Yoga
Background</span></a></li><li class="item56"><a href="/joomla
```

2. We can see that this is all HTML and CSS. The menu is generated using the `<ul>` and `<li>` tags. The formatting is done via `menu`, `active`, and `item` CSS classes. This means if we edit the CSS file, we can change its appearance.

3. In the same HTML source view, go to near the top. Locate lines pointing to the CSS files. Our code shows these four templates used by the Jamba template. Looking at the names, we can guess that we will need to change either the `nav.css` or the `style1.css` file.

```
<link href="/joomla/templates/js_jamba/css/template_css.css" rel="stylesheet"
type="text/css" media="screen" />
<link href="/joomla/templates/js_jamba/css/nav.css" rel="stylesheet"
type="text/css" media="screen" />
<link href="/joomla/templates/js_jamba/css/style1.css" rel="stylesheet"
type="text/css" media="screen" />
<link href="/joomla/templates/js_jamba/css/j15.css" rel="stylesheet"
type="text/css" media="screen" />
```

4. Go to Joomla! Administration. Come to the template editing screen for **js_jamba**. This will show a toolbar like following image.

5. Click on **Edit CSS**.

6. Select the **nav.css** file and click on the **Edit** button. Go through the CSS code. It does not seem to contain any styling information for the left menu.

7. Go back and select the **style1.css** file, and **Edit** it.

8. Near the end of that file, we see some styling information for the left column. It does not contain the exact styles that we want. But this seems like the right place to put in our own definitions.

```
div#navmenu li.active a {
        background: url(../images/style1/nav_active_r.png) no-repeat bottom right;
        color: #FFF;
}

/* @end */


/* @group Left Nav */

#leftcol ul#mainlevel,#rightcol ul#mainlevel,
#leftcol ul#mainlevel-sidenav,#rightcol ul#mainlevel-sidenav {
        list-style: none;
}
```

9. We are editing the CSS for `Style 1`. The `images` folder for this style already contains three images that we can use as background for the left menu: a normal state, a hover state (when the mouse cursor is hovering over an item), and an active state (when an item is clicked). Let's add the CSS to add background images to the left menu in `style1.css`, just above the other left column styles.

```
/* @group Left Nav */

ul.menu li {
        padding: 5px 10px 10px 5px;
        background: url(../images/style1/leftnav_norm.png) no-repeat;
}
ul.menu li:hover, ul.menu li.iehover {
        background: url(../images/style1/leftnav_over.png) no-repeat;
}
ul.menu li.active{
        background: url(../images/style1/leftnav_active.png) no-repeat;
}
```

10. The CSS that we added simply defines background images for the three states. This should be sufficient for now. Click on **Save** to save the CSS.

11. Let's preview the site now to see how it looks.

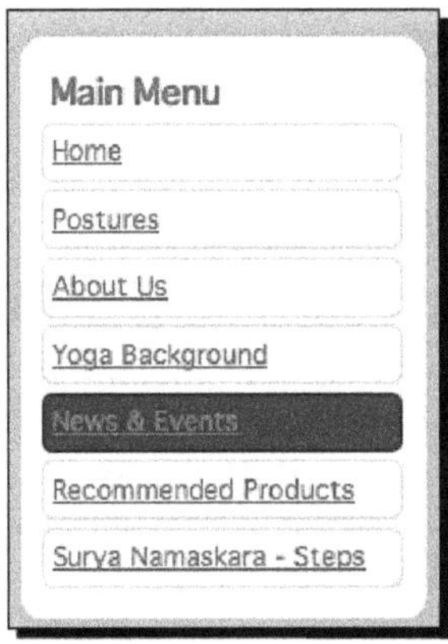

12. Wow! It looks beautiful! Our left menu has a completely different—and a much better—look.

What just happened?

We found and edited a CSS file to change the appearance of the left menu. We first looked at the HTML source code to understand how the menu was formatted. If it was using the `<table>` tag or some other HTML code to create the menu, we would have had to go to the template's PHP code and change its formatting. Thankfully, our template uses a CSS. **CSS** (**Cascading Style Sheet**) unifies styling information and simplifies the process to change the entire site's appearance.

We then located the CSS files used in our template via the HTML source. We went in to edit the CSS and added new styles for the `<li>` tag, which has the `menu` class. We also added styles for active and hover states.

We can **Apply** or **Save** changes and preview until we get it right. We can also add our own images, and any other formatting we want, through this CSS file.

Have a go hero-fixing submenus

The change we made is not yet perfect. If a menu has a submenu within, our design breaks. This is a good lesson. The changes we make to a CMS may affect some other features as well. So, it's always wise to test thoroughly after making changes. It's a bad practice to make changes on a live or production site.

Go ahead and fix this. You could try margin or padding properties in the CSS to start.

Customizations may need code changes

You did not have to edit any code to replace the site logo. But some customizations may need you to edit a CSS, an HTML file, or actual CMS source code. In such cases, it i s important to understand the programming language and architecture of your CMS.

What is a programming language? Is it easy?

When you select a CMS, make sure that you understand the programming language it uses. Open source CMSs are written in a variety of languages. A majority of them use PHP. PHP is easy to learn and you will find lots of PHP experts if you need customizations beyond your skills. Ruby and Python experts would be hard to find. Although Java and .Net experts are plentiful, there are not many open source CMSs written in Java and for .Net.

If you need professional support in setting up or running your CMS, it is wise to stick with a PHP-based CMS. Consider other languages only if you have a technology constraint, or experts to help.

If you are going to manage the CMS yourself, make sure you pick up something that you are comfortable with. If you have worked with .Net all along, it is wise to pick up a .Net CMS.

That brings us to the code. If you understand programming, it's a great time to take a peek inside the CMS.

Understanding the code architecture

If you want major customizations to a CMS, you must understand its architecture. If you want to add an extension, you will need to grasp the API and coding standards. A quick look at folder structure can tell you whether the CMS code is well-organized or not. If the folder or file names look inconsistent or illogical, stay away from that CMS. If you can glance through the code and understand what's going on, it's a big plus.

Take a look at the screenshot below. It shows the folder structure of Joomla! on the left, and a code sample on the right. Things look logical overall, and seem to follow a good coding standard. This is a good sign.

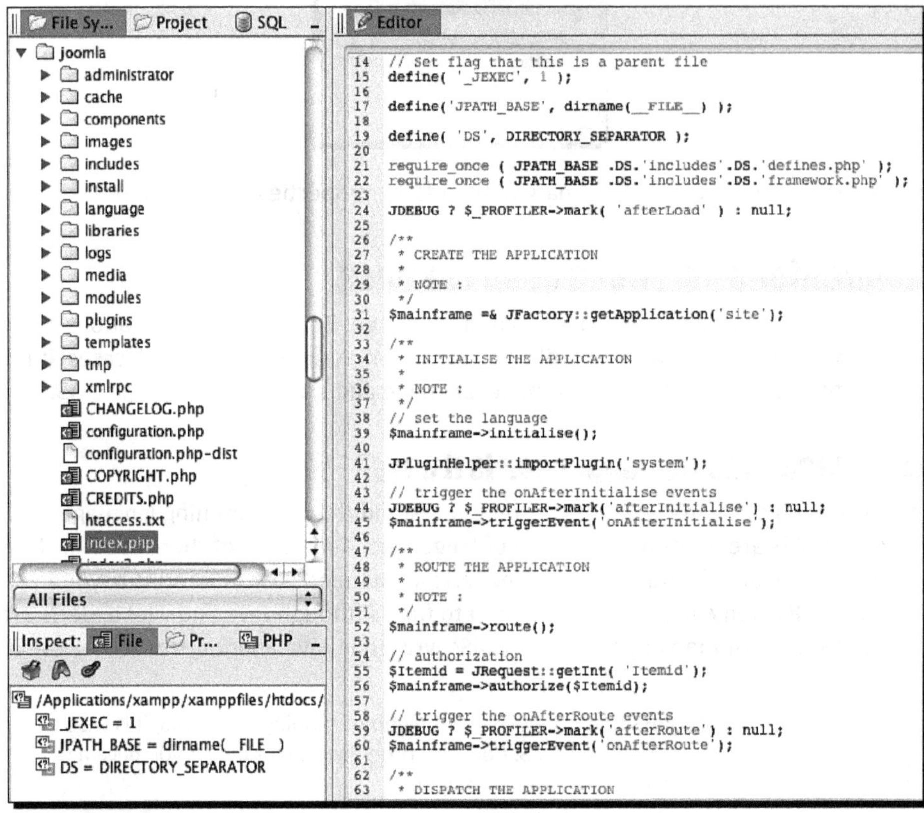

The following are a few items you should check while evaluating a CMS's architecture:

- Does the folder structure seem logical?
- Are the file names logical and consistent?
- Does the CMS follow a strict and understandable coding standard?
- Are the function names and class names understandable? Can you make out what they do just by glancing through the code?
- Can you guess how to make a change you need to make? Or where to make it?
- Does the database structure seem logical?

Once you have taken a look at code structure, you should also evaluate the documentation and the support available. What will you do if you get stuck adding that cool new feature you want?

Understanding the level of support

How can you learn more about a CMS? Are the internals documented? Does it have well-written documentation for both users and developers? Go to the CMS's site and look around for documentation. Evaluate what you see—don't just make a quick scan.

The following screenshot shows a page in the developer documentation of Joomla!. This wiki page describes **Joomla! Framework**. Read through and see if it makes sense to you.

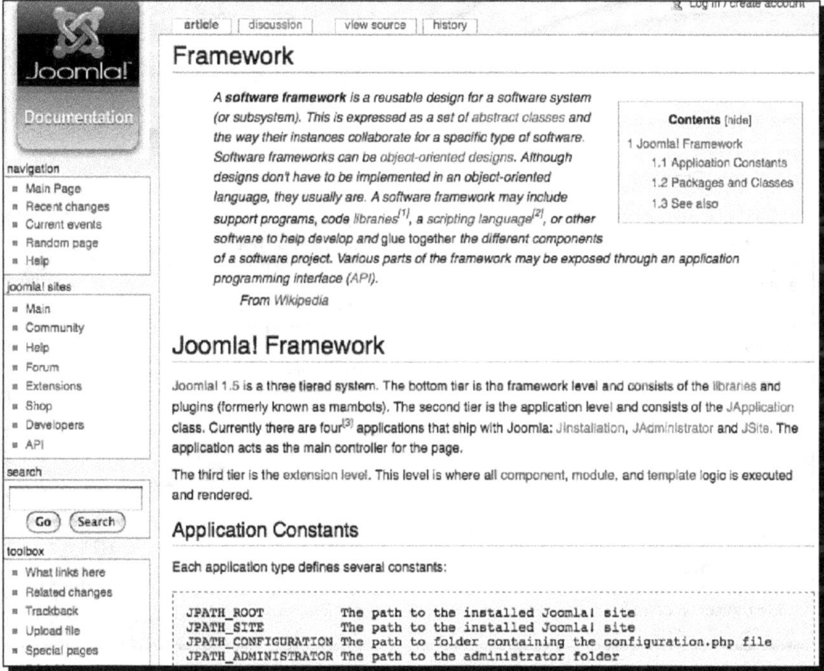

The top CMSs will have a variety of user documentation available. They may have articles and guides grouped by subject. There will also be community forums and mailing lists that can answer your most common questions.

Drupal (another top CMS) has very good handbooks on varying topics—from theme customization to API guides.

Wordpress (the most popular blog engine) has lessons that are easy to follow even for novice users.

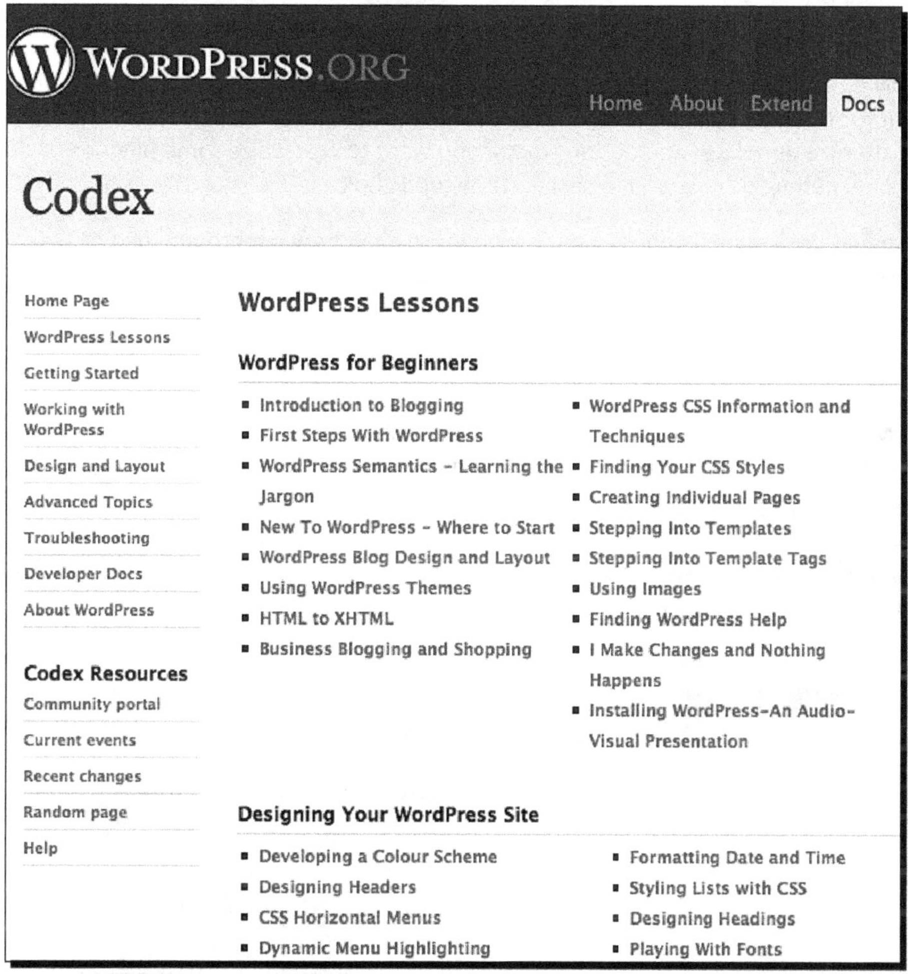

And there are books!

Apart from documentation, tutorials, and forums, there are also some excellent books. Packt itself has one of the best collections of books on open source CMSs. You will find these books at `http://www.packtpub.com/content-management`.

If you have done all this and feel you will still need some help, you will have to turn to professionals. Whether you are busy with other projects or need someone with more experience to take care of your CMS, you will find a lot of experts online.

Finding professional help

If you need professional help in setting up or managing a CMS, don't worry! Help is readily available.

You may find experts who will install the CMS for you. WordPress even has a team that will install it for free—`http://install4free.wordpress.net/`. Experts can help you install and customize templates and designs too. If you want to customize some plug-ins or develop a new one, getting professional assistance is a good choice.

You can find professional help by asking around. You can browse through the CMS's web site for a listing of companies providing professional services. You can even try freelance sites such as Elance, oDesk, and Guru.

A quick search for **joomla** found **2,568** service providers on **Elance**! That's a large number. The number of service providers is a good indication of the support levels you can expect for a CMS. Go ahead and try a search. And if you wish, post a project. You will see responses come in quickly. You can then evaluate and select a vendor you like.

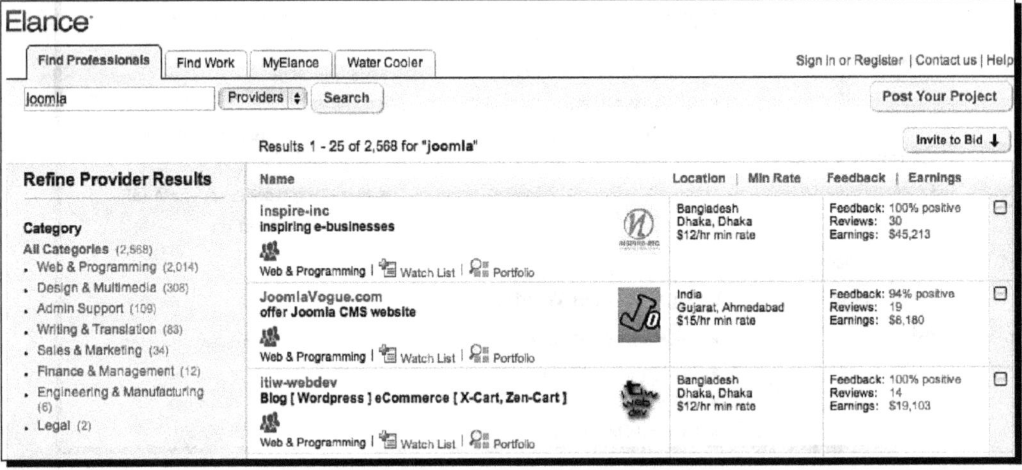

Happy customizing!

Summary

We have looked at how to customize templates further, and how to evaluate the support options of a CMS. We even touched upon how to find professional help.

In this chapter, we specifically learned how to:

- Change the design via CMS's template editing features
- Edit the actual CSS files
- Look at file and code structure to evaluate a CMS's quality
- Go through the available documentation
- Find experts to help you customize the design to what you like

This brings us to the end of this book's first section. We started with understanding the basics of CMSs and went on to refine our needs. Next, we looked at various evaluation criteria. In the process, we implemented the most common CMS tasks using Joomla!.

Now we can jump to reviews. Over the next few chapters we will look at CMSs in a specific category, and evaluate the top contenders. Ready for it?

Section III

CMSs by breed

Blog CMSs

Web CMSs

CMSs for E-Commerce

Team Collaboration CMSs

Specialized CMSs

8

Blog CMSs

So far, we have evaluated our requirements and analyzed the selection criteria for a CMS. We have also learned how we can organize content, set up design, and extend a typical CMS. It's now time to look at the specific uses of CMSs, and evaluate a few of them.

In this chapter, we will take a look at top blog CMSs. We will:

- *Learn about different blog CMSs*
- *Evaluate how to perform typical content management operations using the top three blog CMSs*
- *Review flexibility and extensibility*
- *Consider other options available*

Let's get started.

The first question-do I need a self-hosted or service-based CMS?

Blogs have taken the Internet by storm. They started like simple diaries and have grown to be full-fledged CMSs now. If you want to start a blog, you have the following two options:

- Sign up with a hosted blog service such as WordPress.com, Typepad.com, Blogger.com, or any other similar services available
- Set up blogging software, such as WordPress, Movable Type, ExpressionEngine, and so on, on your own server

If you are a casual blogger, signing up with a hosted service is a suitable choice. But if you want full control of your blog, setting up your own system is the best option. It's not very difficult. In Chapter 4, we saw how easy it was to set up WordPress—you could do it within five minutes.

We will cover only self-hosted solutions for this chapter. But you can easily apply this knowledge to a blog service.

Top blogging CMSs

WordPress (`www.WordPress.org`) is the most popular self-hosted blogging software. Hundreds of thousands of sites run on WordPress, and tens of millions of people see WordPress-driven content every day.

The following images are of the PlayStation (`http://blog.us.playstation.com/`) and the People (`http://offtherack.people.com/`) blog sites, which use WordPress:

Movable Type (`www.movabletype.org`) is another longtime favorite. It's very easy to use and has a strong fan following.

There are many contenders after the top two blogging CMSs. All general-purpose CMSs have a blogging component. Many old blog software applications are no longer actively maintained. There are new entrants on the scene that focus on niches, such as photo blogging.

Let us cover the top choices

We can't cover all of the blog software in this chapter. So, we will only cover WordPress at length. We will talk about Movable Type and ExpressionEngine briefly. At the end, we will touch upon other blogging software.

What we are interested in is to find out answers to the following questions:

- What sort of a site is that CMS good for?
- How easy is it to build a site?
- How easy is it to edit content?
- What's its plug-in/template support like?
- How extensible/customizable is it?
- What are the interesting or high-profile examples of that CMS?

Taking WordPress for a test drive

We already installed WordPress (`http://WordPress.org/`) in Chapter 4. We saw that installation can be completed in about five minutes. From Chapters 5 to 7, we used Joomla! to create site structure, add and edit content, apply design templates, and make a few customizations. Let's try out some of that with WordPress to see how it performs.

Time for action-managing content with WordPress

1. Log in to the administration panel of your WordPress installation.
2. Click on the **New Post** link in the top bar. This opens the **Add New Post** page. Enter a title for your first blog post where your cursor is blinking. We will enter a definition of the word **Yoga** for our Yoga Site.
3. Start writing your text in the large text entry box. It's a WYSIWYG editor. You can use buttons in the toolbar to format text, insert links, and so on.
4. Let's insert an image into our post. Click on the first icon next to **Upload/Insert**. When you move your mouse over it, you will see **Add an Image** in the tooltip. Click on that icon.
5. Upload a file from your computer.
6. Once a file is uploaded, you can enter additional parameters for this image. This includes **Title**, **Caption**, **Alignment**, a link to open when an image is clicked, and so on. Here's how your screen may look at this stage.

7. Click on **Insert into Post** to add this image to your post.

8. Complete writing the blog entry.

9. If you want to add tags (keywords) to this post, you can do that from the **Tags** section at right. WordPress will autocomplete long tags and will create new ones as you **Add** them.

10. We have not yet created any categories for our blog. Navigate to the **Categories** section below **Tags**. Click on the **+ Add New Category** link.

11. Enter **Background** as your category name and **Add** it. Any new categories you add are selected automatically. Notice that you can post a blog entry in multiple categories at once.

12. There are a few other options too. There are the settings for **Discussion**. We want to allow both comments and trackbacks, so keep both options checked.

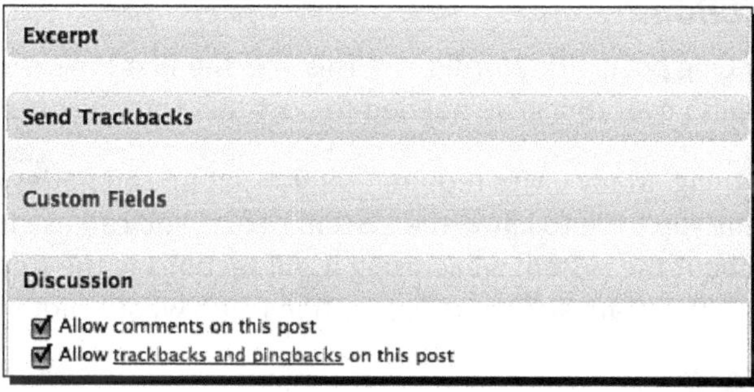

13. Scroll up and click on the **Publish** button on the right to make this post live.

14. Click on **View Post** at the top left to see how your site looks at the moment.

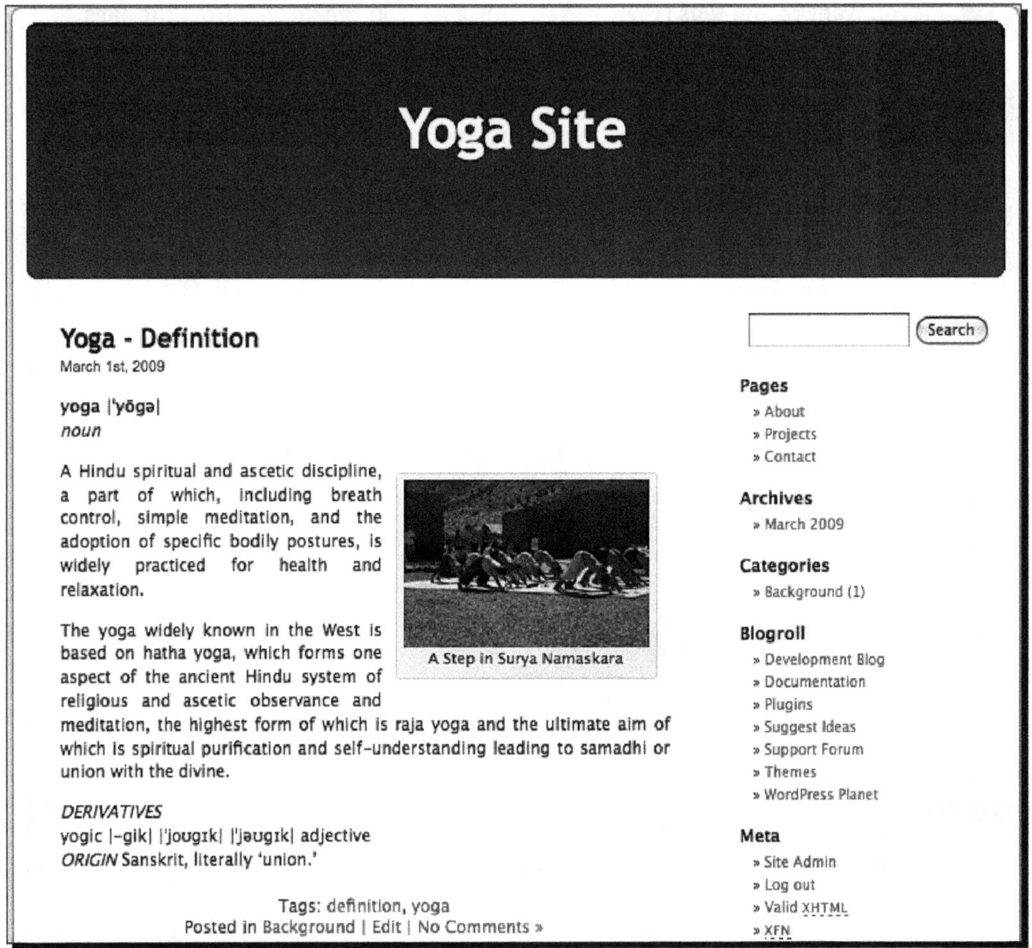

What just happened?

We published a new blog post with WordPress! This was the first time we used WordPress, but we could accomplish everything we needed to post this entry just from one screen.

This is an important thing. Many CMSs require that you set up categories and images separately. This means you have to know the system before you can use it! WordPress allows you to learn about the system while using it. All sections in the **Add New Post** page are well-labeled. There are sufficient descriptions, and what is not needed is hidden by default.

Here are the highlights of what happened:

- Our title automatically became a search engine friendly permalink for this post.
- We could format our text with a simple WYSIWYG editor. It was packed with features—spell check, full screen editing, and further formatting options via **Kitchen Sink**.
- The editor allowed advanced editing by switching to the **HTML** mode.
- Adding an image was very easy. Upload, set options, and insert. We could select a previously uploaded image from the gallery, too.
- We could enter keyword tags for a post quickly.
- Selecting a category and adding new categories was simple. We created a new category on the **Add New Post** page itself. WordPress is intelligent enough to understand that if we added a new category on a post page, we would want to use it for that post. So, it was selected automatically.
- Advance options were available, but were hidden by default.
- We could publish the post right away, or at a later date.
- WordPress could also keep history of all the revisions we make to a post, could preview the post, and would auto-save it frequently.

WordPress looks easy and powerful so far. Let us look at how we can harness it further.

Surviving blog jargon and benefitting from it

Blogs have their own terminology. You may not have heard of trackbacks, pingbacks, tags, or permalinks. You can learn more about these terms from `http://en.wikipedia.org/wiki/List_of_blogging_terms` and `http://www.dailyblogtips.com/the-bloggers-glossary/`. Similarly, there are excellent features that blogs have—comments, aggregating content from other sources, ability to get updates via RSS feeds, and so on. I recommend you to go through these glossaries to learn more about blogs.

Extending WordPress

Managing content with WordPress seems easy. We want to see how easy is it to customize its design and extend its features. Let's begin with the action.

Time for action-customizing the design

1. Find some themes you like. You can browse through theme galleries at `http://WordPress.org/extend/themes/` or Google **WordPress themes**. There are thousands of free and paid themes available for WordPress.
2. Download some themes that you like. Unzip each theme's ZIP file. Each theme should create a new folder for itself.
3. Upload all these folders to the `wp-content/themes` folder on your server.
4. In WordPress, go to **Admin | Appearance**. You should see new themes you uploaded in the **Available Themes** section. The page also lists the **WordPress Classic** and **Default** themes.

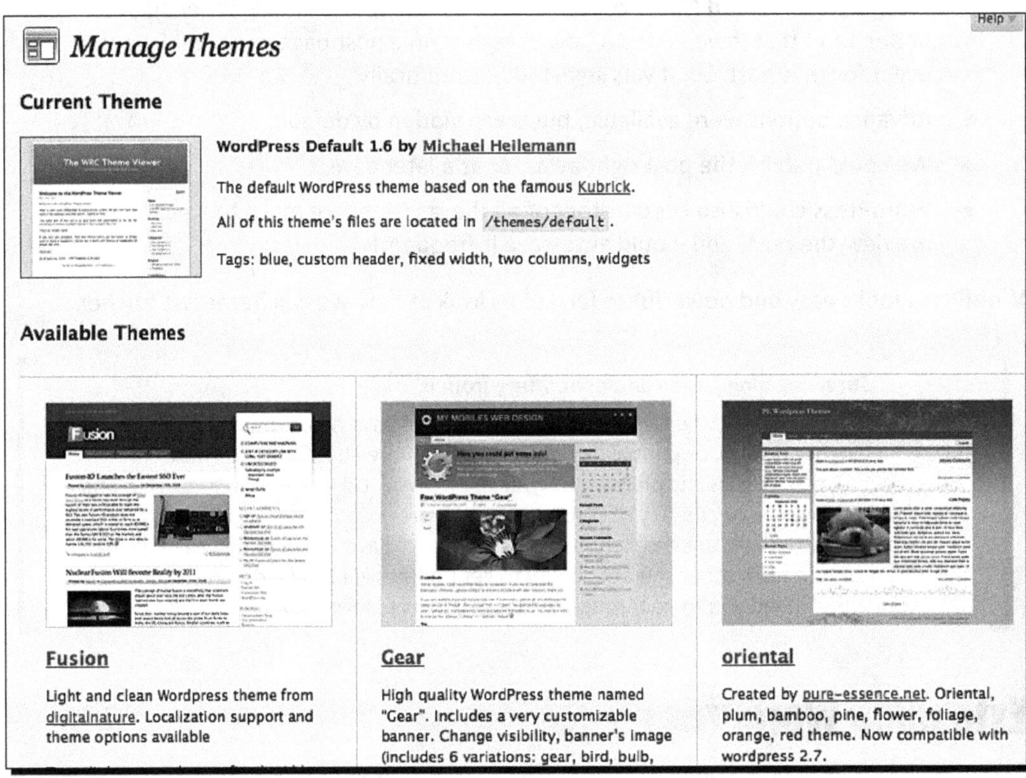

5. We have three new themes showing up.
6. Click on one of the themes to see a live preview. This is how it will look.

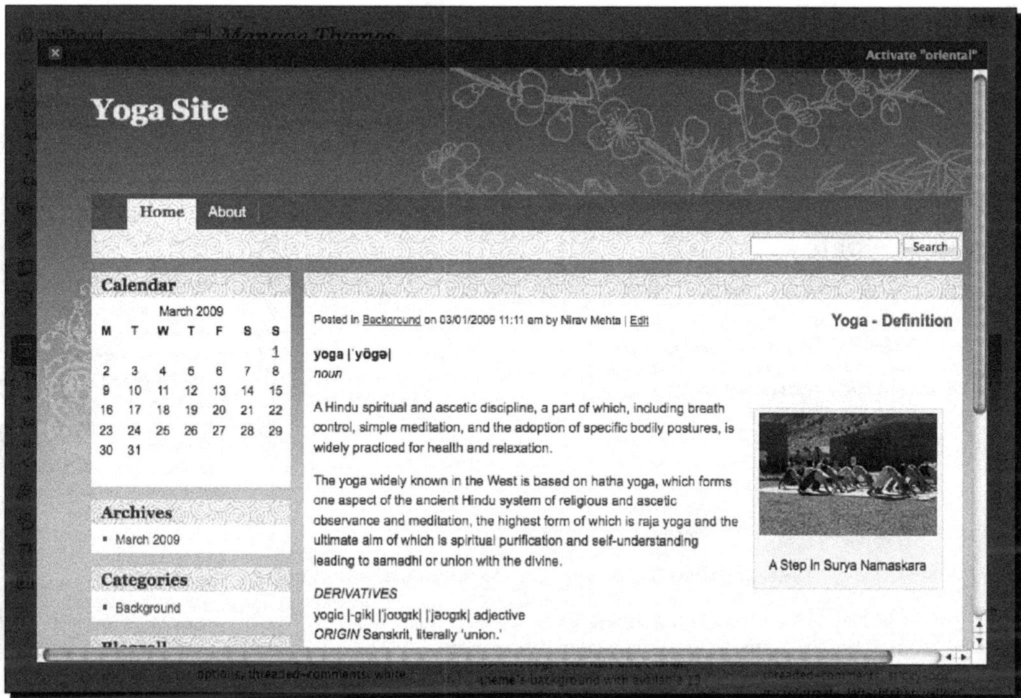

7. Review all themes. Activate the one you like the most by clicking on the **Activate** link at the top right in the preview window. We liked **oriental** and activated it. Our site now shows up just like the live preview.

What just happened?

We installed a new design theme for our WordPress blog. We downloaded three themes from the Web, unzipped them, and uploaded them to our WordPress themes folder.

The themes showed up in WordPress admin. Clicking on a theme showed a live preview. This made our decision easy. We activated the theme we liked. That's how easy it was to change the design of our blog!

If you recall, installing a new design was similar in Joomla!, except that Joomla! allowed us to upload a ZIP file using its administration interface itself. The tricky part in giving a new design to your site was shortlisting and selecting a design, not setting it up.

Customizing the theme

Consider the following theme editor in WordPress

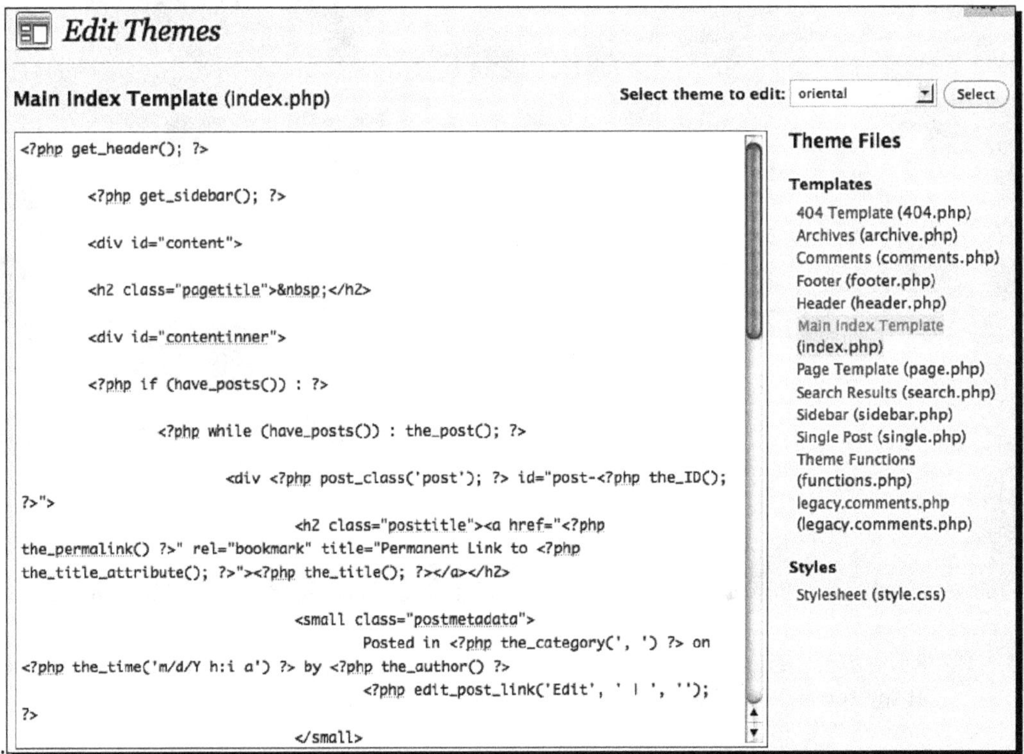

If you want to further customize your theme, you can do that. In fact, you have full control over how your site looks with WordPress. You can use **Appearance | Editor** to change individual theme files.

We recommend making template customizations on a local installation of WordPress first. Once you get everything done according to your choice, you can upload the changed files to the theme's folder and activate it.

WordPress widgets

Widgets are content blocks that can be used in a theme. Search, RSS feeds, Blog Post Archives, Tag Cloud, and Recent Posts are some of the built-in widgets available in WordPress. You can turn them on or off independently, determine their position in the sidebar, and also change their settings. Go to the **Appearance | Widgets** page to take over the control of WordPress widgets.

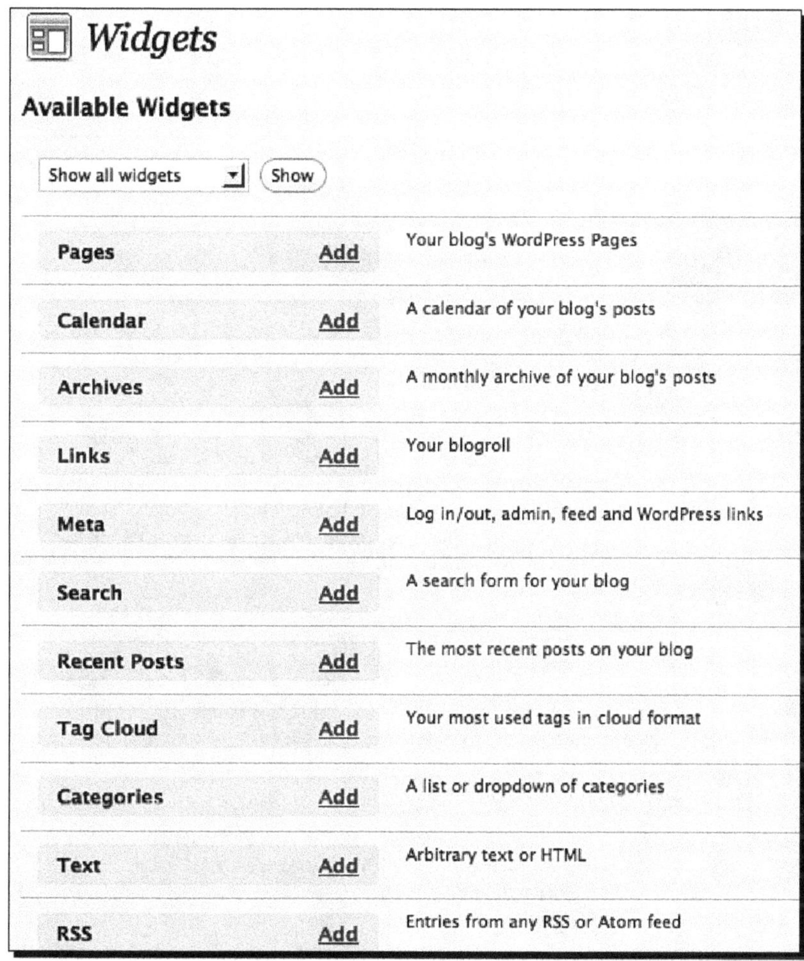

Add unlimited power with plug-ins

Our Yoga Site needs a lot more than just the core content management. How can we achieve that with WordPress? And will it be wise to use WordPress for our Yoga Site?

The WordPress plug-in architecture is solid. You will find hundreds of high-quality plug-ins from photo galleries to e-commerce. But remember that the core of WordPress is a blog engine, which chronologically displays content under set categories. It encourages sharing and contribution. Theoretically, you can customize WordPress to any need you have. But we recommend you to evaluate the most important features for your site and then decide whether you want to use WordPress as a base, or something else.

I use WordPress for my blog and have a range of plug-ins installed. WordPress is painless, and it allows me to focus on the core goal of my blog—sharing knowledge. Take a look at the list of plug-ins on my blog at www.mehtanirav.com.

Currently Active Plugins

Bulk Actions | Apply

Plugin	Version	Description	Action
AdSense Manager	3.2.13	Control and arrange your AdSense & Referral blocks on your Wordpress blog. With Widget and inline post support, configurable colours. By Martin Fitzpatrick.	Deactivate
Akismet	2.2.3	Akismet checks your comments against the Akismet web service to see if they look like spam or not. You need a WordPress.com API key to use it. You can review the spam it catches under "Comments." To show off your Akismet stats just put <?php akismet_counter(); ?> in your template. See also: WP Stats plugin. By Matt Mullenweg.	Deactivate
AutoMeta	0.8	Automatically generate and include HTML Meta Tags and Technorati Tags based on the full text of your post. By Rich Boakes.	Deactivate
FeedBurner FeedSmith	2.3.1	Originally authored by Steve Smith, this plugin detects all ways to access your original WordPress feeds and redirects them to your FeedBurner feed so you can track every possible subscriber. By FeedBurner.	Deactivate
Google XML Sitemaps	3.1.2	This plugin will generate a sitemaps.org compatible sitemap of your WordPress blog which is supported by Ask.com, Google, MSN Search and YAHOO. Configuration Page By Arne Brachhold.	Deactivate
iG:Syntax Hiliter	3.5	Syntax Highlighter for various programming languages, using the GeSHi engine. See the MANUAL for more instructions. [Plugin Home] [Plugin Feed (RSS2)]. By Amit Gupta.	Deactivate
Math Comment Spam Protection	2.2	Asks the visitor making the comment to answer a simple math question. This is intended to prove that the visitor is a human being and not a spam robot. Example of such question: *What is the sum of 2 and 9?* By Michael Woehrer.	Deactivate

You may have noticed a few plug-ins to handle comments and spam. Why would you need that? Well, because you will end up spending all your time removing spam comments from your system if you don't have them activated.

Comments or spam

Comment spam is a real pain with all blogs. Spammers have written spam-bots (automatic software) that keep posting junk comments on your blog. If you don't protect comment submission, your blog will soon be flooded with advertisements of pills you don't want to take and a lot of other things you don't want your visitors to attend to.

Comment protection plug-ins are the first you should install. I use **Akismet** with **Simple Math**. Simple Math poses a simple mathematical question to the comment writer. A human can easily answer that. This takes care of most of the spam comments. Comments that pass through this test need to pass through Akismet. Askimet is an excellent spam-protection plug-in from the WordPress team. These two plug-ins kill almost 99.99% of spam comments on my blog.

Once I am left with legitimate comments, I can go to WordPress's **Admin | Comments**, and **Approve**, **Unapprove**, **Delete**, or **Mark as Spam** all comments. The **Edit Comments** screen looks like the following screenshot:

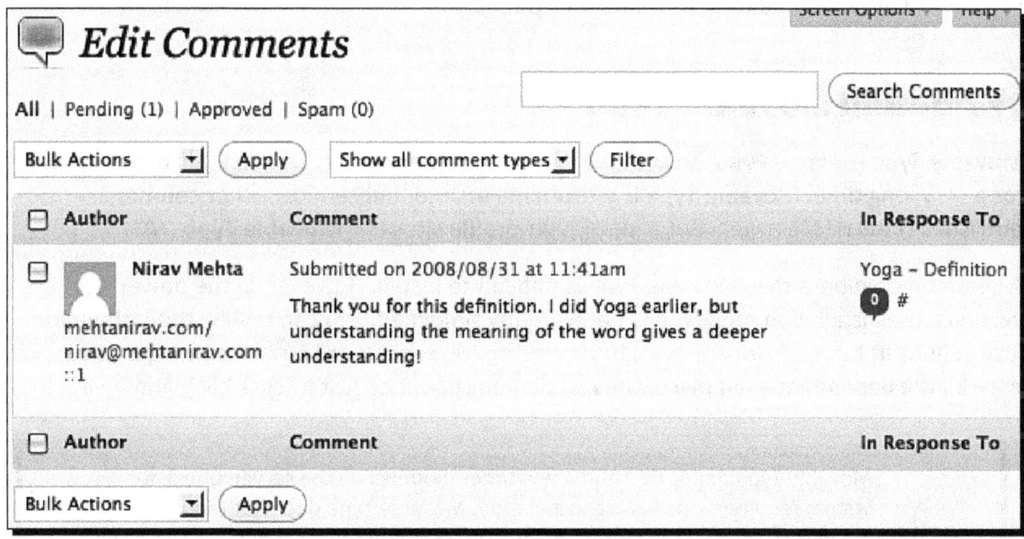

WordPress is a superb choice for creating a blog. It can be used as a general-purpose CMS as well. We have covered most of the day-to-day operations with WordPress so far. Here are some additional resources for you.

Additional resources

Here are some web-sites that will guide you in your WordPress adventures:

- Start with WordPress Codex: `http://codex.WordPress.org/`
- Official support forums: `http://WordPress.org/support/`
- Some excellent How-Tos, which are categorized: `http://tamba2.org.uk/WordPress/`
- Great resources, themes, and articles: `http://wpcandy.com/`
- A showcase of WordPress-powered sites: `http://welovewp.com/`
- The WordPress resource blog: `http://lorelle.WordPress.com/`
- Free themes, tips, and more: `http://www.themelab.com/`
- The WordPress podcast: `http://wp-community.org/`

You should be able to manage a WordPress site now. But is it the best blogging software you can have? Let's continue to review further options.

Evaluating Movable Type

Movable Type (`http://www.movabletype.org/`) is extremely popular. It's been around for a very long time. Movable Type is written in Perl and, unlike most other solutions, publishes static HTML pages. But a lot of high-profile sites use **Movable Type** (**MT**).

A common opinion is that Movable Type is difficult to install. However, in the newer versions, the installation process has been greatly simplified. You can review the installation instructions at `http://www.movabletype.org/documentation/`. Assuming that you have all the dependencies in place, the installation should be just a "click-click-and-away" job!

Movable Type needs Perl and a few other modules on the server. Check for system requirements before installation. Movable Type does not require a database—it can use an internal database. But it will work happily with MySQL, or other databases, if you wish.

Let's assume we have installed Movable Type and created a blog in it. Let's now evaluate how easy it is to use.

Time for action-managing content with Movable Type

1. Log in to the MT administration panel. The screen looks like this.

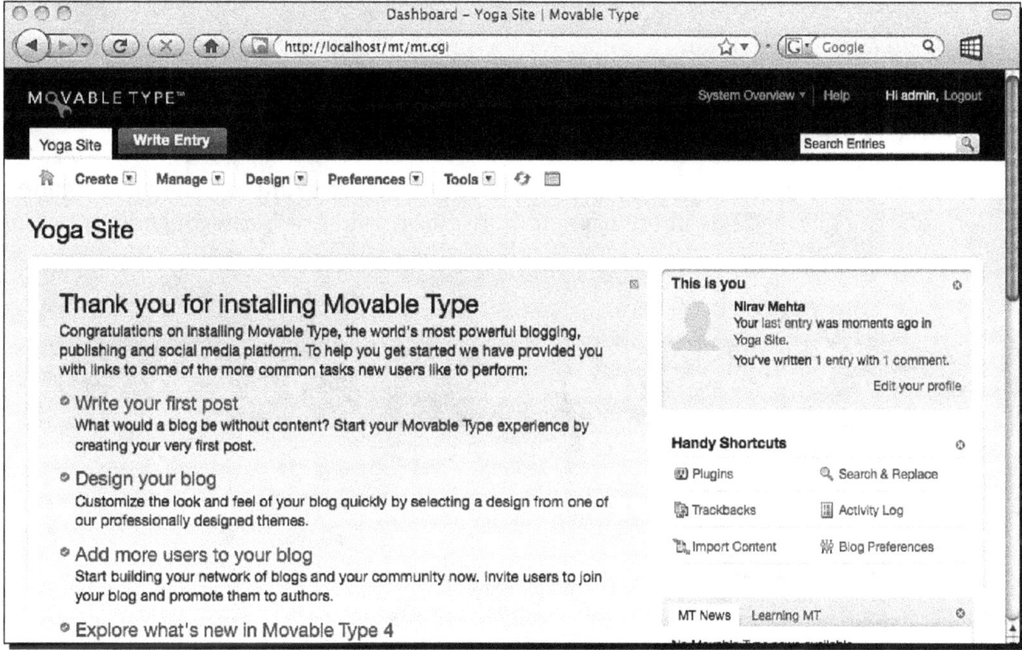

2. Click on the **Write Entry** button at the top of the page.

3. This brings you to a WYSIWYG editor. Enter a blog title and post content here. This is very similar to WordPress.

4. Once we have added some text, we want to add an image. Click on the picture icon in the editor's toolbar. This brings up the **Insert Image** panel.

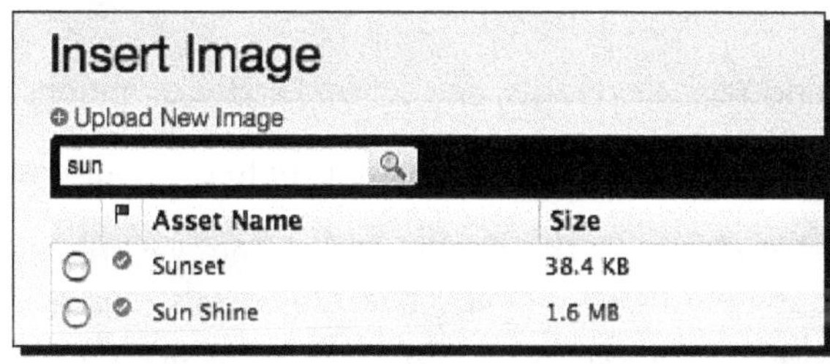

5. Click on **Upload New Image**. Browse and select a file to upload, enter a folder location where you want to save the file. A good option is the current date, which shows up in the dropdown for quick selection. Click on the big **Upload** button to save this image.

6. Add **Name**, **Description**, and **Tags** for this image. Also select the right-alignment option. Keep **Display image in entry** checked.

7. The image automatically comes up in the content text.

8. We need to create a new category for this entry. Click on **Add new** under **Categories** on the righthand side of the page. You can quickly add a new category here.

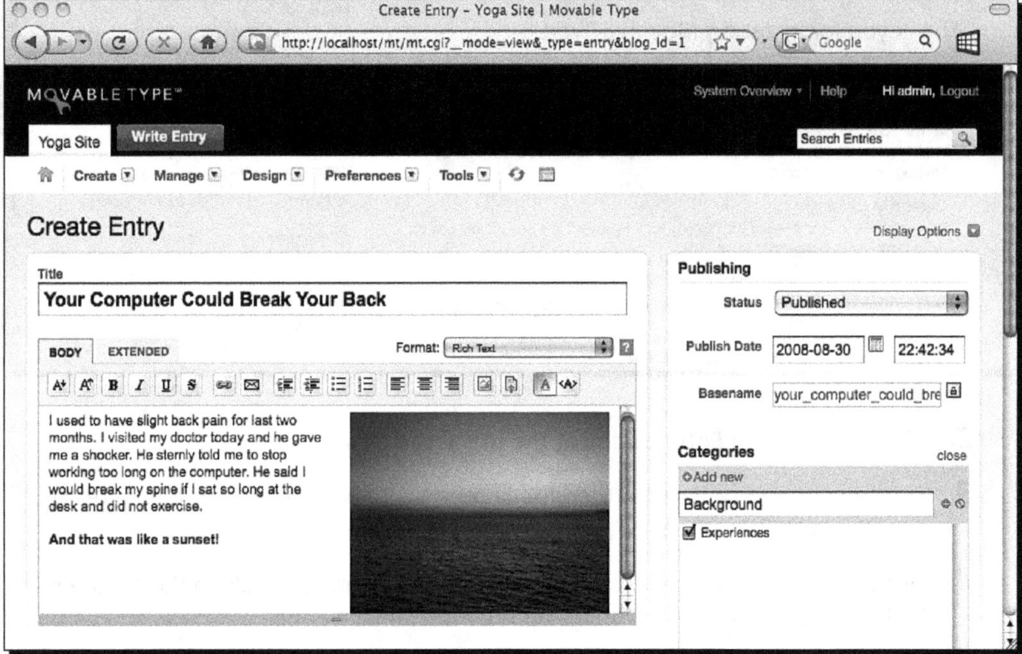

9. You can also add **Tags**, **Keywords**, and set up **Feedback** options from there.

10. Click on the **Save** button at the end of this form to save our entry.

11. MT will publish our entry to the site. If you have not yet created a folder to publish the site in, do so now. Make sure you give 777 permissions on the folder. To manually publish your blog, click on the two circling arrows in the menu bar.

12. This opens up a **Publish** window. Select **All Files** and click on **Publish**.

13. The site will publish, and you will see a message like this.

14. Click on the icon next to the **Publish** icon in the menu bar to **View Site**.

15. Congratulations, our beautiful site is live!

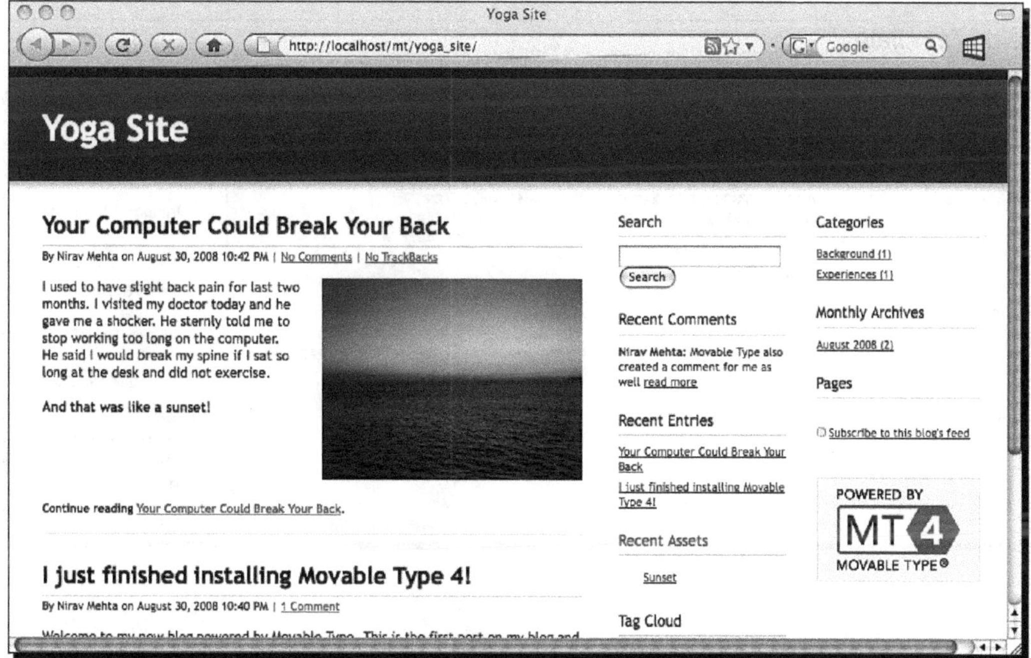

What just happened?

We posted our first blog entry with Movable Type. Writing an entry was very similar to doing so in WordPress. We could enter a title and an entry text, add an image to the entry, create a new category, and associate metadata—all from a single page.

The look and feel of MT was intuitive, yet solid. It did not require much learning. The image upload process was just as we would have expected—or even better! Category creation happened in a jiffy. Movable Type is certainly one of the easiest CMS to use.

MT automatically publishes the blog as static HTML pages. But we also saw how we could do it manually if needed. We had full control over the publishing process and could select **All Files**, or only specific types of pages to publish. The advantage of publishing static pages is that it significantly reduces load on your server. On the other hand, if you have a lot of posts, publishing may take longer.

Customizing Movable Type

The default template that MT uses is professional. But if we wanted to make changes, we could easily make them. One of the other benefits of MT is that its template language is like HTML. You don't need to know programming to edit MT templates. You can go to **Design | Templates** to see a list of templates that MT uses. Click on **Main Index** to see how the index page of your blog is created. This shows up a page like the following screenshot:

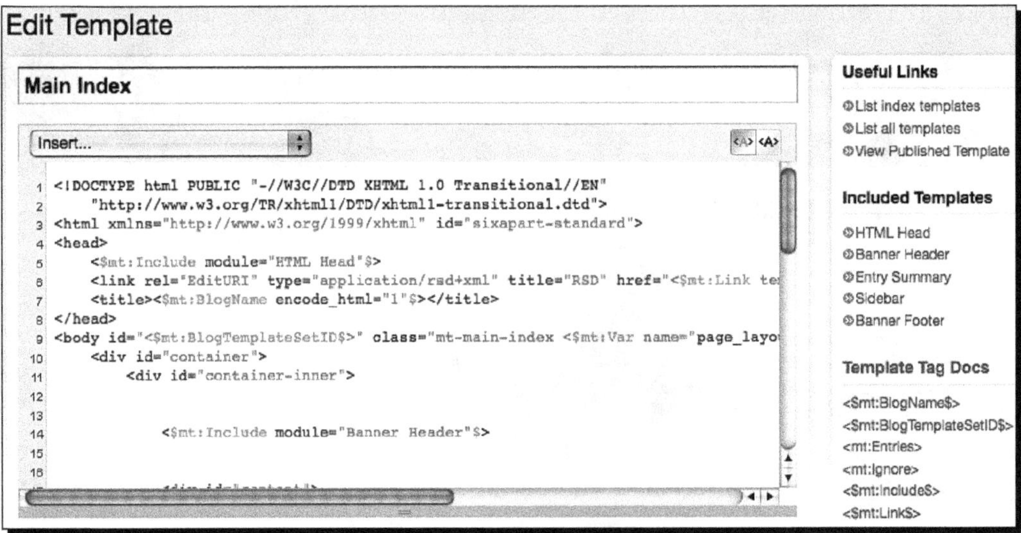

As you see, much of this is HTML. The rest is `<$mt:something$>` tags—MT's magic blocks that insert content within the HTML design. You can even set up advanced options for each template—including whether it should be published dynamically or statically. (Yes, MT can even publish blog content dynamically.)

Styles allow you to control the overall look of the design, much like Themes do in WordPress. Widgets control the elements that appear on different layouts and are similar to WordPress Widgets.

MT also has a plug-in support. Here, you may not find as much variety of plug-ins as you would in WordPress. But everything you may need for a blog is available.

If you want further customizations, you can modify the Perl source code. If you are publishing your blog dynamically, you can even use PHP for needed customizations. Finding a programmer for MT is harder than for a PHP-based CMS, but you won't really need one to run a blog site.

Additional resources

We saw that MT is a really easy blog system. It allows running multiple blogs out of the box, comes with nice templates, and is flexible enough. It is also available under commercial license. You can pick the version that suits you the most. Here are some additional resources for you:

- Plug-ins for MT: `http://plug-ins.movabletype.org/`, `http://plug-ins.movalog.com/`
- Documentation: `http://www.movabletype.org/documentation/`
- Helpful screen casts: `http://www.movabletype.org/screencasts/`
- Hosted MT: `http://www.typepad.com`, `http://www.vox.com`
- Developer resources: `http://www.sixapart.com/developers/movabletype.html`
- Learning MT: `http://www.learningmovabletype.com/`

We are now ready to quickly review another blog CMS. The chosen one is ExpressionEngine.

Expressing opinions with ExpressionEngine

ExpressionEngine (`http://expressionengine.com/`) is a CMS system with a blog at its core. It was called pMachinePro earlier, and comes from the same company that makes the CodeIgniter development framework. ExpressionEngine's core is a blog system and you can purchase extensions to enhance its features. Its code quality is good. Though the number of users is not very high now, some people have made very good use of ExpressionEngine.

Here are a couple of examples:

- `http://nelsonmandela.org/`
- `http://www.truthdig.com/`

Time for action-managing content with ExpressionEngine

Let's see how ExpressionEngine manages our content. Let's put it through the same process we applied to WordPress and MT.

1. Download and install ExpressionEngine. The steps are easy to follow.
2. Log in to the administration panel.
3. Click on the first menu item—**Publish**.
4. This brings you to the now-familiar blog post screen. Enter a title. **EE** (**ExpressionEngine**) will automatically create a URL title and allow modifying it, just like other systems.
5. Enter text for the blog post. Notice that the text area does not have a WYSIWYG editor. If you know XHTML, you can add your post with full XHTML markup.

6. Click on **Upload File** to add an image to the post. Follow the onscreen prompts to upload, re-size, and place an image in the main body.

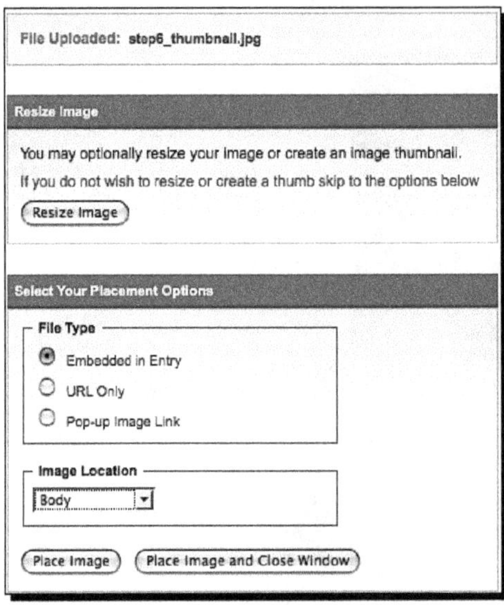

7. You can use formatting buttons to select and format a portion of text. Select **Normal** in **Button Mode**. Select the portion of text you want to make bold. Then click on the **<b>** button to make it bold. The guided mode prompts you to type the text in bold when you click on it.

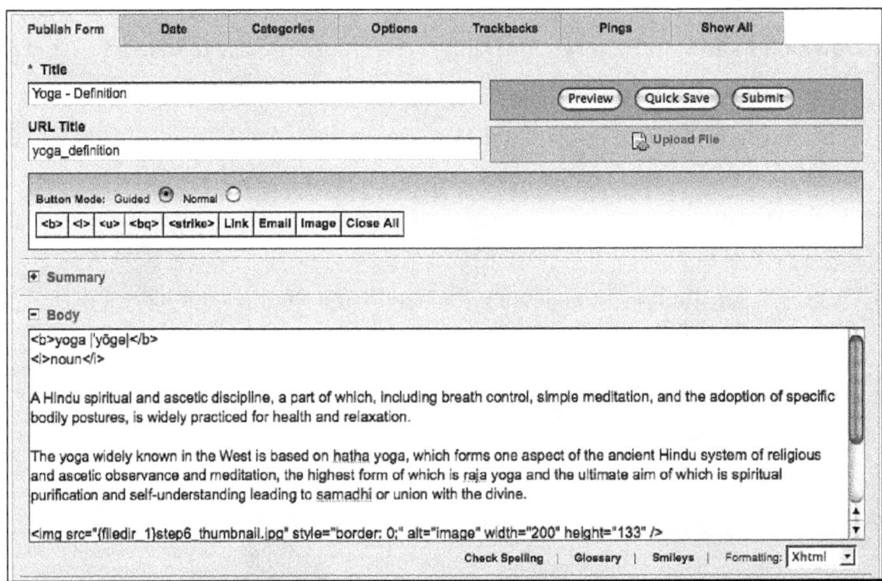

8. Click on the **Categories** tab from the top bar. Click on **Edit Categories**. This opens up a new window. Create a new category called **Background** here. Click on **Close Window and Update Categories in PUBLISH Page**.

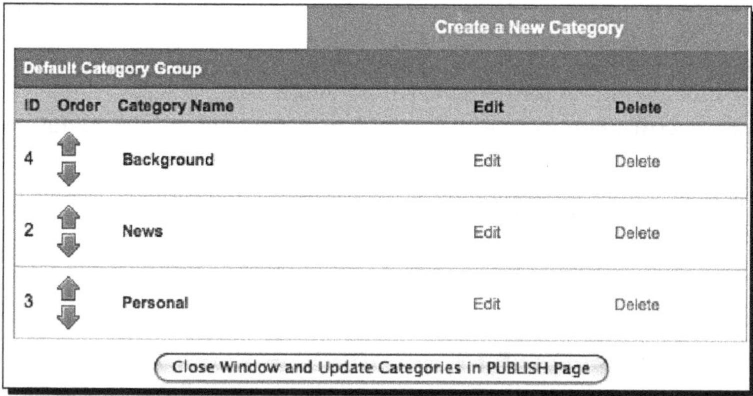

9. Now select **Background** as category. You can shift-click another category to post this entry in multiple categories.

10. Click on the other tabs such as **Date**, **Options**, **Trackbacks**, and **Pings** to evaluate options there.

11. Click on the **Submit** button in the main **Publish** form to save this post.

12. Click on the **My Site** link in the top right menu to view our site. As you can see, it's all ready to go!

What just happened?

We created our first blog post with ExpressionEngine. The process was similar to that with WordPress and MT. It was not as easy as with the earlier two, but we could get the job done in a logical way.

We added content, an image, and did basic formatting on content. We could also add categories and modify options for the post from a single page. EE gave us full freedom to use XHTML in blog posts. But this makes it a bit harder for people who do not know XHTML markup.

The administration panel allows you to manage templates, modules, and account settings. An interesting feature is communicating with members, much like a newsletter system from within EE.

Customizing ExpressionEngine

Of course, you get full control over design. Template editing is tag-based, and a template looks as follows:

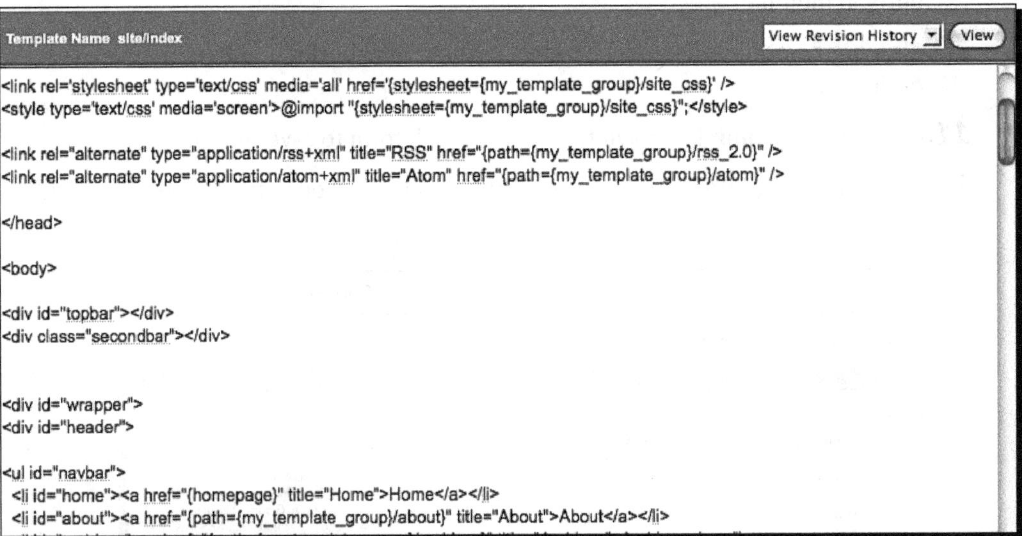


```
<link rel='stylesheet' type='text/css' media='all' href='{stylesheet={my_template_group}/site_css}' />
<style type='text/css' media='screen'>@import "{stylesheet={my_template_group}/site_css}";</style>

<link rel="alternate" type="application/rss+xml" title="RSS" href="{path={my_template_group}/rss_2.0}" />
<link rel="alternate" type="application/atom+xml" title="Atom" href="{path={my_template_group}/atom}" />

</head>

<body>

<div id="topbar"></div>
<div class="secondbar"></div>


<div id="wrapper">
<div id="header">

<ul id="navbar">
  <li id="home"><a href="{homepage}" title="Home">Home</a></li>
  <li id="about"><a href="{path={my_template_group}/about}" title="About">About</a></li>
```

The markup is simple. All dynamic blocks are in curly braces.

EE comes with useful modules. You may notice that even the core blog functionality is implemented as a module. This tells us that its add-on architecture is solid, and it should be easy to build custom modules. Here's a list of default modules that get installed.

CP Home › Modules

	Module Name	Description	Version	Status	Action
1	Blacklist/Whitelist	Blacklist and whitelist module	--	Not Installed	Install
2	Blogger API	Blogger API Module	--	Not Installed	Install
3	Comment	User commenting system	1.2	Installed	Remove
4	Emoticon	Emoticon (smiley) module	1.0	Installed	Remove
5	IP to Nation	Utility for associating IP addresses with their country	--	Not Installed	Install
6	Metaweblog API	Metaweblog API Module	--	Not Installed	Install
7	Referrer	Referrer tracking module	1.3	Installed	Remove
8	RSS	RSS page generating module	1.0	Installed	Remove
9	Search	Search module	1.2	Installed	Remove
10	Statistics	Statistics display module	1.0	Installed	Remove
11	Trackback	Trackback module	1.1	Installed	Remove
12	Weblog	Weblog module	1.2	Installed	Remove

We can judge that EE is a solid system, but will have a learning curve. It's great for programmers as they can get into PHP code and extend all the functionality that they want. EE is very flexible and if you want more than just a blog, there are some excellent add-ons available from `http://expressionengine.com/downloads/addons/`.

Additional resources

If you opt to use EE for your site, here are some additional resources that may help you.

- EE templates: `http://expressionengine.com/templates/`
- Documentation, excellent Wiki and support forums, and so on: `http://expressionengine.com/support/`
- Developer resources: `http://expressionengine.com/developers/`
- EE templates: `http://www.eetemplates.com/`

Searching for more alternatives

We have taken a detailed look at the top two blogging CMSs and one upcoming choice. There are many more blogging engines available. Let's take a quick look at some noteworthy contenders.

- Take a look at Wikipedia's blog software page for a longer list: `http://en.wikipedia.org/wiki/Weblog_software`
- Review the blog software demos at: `http://www.opensourcecms.com/`

- Pebble, a Java-based simple blogging software application: `http://pebble.sourceforge.net/`
- Roller—`http://rollerweblogger.org/`—is another good choice.
- Mephisto, a Ruby-based blog engine: `http://mephistoblog.com/`
- Thingamablog, an offline desktop-based blog engine that publishes static pages to your site: `http://thingamablog.sourceforge.net/`
- LifeType, an open source blogging platform: `http://lifetype.net/`
- Hosted blog solutions: `http://www.WordPress.com`, `http://www.typepad.com`, `http://www.blogger.com`, and many others
- Generic CMS systems, such as Joomla! and Drupal, have blogging components as well.

Additional help is also available

If you select one of the top blogging software application for your site, there is enough help available on the Internet. Packt has a great collection of books on open source CMSs, including blog CMSs.

The following link lists books that will help you get an in-depth knowledge of blog CMSs:

`http://www.packtpub.com/content-management`

Now that we have covered all the details, let's review what we did.

Summary

We reviewed WordPress, Movable Type, and ExpressionEngine in this chapter. We looked at how easy is it to add and manage content. We also saw how templates and functionality can be customized to our needs.

By overall evaluation, we can say that a blog is great as a general-purpose CMS. It is especially good for sites that post periodic updates or articles. Blogs allow for easy collaboration, syndication, and publishing. Most blogging software also have a range of plug-ins that can convert a blog from a content site to an e-commerce site, or whatever else you want.

We specifically looked at:

- Adding content with WordPress, Movable Type, and ExpressionEngine
- Creating categories
- Adding tags

- Uploading images
- Publishing a blog site
- Customizing the look of a WordPress blog by uploading and activating a theme
- An overview of plug-ins and the template system with these three blog engines
- Examples of some high-profile web-sites using WordPress, Movable Type, and ExpressionEngine

There is lot more to CMSs. We have looked at blog CMSs, and now is the turn of their big cousins—web-based CMSs. Let's take closer look at the top web CMSs in the next chapter.

9
Web CMSs

After understanding our requirements and learning the basics of using CMSs, we evaluated the top Blog CMSs in the last chapter. We are now ready to look at ***Web Content Management Systems*** *(commonly known as* ***WCMS, Web CMS****, or* ***WCM Systems****). Web CMSs allow you to manage your web content easily. They are generic in nature and perform a variety of operations. If you ask someone about a CMS, they will most probably recommend you one of the systems we cover in this chapter. It's important to learn the features of the top web CMSs to make the right choice for your project.*

In this chapter, we will take a look at the top general-purpose Web CMSs. In the process, we will:

- *Cover a variety of top Web CMSs*
- *Perform customizations and content management operations*
- *Discover interesting features in CMSs*
- *Examine which CMS could be right for you*

Let's get started.

Do you want a CMS or a portal?

We are evaluating a CMS for our Yoga Site. But you may want to build something else. Take a look again at the requirements you drafted in Chapter 3. Do you need a lot of dynamic modules such as an event calendar, shopping cart, collaboration module, file downloads, social networking, and so on? Or you need modules for publishing and organizing content such as news, information, articles, and so on?

Today's top-of-the-line Web CMSs can easily work as a portal. They either have a lot of built-in functionality or a wide range of plug-ins that extend their core features. Yet, there are solutions specifically made for web portals. You should evaluate them along with CMS software if your needs are more like a portal.

On the other hand, if you want a simple corporate or personal web site, with some basic needs, you don't require a mammoth CMS. You can use a simple CMS that will not only fulfill your needs, but will also be easier to learn and maintain.

We have used Joomla! in our examples in Chapters 4 through 7. Joomla! is a solid CMS. But it requires some experience to get used to it. For this chapter, let's first evaluate a simpler CMS. How do we know which CMS is simple? I think we can't go wrong with a CMS that's named "CMS Made Simple".

Evaluating CMS Made Simple

As the name suggests, **CMS Made Simple** (`http://www.cmsmadesimple.org/`) is an easy-to-learn and easy-to-maintain CMS. Here's an excerpt from its home page:

> *If you are an experienced web developer, and know how to do the things you need to do, to get a site up with CMS Made Simple is just that, simple. For those with more advanced ambitions there are plenty of addons to download. And there is an excellent community always at your service.*
>
> *It's very easy to add content and addons wherever you want them to appear on the site. Design your website in whatever way or style you want and just load it into CMSMS to get it in the air. Easy as that!*

That makes things very clear. CMSMS seems to be simple for first-time users, and extensible for developers. Let's take CMSMS to a test drive.

Time for action-managing content with CMS Made Simple

1. Download and install CMS Made Simple. Alternatively, go to the demo at `http://www.opensourcecms.com/`.
2. Log in to the administration section.
3. Click on **Content | Image Manager**. Using the **Upload File** option, upload the Yoga Site logo.
4. Click on **Content | Pages** option from the menu. You will see a hierarchical listing of current pages on the site.

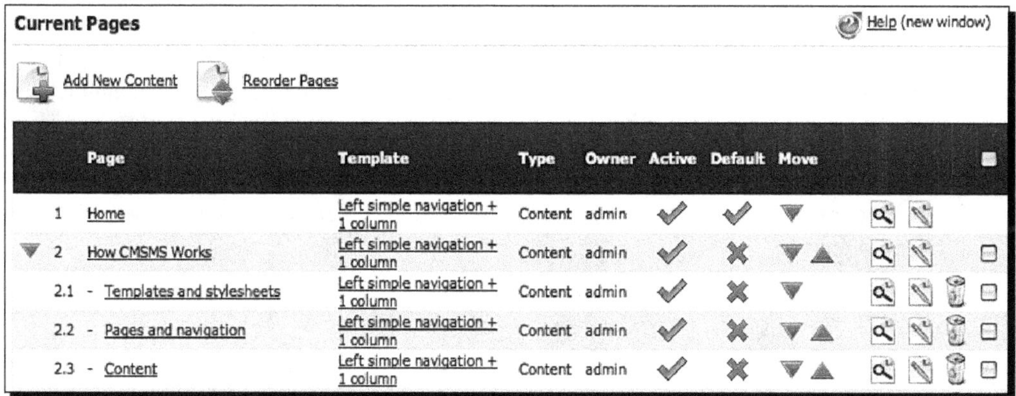

5. The list is easy to understand. Let's add a new page by clicking on the **Add New Content** link above the list.

6. The content addition screen is similar to a lot of other CMSs we have seen so far. There are options to enter page title, category, and so on. You can add page content using a large WYSIWYG editor.

7. Notice that we can select a template for the page. We can also select a parent page. Since we want this page to appear at the root level, keep the **Parent** as **none**.

8. Add some Yoga background information text. Format it using the editor as you see fit.

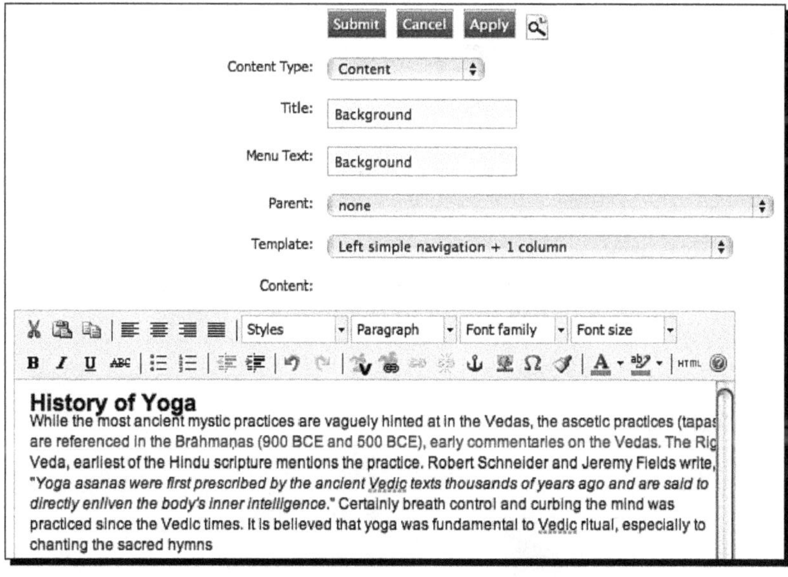

9. There are two new options on this editor, which are indicated by the orange palm tree icons. These are two special options that CMSMS has added: first, to insert a menu; and second, to add a link to another page on the site. This is excellent. It saves us the hassle of remembering, or copying, links.

10. Select a portion of text in the editor. Click on the orange palm icon with the link symbol on it. Select any page from the flyout menu. For now, we will link to the **Home** page.

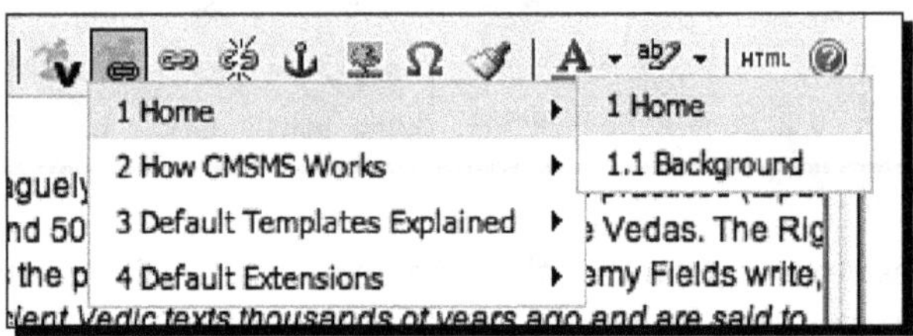

11. Click on the **Insert/edit Image** icon. Then click on the **Browse** icon next to the **Image URL** field in the new window that appears.

12. Select the logo we uploaded and insert it into content.

13. Click on **Submit** to save the page.

14. The **Current Pages** listing now shows our **Background** page. Let's bring it higher in the menu hierarchy. Click on the up arrow in the **Move** column on our page to push it higher. Do this until is at the second position—just after **Home**.

15. That's all. We can click on the magnifying glass icon at the main menu bar's right side to preview our site. Here's how it looks.

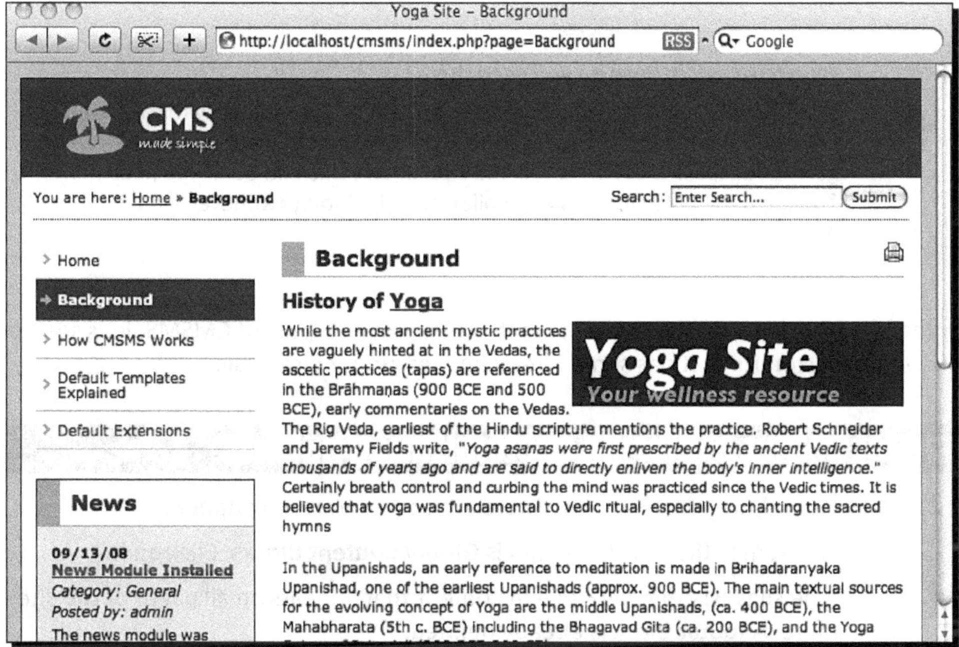

What just happened?

We set up the CMSMS and added some content to it. We wanted to use an image in our content page. To make things simpler, we first uploaded an image. Then we went to the current pages listing. CMSMS shows all pages in the site in a hierarchical display. It's a simple feature that makes a content administrator's life very easy. From there, we went on to create a new page.

CMSMS has a WYSIWYG editor, like so many other CMSs we have seen till now. The content addition process is almost the same in most CMSs. Enter page title and related information, type in content, and you can easily format it using a WYSIWYG editor. We inserted the logo image uploaded earlier using this editor.

CMSMS features extensions to the default WYSIWYG editor. These features demonstrate all of the thinking that's gone into making this software. The orange palm tree icon appearing on the WYSIWYG editor toolbar allowed us to insert a link to another page with a simple click. We could also insert a dynamic menu from within the editor if needed.

Saving and previewing our site was equally easy.

Notice how intuitive it is to add and manage content. CMS Made Simple lives up to its name in this process. It uses simple terms and workflow to accomplish tasks at hand. Check out the content administration process while you evaluate a CMS. After all, it's going to be your most commonly used feature!

Hierarchies: How deep do you need them?

What level of content hierarchies do you need? Are you happy with two levels? Do you like Joomla!'s categories → sections → content flow ? Or do you need to go even deeper? Most users will find two levels sufficient. But if you need more, find out if the CMS supports it. (Spoiler: Joomla! is only two-level deep by default.)

Now that we have learned about the content management aspect of CMSMS, let's see how easily we can customize it. It has some interesting features we can use.

Time for action-exploring customization options

1. Look around the admin section. There are some interesting options.
2. The third item in the **Content** menu is **Global Content Blocks**. Click on it.
3. The name suggests that we can add content that appears on all pages of the site from there. A **footer** block is already defined.
4. Our Yoga Site can get some revenue by selling interesting products. Let's create a block to promote some products on our site. Click on the **Add Global Content Block** link at the bottom.
5. Let's use **product** as the name.
6. Enter some text using the editor.
7. Click on **Submit** to save.
8. Our new content block will appear in the list. Select and copy **Tag to Use this Block**.

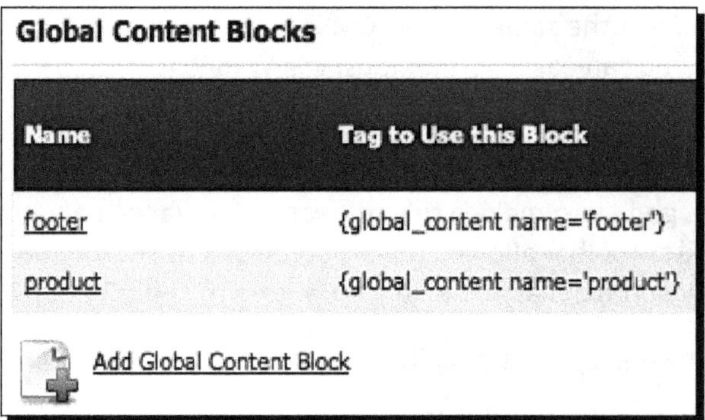

9. Logically, we need to add this tag in a template. Select **Layout | Templates** from the main menu. If you recall, we are using the **Left simple navigation + 1 column** template. Click on the template name.

10. This shows a template editor. Looking at this code we can make out the structure of a content page. Let's add the new content block tag after the main page content.

11. Paste the tag just after the **{* End relational links *}** text. The tag is something like this.

```
{* Start Content Area *}
<div id="main">
   <div style="float: right;">{print showbutton=true script=true}</div>
   <h2>{title}</h2>
   {content} <br />

   {* Start relational links *}
   <div class="hr"></div>
   <div class="right49">
        <p>{anchor anchor='main' text='^ Top'}</p>
   </div>
   <div class="left49">
      <p>{cms_selflink dir="previous" label="Previous page: "} <br />
      {cms_selflink dir="next"}</p>
   </div>
   {* The label parameter doesn't need to be there if you're using Engli
it's used if you don't want the English text "Previous page" *}
   {* End relational links *}

{global_content name='product'}

<hr class="accessibility" />
</div>
   {* End Content Area *}
```

12. Save the template. Now preview the site. Our content block shows up after main page content as we wanted. Job done!

Previous page: Home ^ Top
Next page: How CMSMS Works

A product that we want to promote throughout the site. Can be easily updated later on!

What just happened?

We used the global content block feature of CMSMS to insert a product promotion throughout our site. In the process, we learned about templates and also how we could modify them.

Creating a global content block was similar to adding a new content page. We used the WYSIWYG editor to enter content block text. This gave us a special tag. If you know about PHP templates, you will have guessed that CMSMS uses Smarty templates and the tag was simply a custom tag in Smarty.

Smarty Template Engine

Smarty (`http://www.smarty.net/`) is the most popular template engine for the PHP programming language. Smarty allows keeping core PHP code and presentation/HTML code separate. Special tags are inserted in template files as placeholders for dynamic content. Visit `http://www.smarty.net/crashcourse.php` and `http://www.packtpub.com/smarty/book` for more.

Next, we found the template our site was using. We could tell it by name, since the template shows up in a dropdown in the add new pages screen as well. We opened the template and reviewed it. It was simple to understand—much like HTML. We inserted our product content block tag after the main content display. Then we saved it and previewed our site.

Just as expected, the product promotion content showed up after main content of all pages.

This shows how easy it is to add global content using CMSMS. But we also learned that global content blocks can help us manage promotions or commonly used content. Even if you don't go for CMS Made Simple, you can find a similar feature in the CMS of your choice.

Simple features can make life easier

CMS Made Simple's Global Content Block feature made it easy to run product promotions throughout a site. A simple feature like that can make the content administrator's life easier. Look out for such simple things that could make your job faster and easier in the CMS you evaluate.

It's good time now to dive deeper into CMSMS. Go ahead and see whether it's the right choice for you.

Have a go hero-is it right for you?

CMS Made Simple (**CMSMS**) looks very promising. If we wanted to build a standard web site with a photo gallery, newsletter, and so on, it is a perfect fit. Its code structure is understandable, the extending functionality is not too difficult. The default templates could be more appealing, but you can always create your own.

```
#Perform the content postrender callback
reset($gCms->modules);
while (list($key) = each($gCms->modules))
{
    $value =& $gCms->modules[$key];
    if ($gCms->modules[$key]['installed'] == true &&
        $gCms->modules[$key]['active'] == true)
    {
        $gCms->modules[$key]['object']->ContentPostRender($html);
    }
}

Events::SendEvent('Core', 'ContentPostRender', array('content' => &$html));

header("Content-Type: " . $gCms->variables['content-type'] . "; charset=" . (i

echo $html;

@ob_flush();

$endtime = microtime();

$db =& $gCms->GetDb();
```

The gentle learning curve of CMSMS is very impressive. The hierarchical display of pages, easy reordering, and simplistic content management approach are excellent. It's simple to figure out how things work. Yet CMSMS is a powerful system—remember how easily we could add a global content block? Doing something like that may need writing a plug-in or hacking source code in most other systems.

It's the right time for you to see how it fits your needs. Take a while and evaluate the following:

- Does it meet your feature requirements?
- Does it have enough modules and extensions for your future needs?
- What does its web site say? Does it align with your vision and philosophy?
- Does it look good enough?
- Check out the forums and support structure. Do you see an active community?
- What are its system requirements? Do you have it all taken care of?
- If you are going to need customizations, do you (or your team) comfortably understand the code?

We are done evaluating a simple CMS. Let us now look at the top two heavyweights in the Web CMS world—**Drupal** and **Joomla!**.

Diving into Drupal

Drupal (`http://www.drupal.org`) is a top open source Web CMS. Drupal has been around for years and has excellent architecture, code quality, and community support. The Drupal terminology can take time to sink in. But it can serve the most complicated content management needs.

FastCompany and **AOL's Corporate** site work on Drupal:

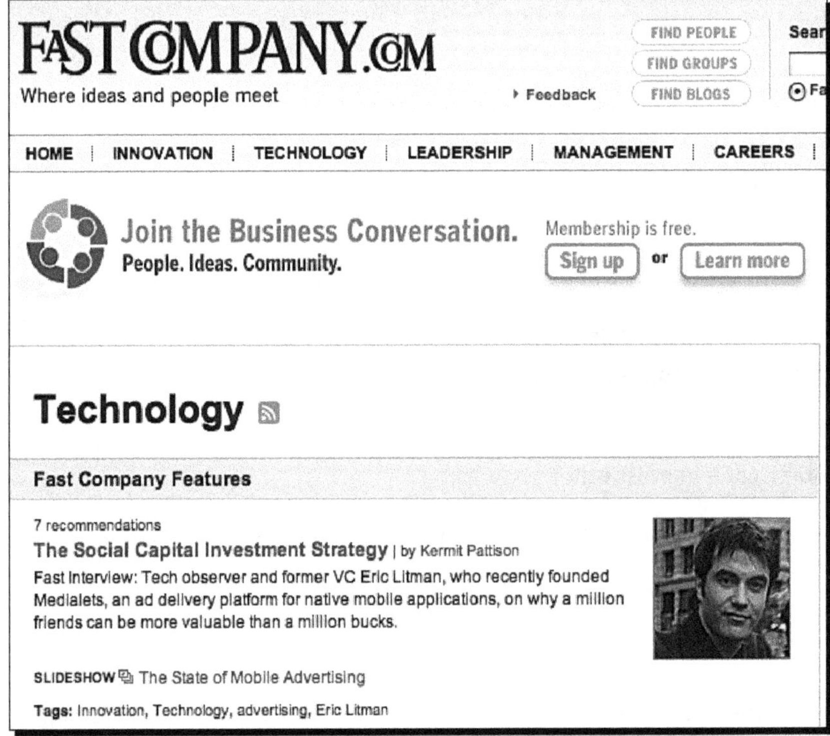

Here is the **About Drupal** section on the Drupal web site. As you can see, Drupal can be used for almost all types of content management needs. The goal is to allow easy publishing and management of a wide variety of content.

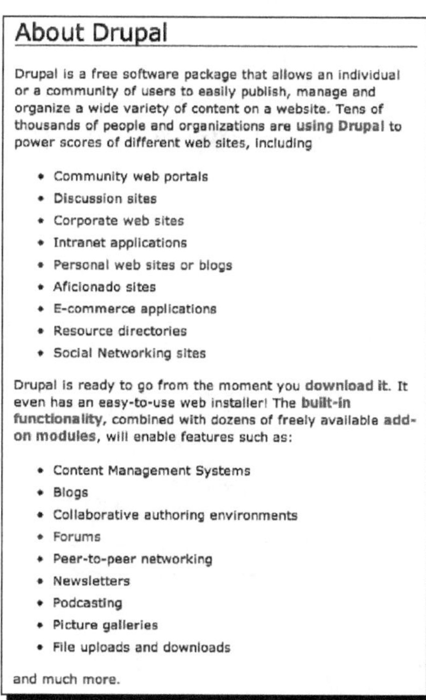

About Drupal

Drupal is a free software package that allows an individual or a community of users to easily publish, manage and organize a wide variety of content on a website. Tens of thousands of people and organizations are **using Drupal** to power scores of different web sites, including

- Community web portals
- Discussion sites
- Corporate web sites
- Intranet applications
- Personal web sites or blogs
- Aficionado sites
- E-commerce applications
- Resource directories
- Social Networking sites

Drupal is ready to go from the moment you **download it**. It even has an easy-to-use web installer! The **built-in functionality**, combined with dozens of freely available **add-on modules**, will enable features such as:

- Content Management Systems
- Blogs
- Collaborative authoring environments
- Forums
- Peer-to-peer networking
- Newsletters
- Podcasting
- Picture galleries
- File uploads and downloads

and much more.

Let's try out Drupal. Let's understand how steep the learning curve really is, and why so many people swear by Drupal.

Time for action-putting Drupal to the test

1. Download and install Drupal.

Installing Drupal involves downloading the latest stable release, extracting and uploading files to your server, setting up a database, and then following the instructions in a web installer. Refer to `http://drupal.org/getting-started/` if you need help.

2. Log in as the administrator. As you log in, you see a link to **Create Content**. This tells you that you can either create a page (simple content page) or a story (content with comments). We want to create a simple content page without any comments. So click on **Page**.

In Drupal, viewing a page and editing a page are almost the same. You log in to Drupal and see site content in a preview mode. Depending on your rights, you will see links to edit content and manage other options.

3. This shows the **Create Page** screen. There is a title but no WYSIWYG editor. Yes, Drupal does not come with a WYSIWYG text editor by default. You have to install an extension module for this.
4. Let's go ahead and do that first.
5. Go to the Drupal web site. Search for **WYSIWYG** in downloads.

6. Find TinyMCE in the list. TinyMCE is the WYSIWYG editor we have seen in most other CMSs.

7. Download the latest TinyMCE module for Drupal—compatible with your version of Drupal.

Releases

Official releases	Date	Size	Links	Status	
6.x-1.1-dev	2008-Mar-31	45.86 KB	Download · Release notes	Recommended for 6.x	✓

8. The download does not include the actual TinyMCE editor. It only includes hooks to make the editor work with Drupal.

9. Go to the TinyMCE web site (`http://tinymce.moxiecode.com/download.php`). Download the latest version.

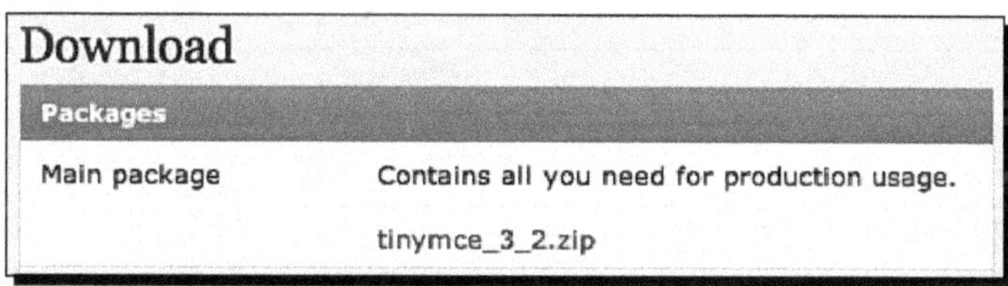

10. Create a new folder called `modules` in the `sites/all/` folder of Drupal. This is the place to store all custom modules.

11. Extract the TinyMCE Drupal module here. It should create a folder named `tinymce` within the `modules` folder.

12. Extract the TinyMCE editor within this folder. This creates a subfolder called `tinymce` within `sites/all/modules/tinymce`.

13. Make sure the files are in the correct folders. Here's how your structure will look:

```
bash-3.2$ pwd
/Applications/xampp/htdocs/drupal/sites/all/modules/tinymce
bash-3.2$ ls
INSTALL.txt              plugins                  tinymce.info
LICENSE.txt              po                       tinymce.install
README.TXT               tinymce                  tinymce.module
plugin_reg.php           tinymce.admin.inc
bash-3.2$ 
```

14. Log in to Drupal if you are not already logged in. Go to **Administer | Site building | Modules**.

15. If all went well so far, at the end of the list of modules, you will find **TinyMCE**. Check the box next to it and click on **Save Configuration** to enable it.

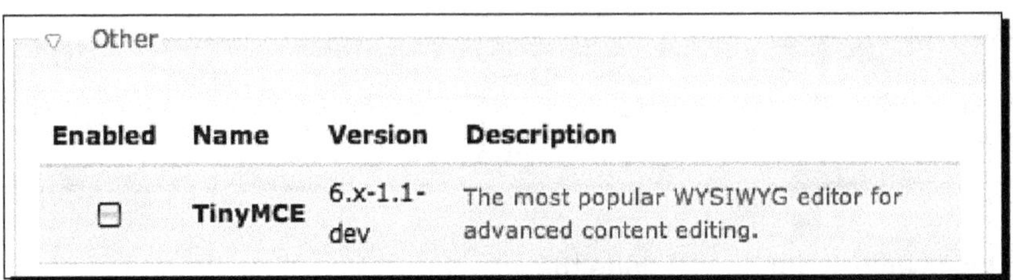

16. We need to perform two more steps before we can test this. Go to **Administer | Site configuration | TinyMCE**. It will prompt you that you don't have any profiles created. Create a new profile. Keep it **enabled** by default.

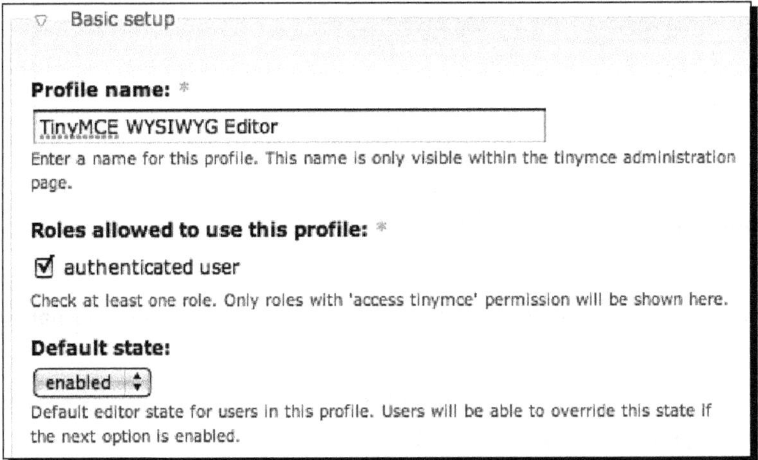

17. Go to **Administer | User management | Permissions**. You will get this link from the TinyMCE configuration page too. Allow authenticated users to **access tinymce**. Then save permissions.

Permission	anonymous user	authenticated user
tinymce module		
access tinymce	☐	☑
administer tinymce	☐	☐

18. We are now ready to test. Go to the **Create Content | Page** link.

19. Super! The shiny WYSIWYG editor is now functional! It shows editing controls below the text area (all the other CMSs we saw so far show the controls above).

20. Go ahead and add some content. Make sure to check **Full HTML** in **Input Format**. Save the page.

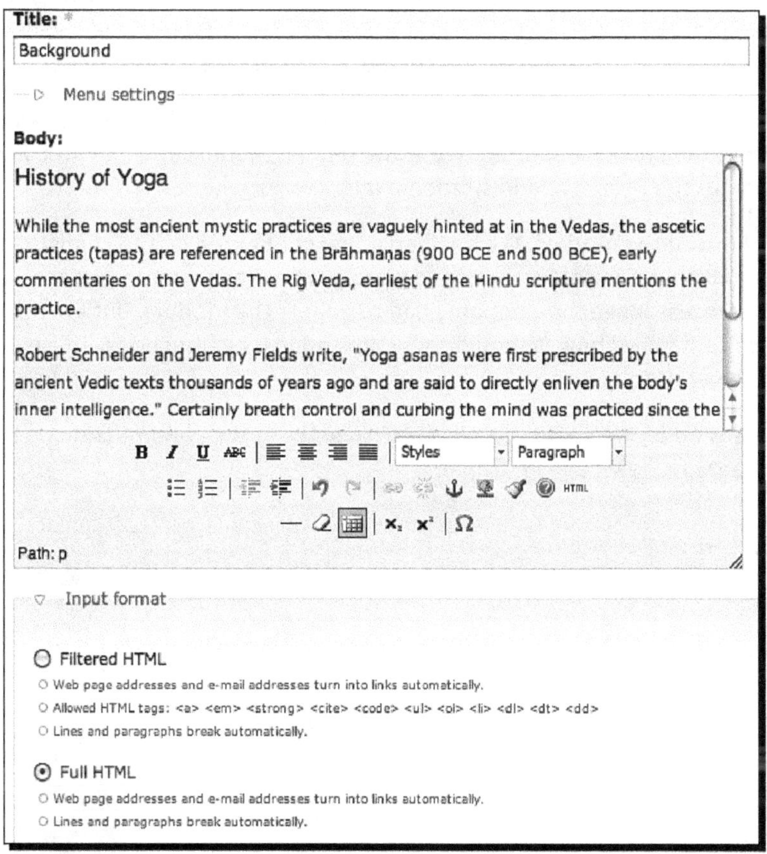

21. You will see the content we entered right after you save it. Congratulations!

What just happened?

We deserve congratulations. After installing Drupal, we spotted that it did not come with a WYSIWYG editor. That's a bit of a setback. Drupal claims to be lightweight, but it should come with a nice editor, right?

There are reasons for not including an editor by default. Drupal can be used for a variety of needs, and different WYSIWYG editors provide different features. The reason for not including any editor is to allow you to use the one that you feel is the best. Drupal is about a strong core and flexibility.

At the same time, not getting a WYSIWYG editor by default was an opportunity. It was our opportunity to see how easy it was to add a plug-in to Drupal. We went to the Drupal site and found the TinyMCE module. The description of the module mentioned that the module is only a hook to TinyMCE. We need to download TinyMCE separately. We did that too.

Hooks are another strength of Drupal. They are an easy way to develop extensions for Drupal. An additional function of modules is to ensure that we download a version compatible with Drupal's version. Mismatched Drupal and module versions create problems.

We created a new directory within `sites/all`. This is the directory in which all custom modules/extensions should be stored. We extracted the module and TinyMCE ZIP files. We then logged on to the Drupal administration panel.

Drupal had detected the module. We enabled it and configured it. The configuration process was multistep. Drupal has a very good access privilege system, but that made the configuration process longer. We not only had to enable the module, but also enable it for users. We also configured how it should show up, and in which sections. These are superb features for power users.

Once all this was done, we could see a WYSIWYG editor in the content creation page. We used it and created a new page in Drupal.

Here are the lessons we learned:

- Don't assume a feature in the CMS. Verify if that CMS has what you need.
- Drupal's module installation and configuration process is multistep and may require some looking around.
- Read the installation instructions of the plug-in. You will make fewer mistakes that way.
- Drupal is lightweight and is packed with a lot of power. But it has a learning curve of its own.

With those important lessons in our mind, let's look around Drupal and figure out our way.

Have a go hero-figure out your way with Drupal

We just saw what it takes to get a WYSIWYG editor working with Drupal. This was obviously not a simple plug-and-play setup! Drupal has its way of doing things. If you are planning to use Drupal, it's a good time to go deeper and figure your way out with Drupal. Try out the following:

- Create a book with three chapters.
- Create a mailing list and send out one newsletter.
- Configure permissions and users according to your requirements.
- What if you wanted to customize the homepage? How easily can you do this? (Warning: It's not a simple operation with most CMSs.)

Choosing a CMS is very confusing!

Evaluating and choosing a CMS can be very confusing. Don't worry if you feel lost and confused among all the CMSs and their features. The guiding factors should always be your requirements, not the CMS's features. Figure out who's going to use the CMS—developers or end users. Find out all you need: Do you need to allow customizing the homepage? Know your technology platform. Check the code quality of the CMS—bad code can gag you. Does your site need so many features? Is the CMS only good looking, or is it beauty with brains? Consider all this in your evaluation.

Drupal code quality

Drupal's code is very well-structured. It's easy to understand and extend it via the hooks mechanism. The Drupal team takes extreme care in producing good code. Take a look at the sample code here. If you like looking around code, go ahead and peek into Drupal. Even if you don't use Drupal as a CMS, you can learn more about programming best practices.

```
/**
 * This function is called by book_export() to generate HTML for export.
 *
 * The given node is /embedded to its absolute depth in a top level
 * section/. For example, a child node with depth 2 in the hierarchy
 * is contained in (otherwise empty) &lt;div&gt; elements
 * corresponding to depth 0 and depth 1. This is intended to support
 * WYSIWYG output - e.g., level 3 sections always look like level 3
 * sections, no matter their depth relative to the node selected to be
 * exported as printer-friendly HTML.
 *
 * @param $nid
 *   An integer representing the node id (nid) of the node to export.
 * @return
 *   A string containing HTML representing the node and its children in
 *   the book hierarchy.
 */
function book_export_html($nid) {
  if (user_access('access printer-friendly version')) {
    $export_data = array();
    $node = node_load($nid);
    if (isset($node->book)) {
      $tree = book_menu_subtree_data($node->book);
      $contents = book_export_traverse($tree, 'book_node_export');
    }
    return theme('book_export_html', $node->title, $contents, $node->book['depth']);
  }
  else {
    drupal_access_denied();
  }
}
```

You may be wondering why we haven't covered Joomla! so far. After all, we used Joomla! for the examples in the initial chapters. Since we have gained a good understanding of how Joomla! can meet our needs, let's do a quick review and see some interesting Joomla! features.

Is Joomla! the best choice?

Joomla! (`http://joomla.org/`) is the most popular open source Web CMS. It's been more than three years since Joomla! was born as a fork of Mambo (`http://mambo-foundation.org/`). Today Joomla! has an active community of more than 200,000 users and contributors. Joomla! has around 4,000 extensions and many themes.

Numerous high-profile sites use Joomla!. The code quality is good enough, but there is a steep learning curve. Many users complain about its template system. Also, the backend administration system could be simpler.

The **Harvard University** web site and the MTV's **Quizilla** web site are both Joomla! based.

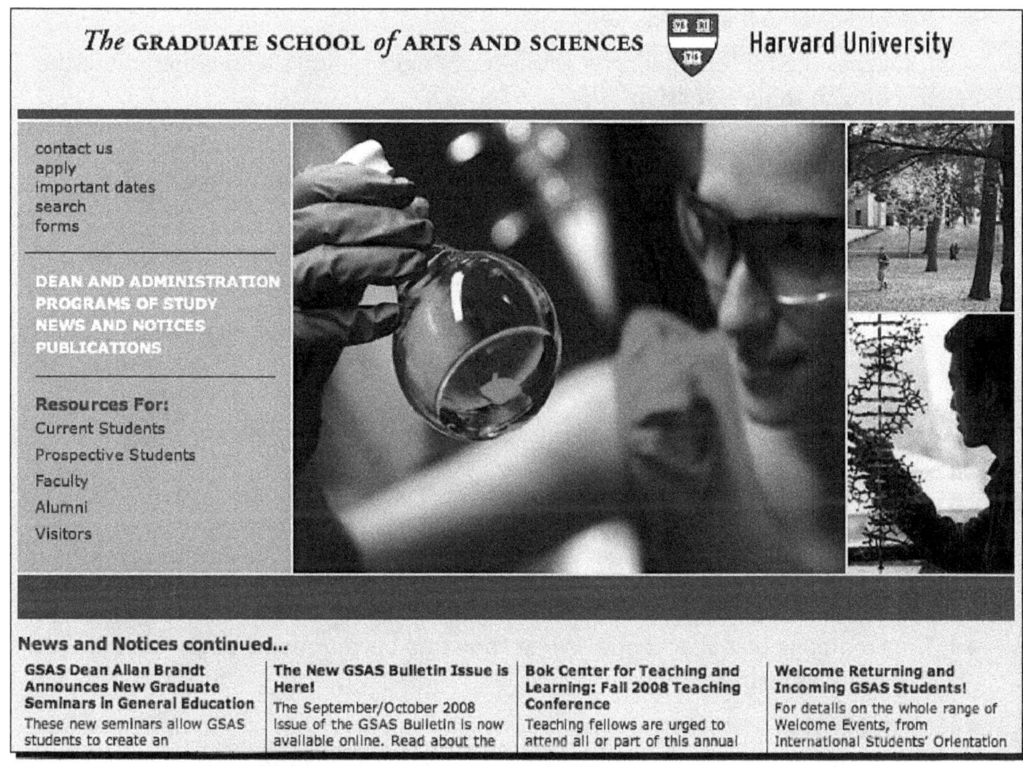

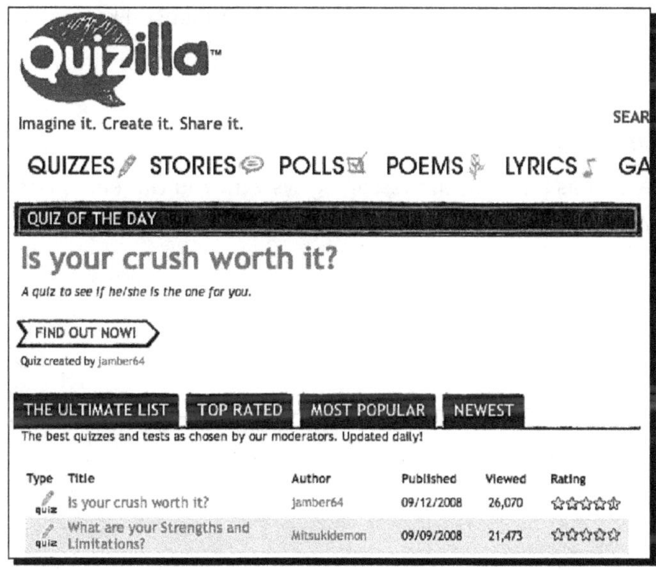

But is Joomla! the best choice? Consider the following:

- Joomla! has the reach and size.
- It satisfies the content management needs of most typical sites—either out of the box or with some extension.
- Since there are so many choices in Joomla!, it can get confusing. Selecting a template can be arduous. Selecting the best extension for your need maybe completely a guess.
- Joomla! does not score too well on usability. But that's the case with most CMSs. Joomla! is also known to be demanding on the server.
- If you are looking for additional modules such as e-commerce, communities, and so on, you won't go wrong with Joomla!.

With this overall feedback, let me show a few useful out-of-the-box features of Joomla!.

Joomla! gives you more

Here are some useful features in the default installation of Joomla!. We did not cover them earlier, since we concentrated on the core content management features.

- The Frontpage Manager controls what shows up on your home page. This gets really important as your site grows.
- Menus control navigation around the site. You can manage them the way you want. You can order items in the priority you wish, and even control access levels.
- Banners let you run advertisements and promotions. They support both text and image ads. This means you can display Google AdSense-like ads on your own.
- News Feeds make it easy to syndicate content from other sites. You can even categorize feeds.
- Polls make it easy to carry out surveys.
- Joomla! even has an internal messaging system. You can easily communicate with all users of your site.

Advertisement

Featured Links:

Joomla!

Joomla! The most popular and widely used Open Source CMS Project in the world.

JoomlaCode

JoomlaCode, development and distribution made easy.

Joomla! Extensions

Joomla! Components, Modules, Plugins and Languages by the bucket load.

Joomla! Shop

For all your Joomla! merchandise.

Ads by Joomla!

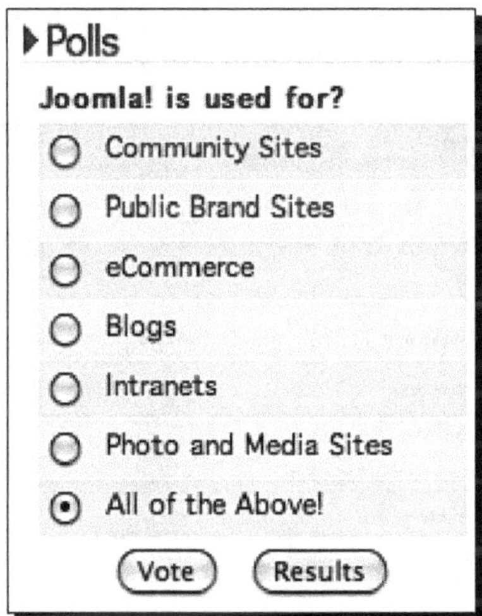

If you use these features creatively, you can build a very powerful site.

Have a go hero-set up a full site with Joomla!

This is a great time to explore Joomla! further. Here's something you can try out:

- Set up a full site with Joomla! along with sample content, images, menus, and homepage.
- Create users and understand how a workflow can be established.
- Install a SEO extension for Joomla! and learn how it can help your site.

I did not answer the question we started with: Is Joomla! the best choice? You are the person who has to decide on that because everyone's needs will be different. Continue to evaluate other CMSs, and then you can make your final decision.

> A small requirement can jeopardize your development. Keep a watch on your requirements and carefully evaluate that the CMS you choose can either fulfill it by default, or allow doing it with custom code. A small requirement (especially if it is not clear at the start) can derail your CMS project if the CMS you select does not accomplish that requirement easily.

SilverStripe—easy and extensive

SilverStripe (`http://www.silverstripe.com/`) is an upcoming CMS. When you see it, you will be impressed. When you try the demo, you will be further impressed! Take a look at the following screen, which shows up right after you log in:

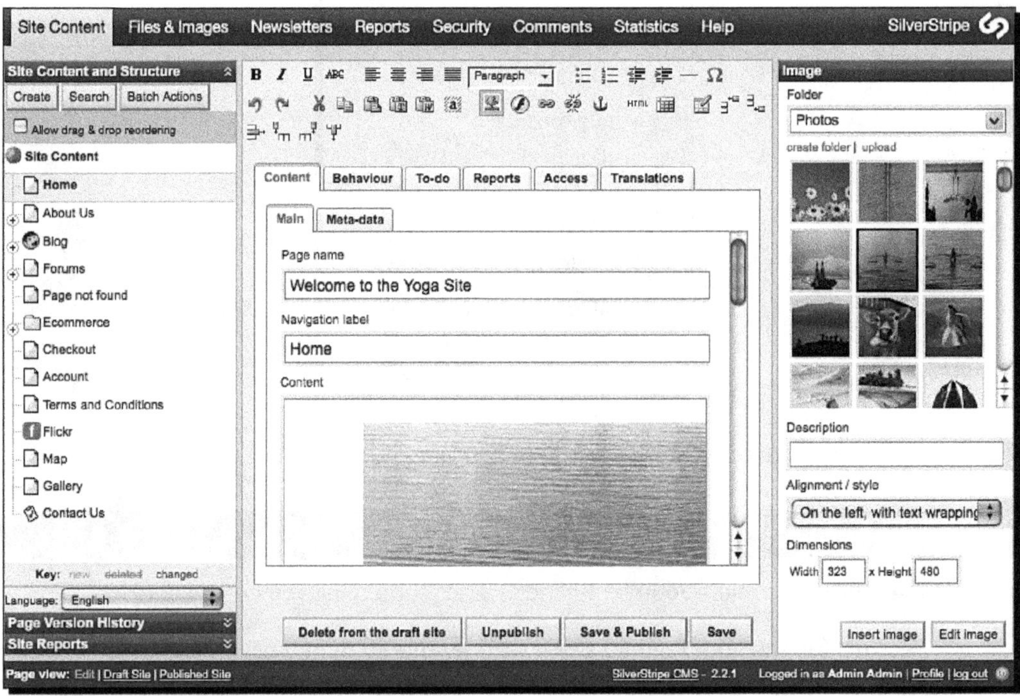

Notable features

Here are the noticeable things in this screen:

- You start in content editing. You don't have to click around menus to get to the content editing screen.
- All the content is easily available on the lefthand side. Click on an item and its content loads on the right side without reloading the page.
- Apart from the standard WYSIWYG editor, you get all other options for this content right here. This includes metadata and page behavior (standard page, forum, blog, e-commerce page, and so on).
- You can control access and translations of content right here.
- When invoked, the image manager shows on the righthand side with thumbnails and quick insertion.
- SilverStripe has an built-in image editor. It allows you to resize and crop images.
- On the left, you also get options for Page Versions and Site Usage Reports.
- The CMS also has other powerful features such as Newsletter, Files, Comments, Reports, and Statistics.

The things that you don't see onscreen, but are worth a mention for SilverStripe, are:

- An RoR-like framework in PHP, based on Sapphire
- An easy template system
- SilverStripe has additional modules for e-commerce, blog, forum, Flickr, and Google Maps
- Thorough documentation for both users and developers

Is it for you?

SilverStripe is a strong contender for any site that needs core content management features. If you don't need all the extensions and overhead, it makes perfect sense. The efforts spent on making the software usable are evident. The terminology is simple, and the workflow even better. Anyone can get started with SilverStripe in minutes. The bottom line is, evaluate SilverStripe before you take your decision.

ezPublish—enterprise CMS

If you are looking for an enterprise class CMS, you should consider **ezPublish** (`http://ez.no/`). High-profile sites such as **MySQL** (`http://www.mysql.com`) and **Zend** (`http://www.zend.com`), and even NASA, National Geographic, and MIT run on ezPublish. The software has more than 2.5 million downloads, at least 230 official partners across the world, and approximately 30,000 community users.

So what makes ezPublish an enterprise-class CMS? Let's review some of its notable features.

Notable features

- A complete workflow control, which includes adding, editing, and publishing content
- An extensive user access and privilege system
- Multilingual support from the ground up
- Content Versioning
- Publishes to multiple sites easily
- Strong SEO features
- Strong controls for media or news publishing
- Imports Word or OpenOffice documents, and even supports WebDAV for uploads
- Supports different content types such as text, images, videos, and so on
- Extensive documentation and partner support
- Many extensions available

The following image shows the different categories of setting options in ezPublish:

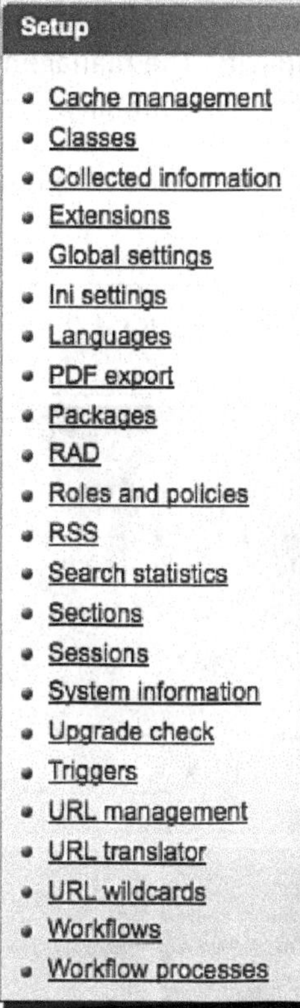

Is it for you?

If you want a strong workflow, ezPublish is one of the best. It comes with all standard CMS features. However, the variety of extensions available is not as good as Joomla!; and the product has a strong corporate feel to it. If you are looking for a quick solution, this may not be your bet. But if you are deploying something for a large organization, ezPublish can top the list.

All the CMSs we have seen up to this point use PHP as the backend programming language. PHP is available on most web servers. But what if you want to use some other environment? Let's quickly review some non-PHP CMSs.

Umbraco—rising high

Umbraco (`http://www.umbraco.org/`) is a simple and easy CMS written for .Net. It's gaining popularity because of its simplicity. The management interface is simple and allows developers to customize the design and functionality.

Hasselblad (`http://www.hasselblad.se/`) is a high-end photography equipment site that runs on Umbraco.

Notable features

- Written in C#, and can be used with any .Net language
- Convenient for custom design, and has full HTML support
- APIs for easy integration with their own applications
- IntelliSense and tight Visual Studio integration
- Outputs content as XML—easily integrates with Flex/SilverLight rich Internet applications
- Out-of-the-box XSLT and AJAX support

- Versioning of content, integration with MS Word
- Multilingual, and easy content translation support
- Simple and easy system that focuses on web site building and content, and not on endless extensions
- Professional support and extensions available

Is it for you?

Umbraco is pretty impressive. You will love its simplicity and integration features. But the documentation needs improvements, and you can't run it without an SQL Server. If your site wants core CMS features, Umbraco is the best .Net system today. Go check it out.

DotNetNuke—the first you may notice

If you are on Windows and want a .Net-based CMS, **dotNetNuke** (**DNN**) (`http://www.dotnetnuke.com/`) is the first CMS you will notice. DNN was inspired from phpNuke—a once very popular CMS—and derived from sample web site code that Microsoft opened up. DNN is advertised as a web application framework. It has well-rounded core features and modules that extend it.

Notable features

- One of the first open source .Net CMSs, DNN has been there for ages
- A good base system, allows extensions via modules
- Many free and commercial modules available
- Feature-rich, extensive support available

Is it for you?

If you want a well-known, well-rounded .Net CMS, DNN is a very good choice. It's not the best when it comes to usability or quality, but it's popular and easy to get developers to review it!

Plone—for Python lovers

If you are into Python, you must have heard of **Zope** and **Plone** (`http://plone.org/`). As a matter of fact, you may have heard of Python because of Plone. Plone is a high-profile (sometimes more hyped) CMS, built on Zope. Zope (`http://www.zope.org/`) is an application server written in Python—with built-in web server and database—to build CMSs, intranets, portals, and community sites.

The magazine Discover and the Free Software Foundation web site are the prime advocates of Plone.

Notable features

- Solid and extensible system
- Enterprise features—workflow engine, security, LDAP, and so on
- Used by many high-profile sites
- Easy to install, powerful template language
- Ability to define its own content types
- Can be used for intranets, community sites, and so on—Plone is not just a CMS!
- Based on Zope, uses ZODB as database—this is also a limitation

Is it for you?

Plone has some great features and some big advocates. It has an equally great learning curve. If you are new to Python, Plone will have a significant learning curve for you. If you don't have a programming background, you may find yourself stuck when you want to enhance the core system. Python is easy to learn, but getting around with Zope and Plone can take a few weeks even for an experienced programmer.

If you are already using Python, Plone is a natural choice for your CMS. It has the elegance and features that satisfy demanding users. Go for Plone if you've got a team to manage it.

dotCMS—enterprise and Java

DotCMS (`http://www.dotcms.org/`) is a J2EE Web CMS. It's packed with features and is in constant development. It's not just a CMS, since it also offers many portal-like components. It has an interesting history, and is from the same company that produced dotProject—an open source project management system.

Notable features

- Excellent core features that match and top similar PHP solutions
- Structured content
- Enterprise features such as caching, rules support, clustering, Amazon EC2 support, WebDAV support, task-based workflow, and so on
- Built-in systems such as calendars, events, CRM, newsletter, and so on
- AJAX used to make things faster and simpler

Is it for you?

If you have a J2EE infrastructure running, dotCMS is a very good choice as a CMS. There are only a handful of Java CMSs, and dotCMS is one of the best. Although setting up dotCMS is not as easy as setting up a PHP CMS, we must remember that they are in different leagues altogether. There are some other popular Java CMSs as well, and most of them are more than just Web CMSs.

Where to find more?

We covered most of the top web CMSs here. If you are still looking for more, here is a quick list:

- XOOPS: `http://xoops.org/`
- Typo Light: `http://www.typolight.org/`
- Apache Lenya: `http://lenya.apache.org/`
- Alfresco: `http://www.alfresco.com/` (we will cover this later in the book)
- OpenCMS: `http://www.opencms.org/`
- mojoPortal: `http://www.mojoportal.com/`
- ImpressCMS: `http://www.impresscms.org/`
- miaCMS: `http://www.miacms.org/`
- MemHT: `http://www.memht.com/`
- WikiPedia's list of CMSs: `http://en.wikipedia.org/wiki/List_of_content_management_systems`

That should satisfy anyone's need for a list of CMSs! We have seen enough CMSs in this chapter. Let's summarize what we learned.

Summary

We reviewed a whole lot of Web CMSs in this chapter. We covered details of only a few, since most have common features and workflow. Doing all these evaluations, we can see that most CMSs are similar. The choice of which to pick depends a lot on factors other than features. The ease of use, platform, integration with other systems, and so on weigh a lot more than just features. At the same time, most CMSs are under constant development. They keep improving on their limitations. Always keep your requirements and situation at the top priority while selecting a CMS.

In this chapter, we specifically looked at:

- Creating structure and content with CMS Made Simple
- Adding a WYSIWYG editor to Drupal
- Using Drupal administration and content addition features
- Drupal's code quality

- Built-in Joomla! features that we can use
- Easy-to-use SilverStripe CMS
- Enterprise features of CMSs
- ezPublish, Plone, Umbraco, DNN, dotCMS— an overview and notable features
- The CMS that could be right for you

We accomplished a lot in this chapter. There is a lot for you to review and think through. Once you are through that, let's go on to e-commerce CMSs in the next chapter.

10

CMS for e-commerce

In the last chapter we evaluated top Web CMSs extensively. Most of the top CMSs are general-purpose CMSs that can take care of the needs of a standard web site. But what if your site is primarily an e-commerce web site? Why should you consider a CMS for e-commerce? Let's answer these questions.

In this chapter we will take a look at some top e-commerce systems. We will:

- *Understand the importance of content in an e-commerce site*
- *Try out one of the best open source e-commerce systems*
- *Evaluate other e-commerce systems*
- *Discover interesting features in these systems*
- *Examine which system could be right for you*

Let's get started.

Content or commerce?

Why do we need to talk about CMS and e-commerce? There are hundreds of open source shopping cart systems. If you want to build an e-commerce site, you could easily pick a shopping cart system and get going. After all, the content on an e-commerce site is limited to terms and policies, right?

Well, not really! Today's customers don't buy a product just looking at the product specifications and price. They also want reviews. They want ratings. They probably want a community around the product. You may even need to build web-based support material for the product—especially if your product too is web-based.

Moreover, products have grown complex. They have different colors and variations. To increase sales, you need to up-sell and cross-sell by showing related products. You also need to show multiple images of a product so that users get a better feel of it. You may need to allow customers to compare products side by side and offer discounts.

Once you have a sale, you need to ensure you retain the customer. Not only that, you want to get more business from that customer. How do you do that? Well, you send out newsletters, write a blog, keep a support forum, and keep sending special offers.

Oh, and what about search engines? You must be ranked high in search engines to get some quality traffic to your site. You must have a good control over the design and metadata of the site.

The point I am trying to make is simple. Online shopping is not simple. You need powerful tools to succeed. Today a good e-commerce system needs to manage not only products and categories, but also a plethora of related content.

So what are your options?

Depending on your requirements, you have the following options:

- Add an e-commerce plug-in to a CMS. Go for this method if your site is more about its content than sales.
- Take an e-commerce system that has good CMS features. Go for this if you mostly have static content.
- Rent a solution. There are hosted e-commerce solutions. You pay a monthly fee and they run the show for you.
- Build your own CMS. If nothing here serves your needs, you can always extend any open source system.

We will look at the first two options here. The primary focus will be e-commerce systems and their store management features. Let's start with one of the best—Magento.

Magento—open source e-commerce evolved

Magento (`http://www.magentocommerce.com/`) is an upcoming e-commerce system. Its tagline is "open source e-commerce evolved". And it is nothing less than impressive. Developers who've been loyal fans of other systems have converted to Magento overnight! It is one of the most advanced, yet one of the easiest e-commerce systems out there.

The **Mia & Maggie** web site (`http://www.miaandmaggie.com/`), providing high-quality dog and puppy supplies, runs on Magento and so does **Myriad Fine Art** (`http://www.myriadfineart.com/`), an online custom art gallery.

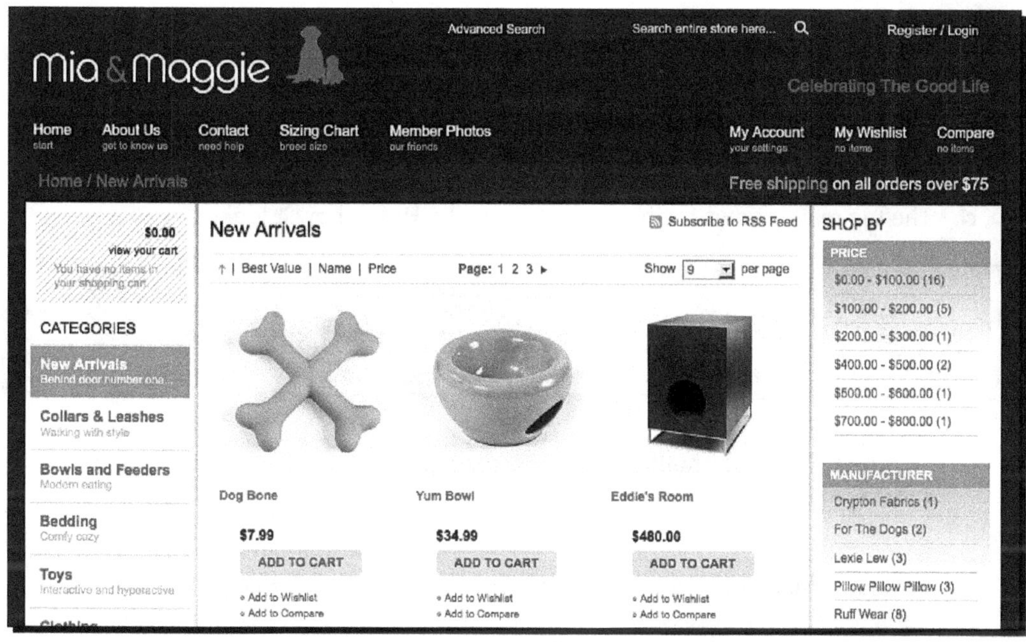

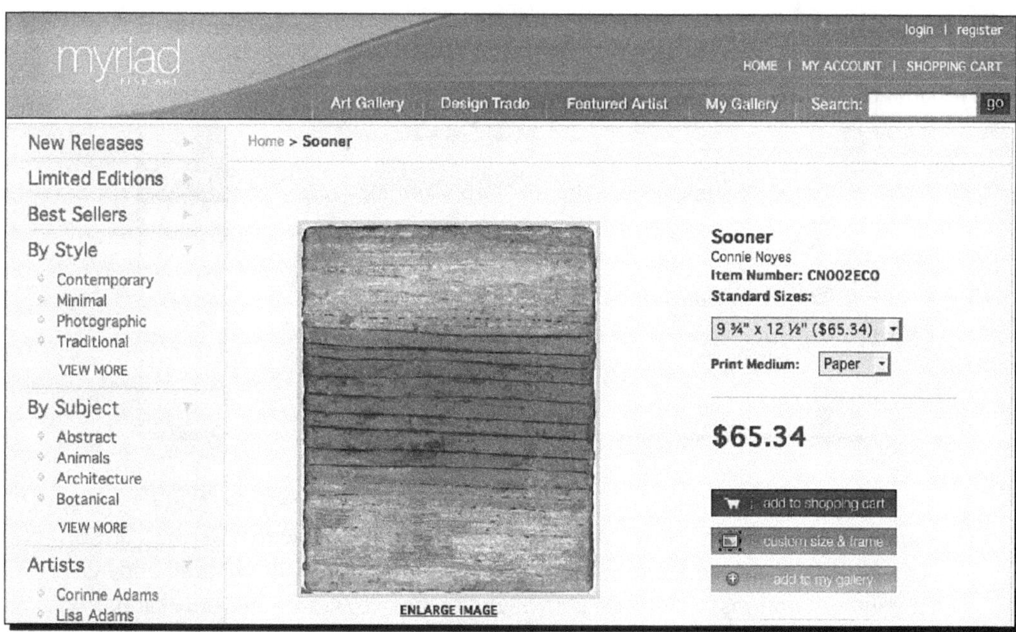

Let's try out Magento to see how good it really is.

Time for action-adding products with Magento

1. Download and install Magento. Alternatively, go to the demo at `http://www.opensourcecms.com/`.
2. Log in to the administration section.
3. The top menu shows the breadth of Magento. Here's how it looks.

4. That's easy to understand. We want to add a product. So we will have to go to the **Catalog** option.
5. Before we add a product, let's add a category for it. It's important to set up a taxonomy that's easy to understand and navigate. Select **Catalog | Manage Categories**. Enter **Accessories** in **Name**, set the **Is Active** field to **Yes**, and enter **accessories** in **URL Key**. Add some **Description** as well.

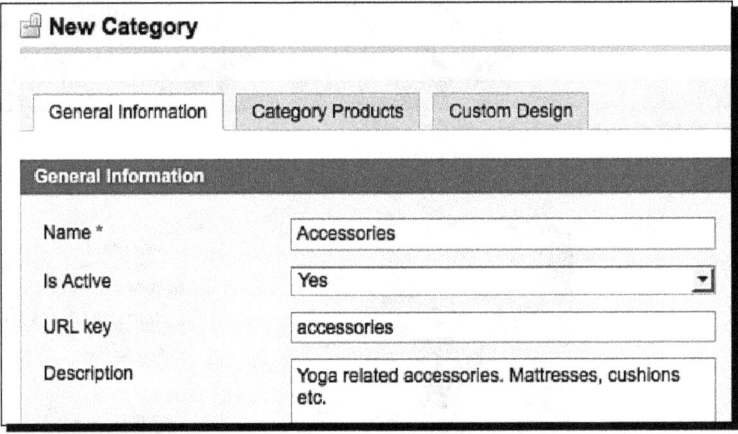

6. You can also add an **Image** for this category. Enter the **Page Title**, **Meta Keywords**, and **Meta Description**. If we want to show some content with a dynamic list of categories, we can select that in the last few options as well. We are happy with the default options, so let's click on **Save Category** to create our new category.

Notice the yellow action bar that shows up at the top of the page as you scroll down. This is one of Magento's beautiful features. You don't need to scroll back to the top in order to click **Save** or other action buttons. The buttons hover over the top of the page as you scroll.

7. You may also create additional categories for **Audio CDs and Tapes** and **Books**.
8. There is a tree navigation for categories in the lefthand column. Drag and drop our newly created **Accessories** category in **Default Category**. This will make it visible on our site later on.

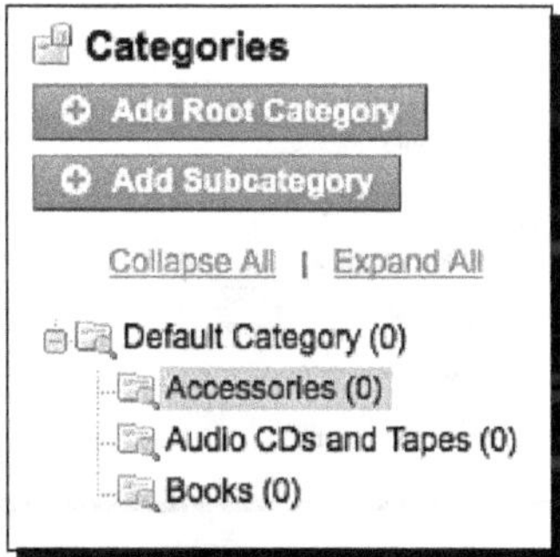

9. We are now ready to add a product. Go to **Catalog | Manage Products**. Click on the **Add Product** button at the right side.
10. Magento asks you about which attribute set you want to use for this product, and what type of product this is. Let's just go ahead with the defaults.

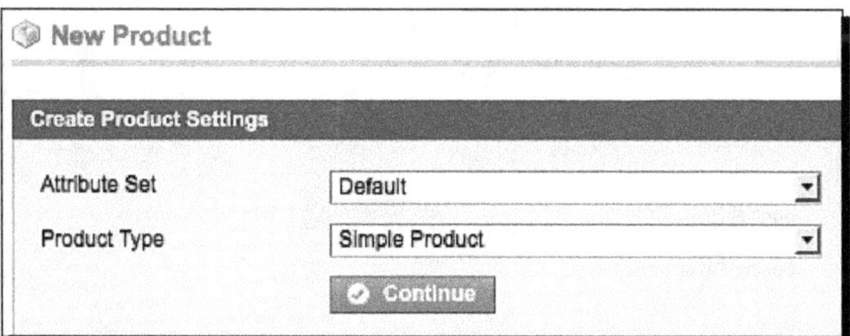

11. This brings you to the product creation screen. We are creating an entry for a yoga mattress. Go ahead and fill in name, description, short description, and so on.

12. Click on the **Save** button.

13. Oops! There is some problem. We forgot to enter pricing information. But look at the left column. We can set many other parameters for a product.

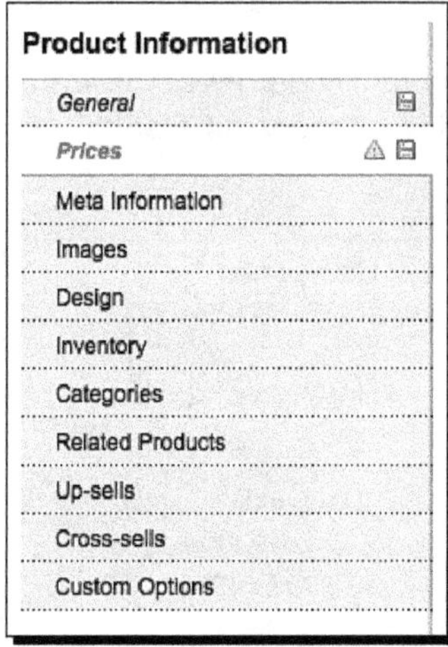

14. Let's first set up pricing. We are selling the mattress at $**12.29**. Its cost is $**4.50** and we want to charge shipping. We don't want to set up any tier pricing or customer-specific pricing yet.

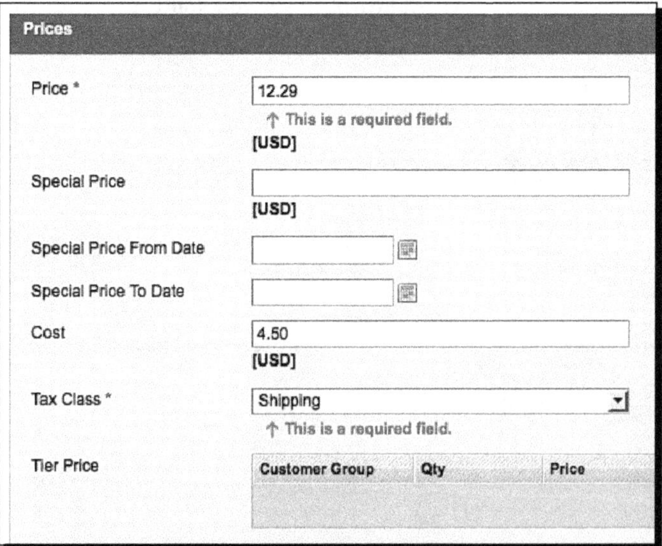

15. Let's add an image for the mattress now. We can browse, select, and upload multiple files. But we will add only one now. Select all three options—**Base Image**, **Small Image**, **Thumbnail**—for that image. Also give it a **Label**. The **Sort Order** will be **1**, as this is the only image for this product.

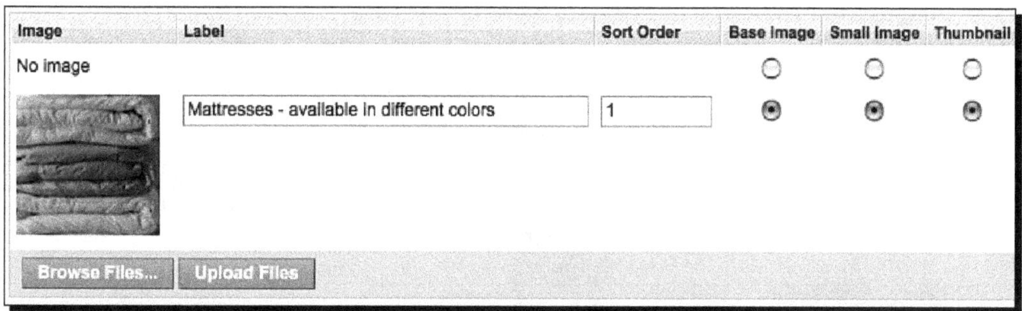

16. Now, let's see what we can set in **Inventory**. Apart from the available inventory, we can also set minimum and maximum order quantities, allow for backorders, and so on. A good thing is that all these options can be set at a global level for all products. If we leave the defaults as they are, Magento will use our global settings.

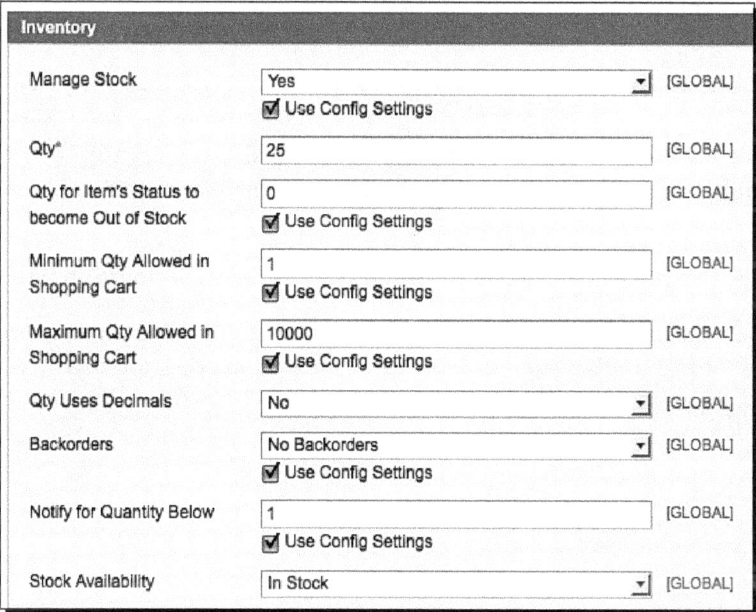

17. Let's go to the next tab—**Categories**. Here we can select categories this product belongs to. Our mattress will go only to the **Accessories** category. But we can show it in as many categories as we want.

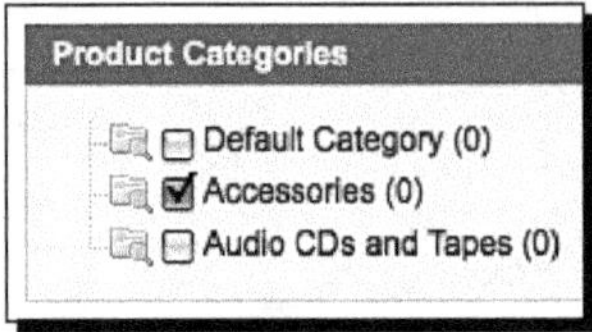

18. This is enough for now. Save the product and come to the **Manage Products** listing. Our new product shows up there very well!

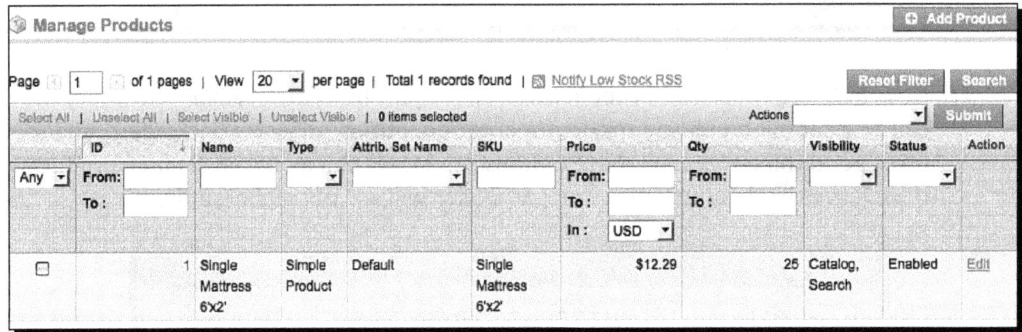

19. There are many options in the header. Magento allows quick sorting and filtering of records along with the listing. This is an interesting feature, isn't it?

20. We want to see our product now. There is no link to view our site from the admin panel, so open a new window and enter your Magento installation URL.

21. This shows our site! Click on the **Accessories** category in the top bar, or search for **yoga** through the search box. Either of these should bring you to a screen similar to the following.

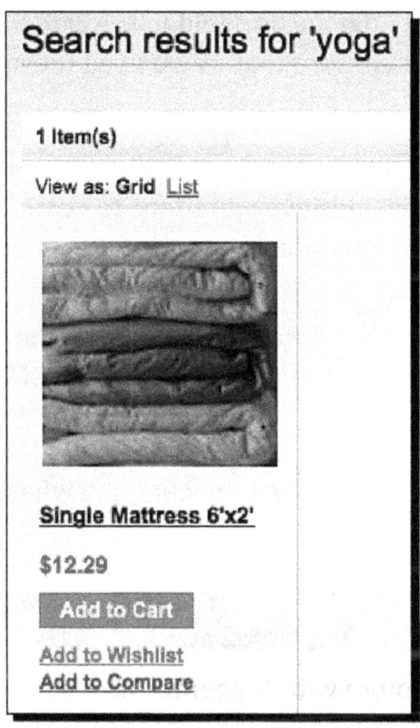

22. Congratulations! We have successfully launched our super-sleek yoga mattresses.

What just happened?

We created a new category and a product using Magento.

Creating a new category was easy and efficient. The drag-and-drop operation on the category tree was a superb way to reorder the hierarchy. Similarly, the hovering action bar would save us a lot of scrolling.

Adding a product was easy, but extensive. We could get away with just the default settings, but Magento's form organization invited us to enter a lot more. We actually set up a lot of detail for our product—basic information, metadata, categorization, images, and inventory info. Never was this process confusing or boring. Taking so much information from a user, without boring him or her, is a great feat!

There were a few things, such as the anchor field in the category options, that we wouldn't understand at the first try. But I am sure that as we used the system more, we would get to know their meanings.

One more advantage with Magento is that its default theme is high on aesthetics. It feels professional. The storefront emits positive vibrations to customers. Even the administration section looks polished. The Magento team's attention to detail has surely paid off.

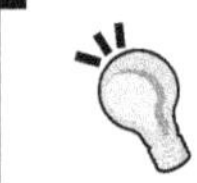

> An e-commerce site should leave a professional impression on customers. You must establish your credibility. Customers won't trust their money with you otherwise.

We now have a functional e-commerce system. Let's see what more we can do with Magento.

Have a go hero

It's time we try out something more with Magento. Take your shot at accomplishing the following tasks with Magento:

- Setting up a discount coupon
- Up-selling a product with another product—for example, selling a yoga book when a customer is buying a mattress
- Setting up a quantity-based pricing—for example one item sells for $10, two for $18, and three for $25

Notable Magento features

Magento is packed with features. Some of them worth noting are given here.

Single page checkout

All the checkout information is collected on a single page. You can even change billing or shipping information, or other details, without going back and forth in the browser. You get a confirmation on the righthand side as you are entering the details. This significantly shortens the checkout time.

Product attributes

Product attributes allow you to create variations of a product. For example, our mattress can have multiple colors. We can charge higher for some colors. Magento allows creating as many attributes as you want, and reusing them across products.

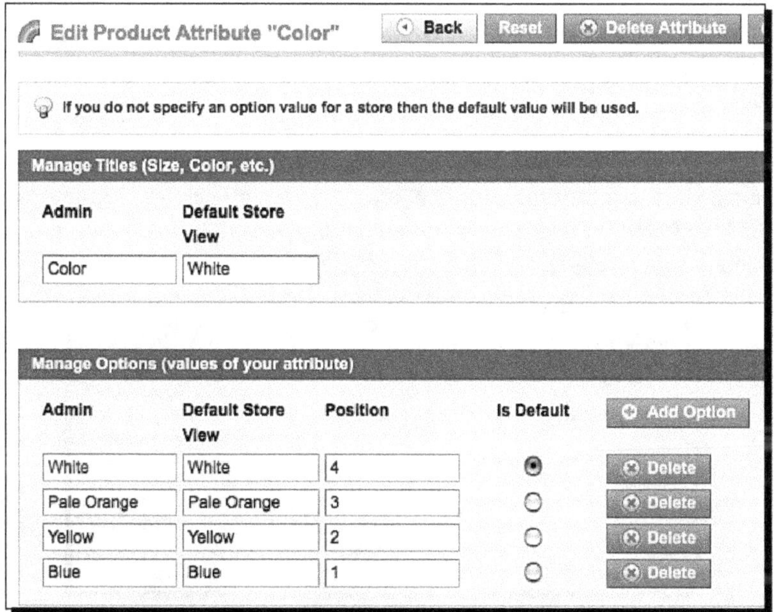

Full control over design

Magento comes with a high-quality template. Some more template varieties are available from Magento Connect, a place to exchange Magento enhancements. You get a complete control over design. You can control a lot of it from the administration interface, too. Magento even watermarks your product images if you want.

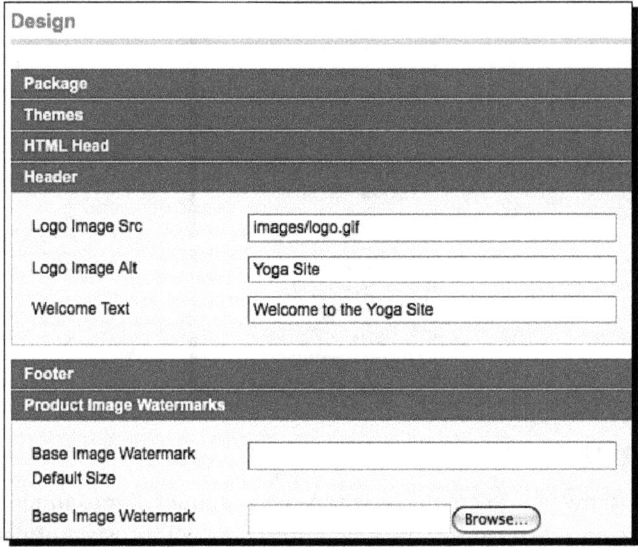

Magento as a CMS

We were talking about CMS and e-commerce. So far, we have seen that Magento is a powerful and flexible e-commerce solution. How can we use Magento to manage the other site content?

Magento offers a good set of basic features to create static pages in your site. Go to the CMS menu to manage static content for your site. From there, you can add, update, and delete pages on your site. A WYSIWYG editor is not enabled by default, but is easy to activate. You can manage the design of pages and also enter metadata for each page.

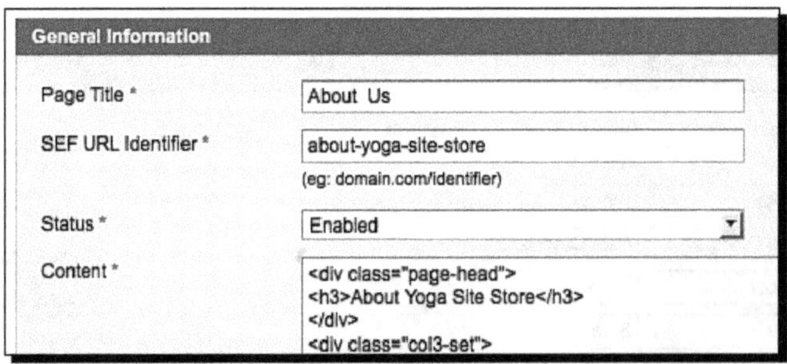

Overall, Magento won't give you blogs, forums, and other nifty CMS features. But it can serve most common needs.

Other features

Some of the other useful Magento features are as follows:

- Solid reporting tools, integration with Google Analytics
- Multiple image support with zooming
- Wish list, newsletter, polls
- Ability to run multiple stores from the same system
- Batch updates
- Extensive SEO features
- Sophisticated pricing rules
- Shipping and Payment Gateway integration

Is it for you?

Magento will serve most of the common e-commerce needs. Some more features are already under development (like an affiliate system) and there is an active community. If you want to sell products, Magento is just about perfect. Evaluate if Magento can serve your requirements before you look for other options.

Alright, what next? How about an e-commerce extension to a CMS? How about an e-commerce extension to Joomla!?

VirtueMart—bringing e-commerce to Joomla!

VirtueMart (`http://virtuemart.net/`) is a Joomla! (and Mambo) extension that gives you a full-blown e-commerce system within Joomla!. VirtueMart gives you advanced options such as product attributes, coupons, newsletters, and so on; and integrates really well with Joomla!. If you are already running a Joomla! site, or think Joomla! is better for your CMS needs, VirtueMart is the extension to check out for your e-commerce needs.

Let's quickly see how we can use VirtueMart with Joomla!.

Time for action-adding products and selling them

1. Download **VirtueMart Complete Package**. You can find it in Joomla!'s extension directory. This will download a ZIP file.
2. Unzip the file. It contains the VirtueMart component, and a collection of other modules and plug-ins that integrate it with Joomla!.
3. Install the necessary packages using Joomla!'s **Extensions | Install/Uninstall** system. Refer to the installation guide that comes with VirtueMart for exact details.
4. Once you have it installed, enable the required modules from **Extensions | Module Manager**. Here, we are enabling **VirtueMart All-In-One** and **VirtueMart Module**.

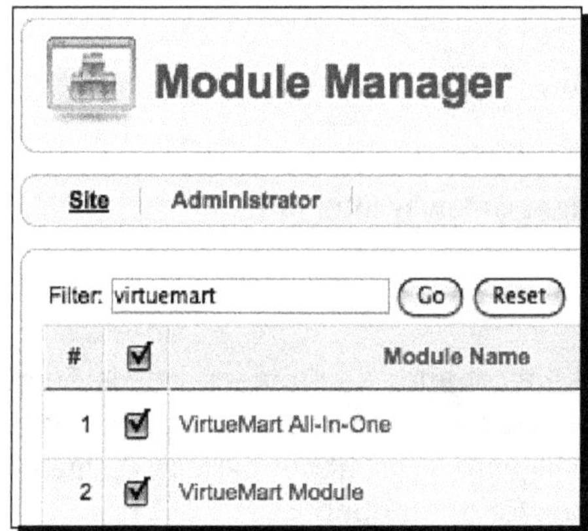

5. Go to **Components | VirtueMart**. This shows you the VirtueMart administration interface. Switch to **Extended Layout**. This hides the Joomla! interface and gives you more space to work with VirtueMart.
6. The VirtueMart top menu may look like this now. It gives you a sense of what's possible with this component!

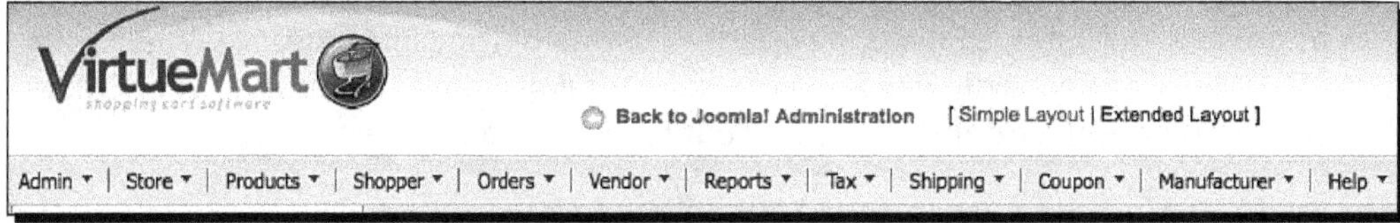

7. Go to **Products | Add Category** to add a category. Create a few categories. **Accessories** and **Books** are good starting points.
8. Click on **Products | Add Product** to add a new product.

9. Enter the product **Name**, **SKU**, **URL** and select which categories it should show up from the left. We can use the same product details that we used while adding a yoga product to Magento—a yoga mattress.

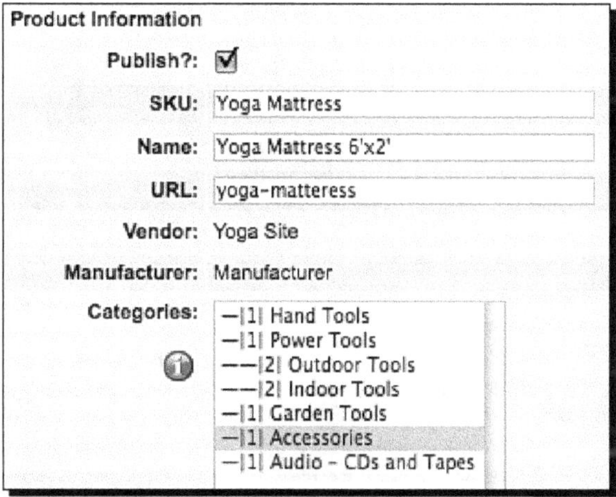

10. Enter pricing information on the right. If you want to apply a discount, you can choose it here.

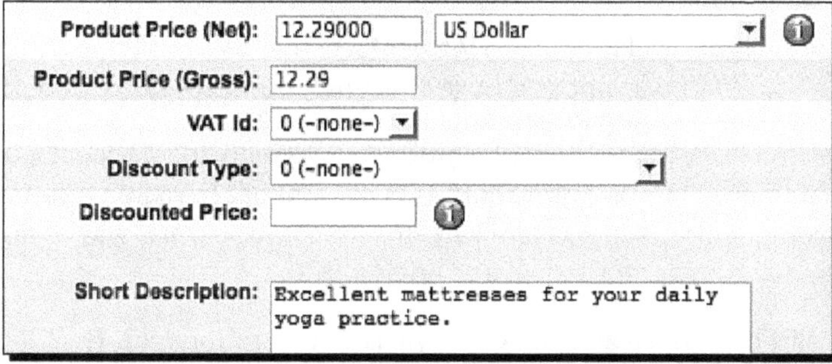

11. You can also enter a long product description using a WYSIWYG editor.

12. Save the product. If you want, add other product-related information from other tabs. You can enter attributes and even create some reviews.

13. Now go to the Joomla! site. Since we enabled the **All-In-One** module, we can see VirtueMart options in the left column. Click on the **Yoga Mattress** product we just entered.

14. That will show you product information like that in the following image.

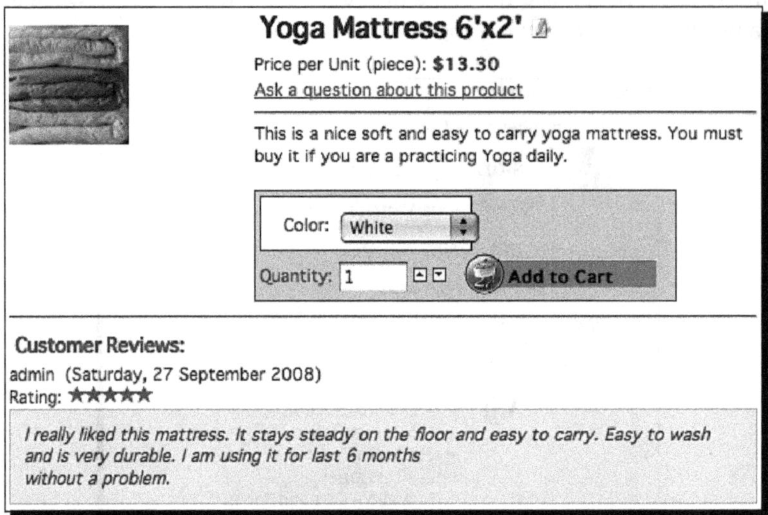

15. This is superb! We can now add it to the cart and proceed to checkout.

What just happened?

We added a new category and product to VirtueMart. The task was the same as what we did with Magento. VirtueMart was not as easy as Magento, but provided a lot of functionality.

We could customize many parameters of a product. We could add discounts, tax, multiple images, and related products. We also could assign a product to multiple categories. The category management interface was familiar—the standard Joomla! way of displaying items, publishing or un-publishing, reordering, and editing.

Overall, VirtueMart's interface and working style is similar to Joomla!. The VirtueMart team has worked hard to make it usable. Some places even use nice JavaScript widgets to ease the operation—such as collapsible trees or a tabbed interface. But the general feeling I got is that it's powerful, but a bit difficult for a typical site owner to use. You can live with it, but it could certainly be better.

Have a go hero

Time to get your hands dirty! Go ahead and implement the following with VirtueMart:

- Add pricing based on customer groups
- Use multiple shipping methods
- Create a discount coupon

Is it for you?

VirtueMart has a good list of features. It is very powerful and the biggest advantage is that it integrates with Joomla!. As I mentioned earlier, if you are on Joomla!, you should try it out. It's certainly not the most user-friendly product out there (neither is Joomla! for that matter), but it's popular and gets the job done.

What about Drupal and WordPress?

VirtueMart works with Mambo, but not with any other CMSs. Fortunately, other CMSs too have e-commerce plug-ins.

- UberCart (`http://www.ubercart.org/`) is a nice e-commerce system that integrates with Drupal.
- WordPress e-commerce Plug-in (`http://www.instinct.co.nz/e-commerce/`), as the name suggests, brings e-commerce to WordPress.

Know what you want to sell!

It's important to know what you want to sell on your site before you start evaluating solutions. Do you want to run promotions and cross-sell items? Do you want to sell services? Knowing your needs will allow you to evaluate solutions quickly. For example, it will be difficult to sell yoga class memberships with Magento (or most e-commerce solutions) as they may involve recurring payments, timing options, and so on. There can be workarounds, but most solutions are designed for products.

If you want to sell services, don't worry. There is a solution.

Freeway—e-commerce for products, events, services, and subscriptions

Freeway (`http://www.openfreeway.org/`) claims to be the most advanced e-commerce solution. It not only supports products but also events, services, and subscriptions. If we are organizing introductory yoga classes every Sunday, we can use Freeway to sell registrations. We could even sell subscriptions to a yoga magazine or charge fees for individual consultation.

Let's try it out then. Let's see how we can register people into our weekly introductory yoga sessions.

Time for action-selling weekly yoga class registrations

1. Download and set up Freeway. Alternatively, go to the demo at `http://www.opensourcecms.com/`.
2. Log in to the administration panel.
3. You will see main admin sections on the left side, and miscellaneous options at the top. We want to add an event. Click on **Events** in the left column.
4. If you imported sample data during installation, you will see some existing event categories. Near the end of this page, you will find a link to add a category.

5. Click on **New Category**. This shows you a progress indicator and opens up a new category form without reloading the page.
6. Enter **Yoga Classes** as **Category Name**, and make it a main category. Enter a title and description. You can also add a category image and decide the sort order.

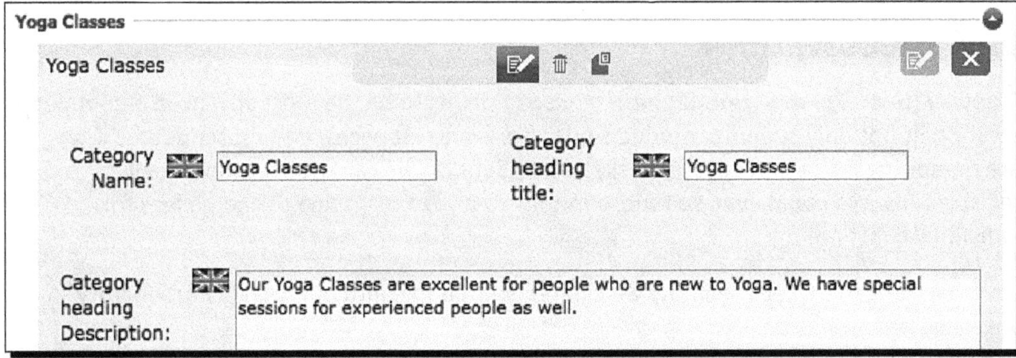

7. Click on the green button on the right to save this entry.

8. Once the category is saved, we can add an event in it. Click on the **Category Name** in the list to open it.

9. Now click on the **New Event** link at the bottom. This opens up the new event form.

10. Select the event **Status**, **Date Available**, and **Categories** it should be visible in. Give it a title—**Yoga Classes**. Also enter a description that visitors can see. This should be your selling pitch.

11. Now comes the interesting part. Below the basic details, we get options to set timings, location, reservation numbers, fees, instructors, and other options for this event. Go ahead and set them up.

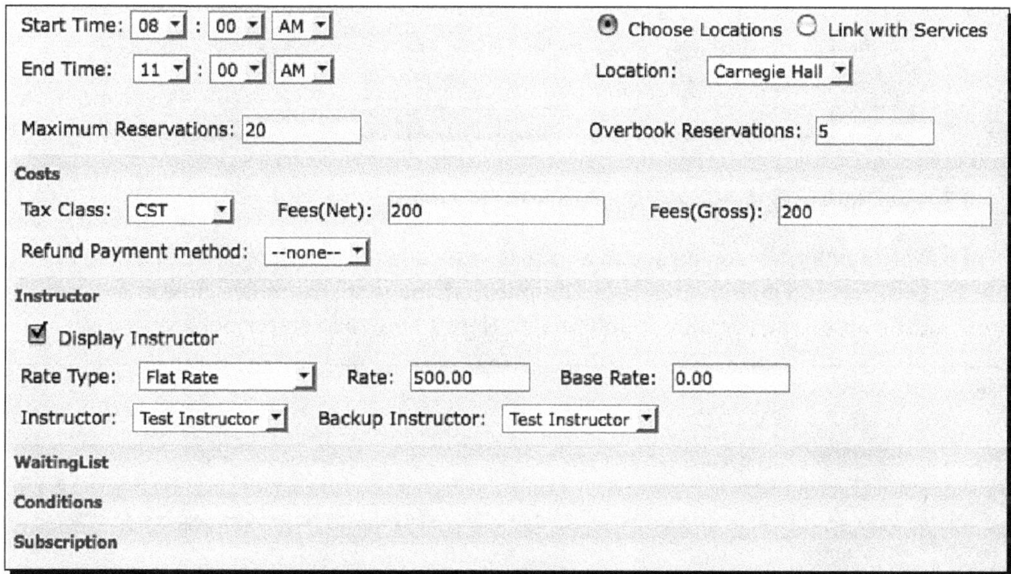

12. An event can have one or more actual sessions. An event session is the actual item to sell. Click on the **Sessions** icon on the event—it looks like a paper with a clock on it.

13. This will show you a **No sessions found** message. Just above the heading of **Sessions in Yoga Classes** is an icon with an arrow. That's the one to click to add a new session. Click on it.

14. Add a new session for **Weekly Yoga Introductions**. Set it to recur every Sunday. This is how the screen will look:

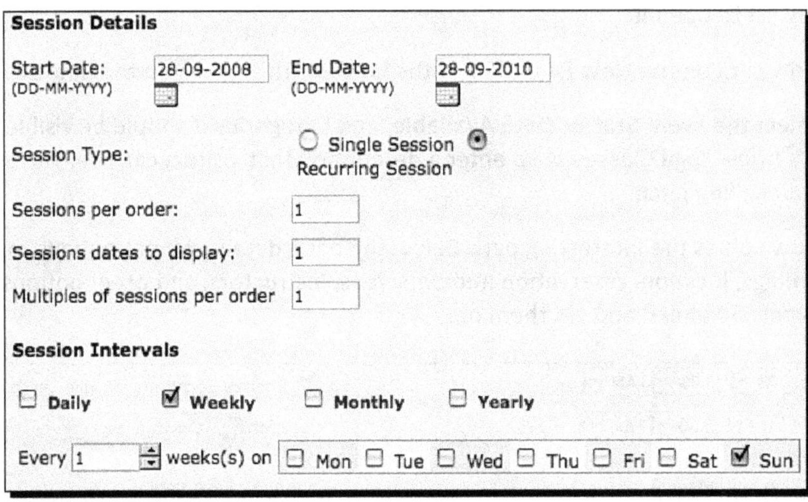

15. Save the entry. Our event is now almost complete!

16. At this point, we can go ahead and customize a few more things—such as the event **Location** and instructor details. Options to manage them are available at the top. Let's set up the **Location** for our event. Here's how this screen looks.

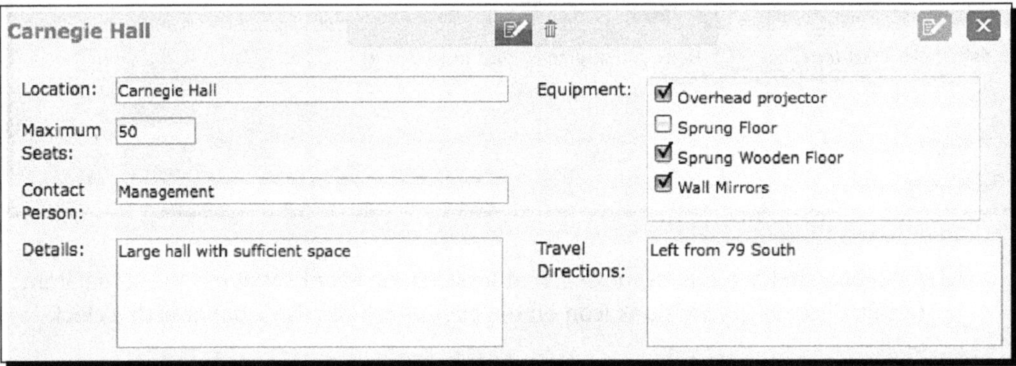

17. Similarly, edit the instructor details. Customers must be aware of our highly-qualified and experienced trainers.

18. We are done now! Go to the site and find the event. This is how it looks:

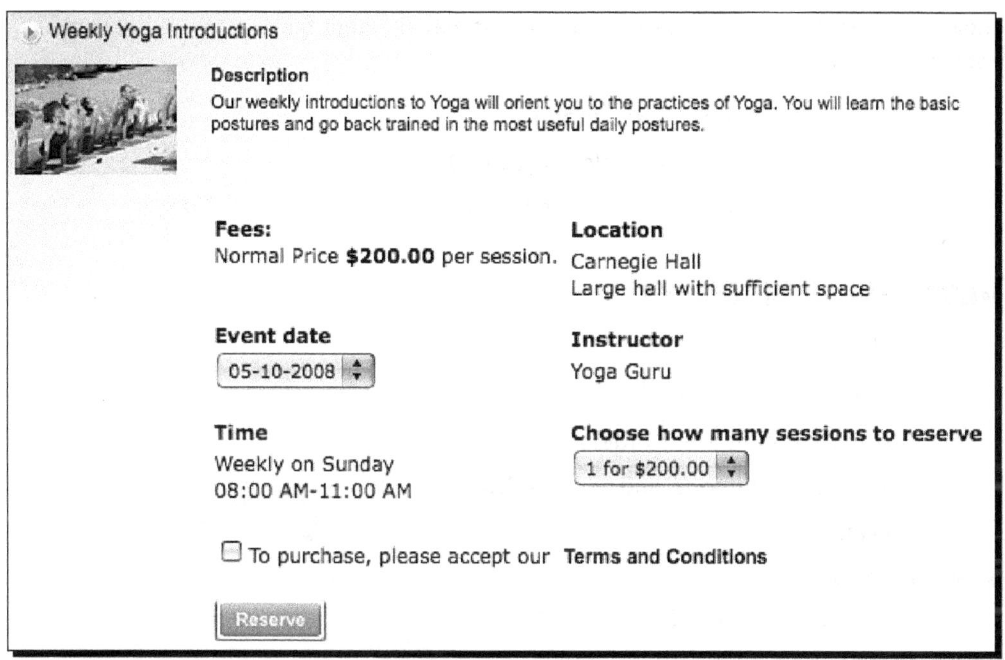

19. You can now add it to your cart and purchase a registration just like any other product. Good job!

What just happened?

We are now selling our weekly introductory yoga sessions online. We created an event category, added an event to it, and then set up sessions for that event. We configured event location, instructor, and costing details too.

Freeway works very logically. It prompted us to enter the right details. Who would've thought about entering instructor and location details otherwise? The process of setting up the event was relatively smooth. Freeway's icons and workflow are non-standard. But after filling in a couple of forms, you will get used to them. Of course, in your installation you can change them if you wish.

Have a go hero

Freeway is quite powerful. We just saw the event management features. Here are some more things to try out:

- Add a magazine subscription product
- Create a one-time product sale—a yoga CD
- Add an appointment booking system for our yoga guru—Oprah Casey

Other notable features

Some other notable features of Freeway are:

- A single-page checkout
- Customer groups, direct orders
- Discounts, promotions, and gift certificates
- SMS marketing, newsletter
- The SEO features
- Joomla! integration, two-level CMS
- A simple template system
- Affiliate program

Now that we have covered some top e-commerce CMSs, let's look at the other choices.

Other notable e-commerce CMSs

The top choices should address most people's needs. But if you are looking for some more variety, here are other notable e-commerce CMSs.

osCommerce and variants

osCommerce (`http://www.oscommerce.com/`) is probably the most famous open source e-commerce solution. It's been around for years and is used on thousands of online shops. It's a huge software application. It does a lot of things and has many extensions, but has not kept up with the times. The osCommerce team is working on a PHP5 version of the system, but it's not out as of this writing. A lot of people complain that osCommerce is crappy. Changing templates is difficult and writing extensions involves hacking the core of the system.

There are a number of osCommerce variants, though. Teams have taken osCommerce source code and added features or simplified the existing features. The following are some implementations worth checking out:

- Zen Cart: `http://www.zencart.com/`
- CRE Loaded: `http://www.getcre.com/`
- OSC Max: `http://www.oscmax.com/`
- xt:Commerce: `http://www.xt-commerce.com/`
- Holbi TrueLoaded: `http://www.trueloaded.com/`

And there are still some more!

PrestaShop—a breath of fresh air

PrestaShop (`http://www.prestashop.com/`) is a beautiful-looking Web 2.0-style e-commerce system. It claims to be light and fast, and scalable and sleek. The interface is refreshing and the features are plentiful. PrestaShop is actively developed, and new features and enhancements are added regularly.

Apart from the interface beauty, I noticed a security feature. When you install any e-commerce solution, you are asked to remove the installation folder. PrestaShop goes one step further. It even asks you to rename the admin URL! This one additional step can boost the security of your store.

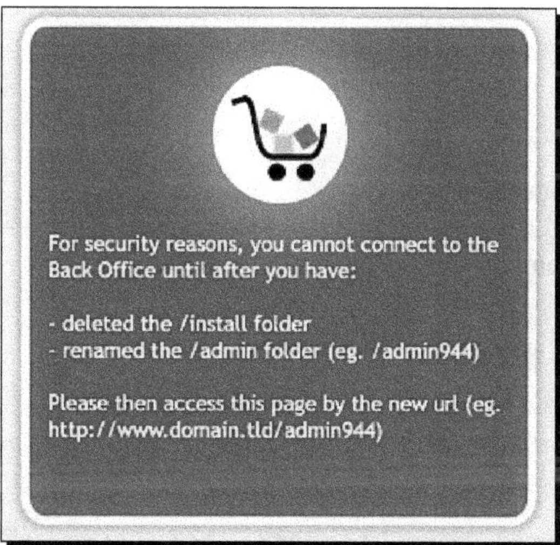

PrestaShop also has a neat AJAX usage. As you add items to your cart, you see an animation and the items get added to the cart display on the right, without reloading the page.

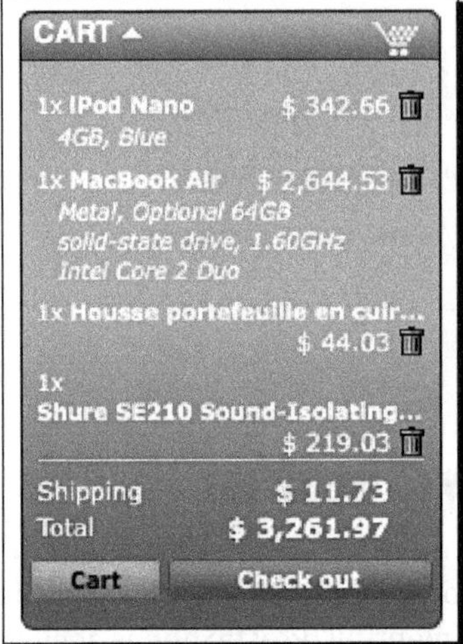

Another noticeable feature of PrestaShop is localization. Not only does it support multiple currencies, but also gives an easy choice to switch currencies and languages. On the admin side, it has a full-blown translation interface as well.

Overall, PrestaShop is a great solution and is highly recommended.

DashCommerce—for .Net

If you are on .Net, **DashCommerce** (`http://dashcommerce.org/`) may be your best bet. It has e-commerce and CMS features. It allows managing products, inventory, shipping, product reviews, and comes with ready support for payment gateways.

Looking for even more?

By now, you should have a fair idea about which e-commerce CMS can fulfill your needs. If you want more options, do a Google search or look around script directories such as `www.hotscripts.com`.

We have now seen enough e-commerce systems. Let's summarize what we learned.

Summary

We reviewed different kinds of e-commerce CMSs in this chapter. We also covered Magento extensively. Then we looked at VirtueMart and Freeway. We followed up with a listing of e-commerce plug-ins to CMSs and popular e-commerce software.

In this chapter, we specifically looked at:

- Creating product categories in Magento and managing them
- Adding product, images, metadata, and setting pricing and inventory with Magento
- Advanced features and customization options with Magento
- Activating VirtueMart for e-commerce within Joomla!
- Managing products and categories with VirtueMart
- Selling services, events, and subscriptions with Freeway
- Other popular CMSs such as osCommerce and variants, PrestaShop, dashCommerce, and so on

The most important thing to remember from this chapter is that having a shopping cart is not sufficient to get customers anymore. Apart from the sleek e-commerce features, one must have solid content. There are many other aspects to e-commerce such as security, payment integration, promotions, and so on. You can learn more about them from your e-commerce software's web site or refer to e-commerce specific books from Packt.

With that squared out, let's see what it will take to please internal customers. Let's evaluate collaboration CMSs in the next chapter.

11
Team Collaboration CMSs

We have looked at many kinds of CMSs so far, but our intent has been building a public-facing web site hosted on the Internet. What if we want to build a site for internal use of our organization or project? Can we use some CMS to manage internal communications, documents, revisions, and approval processes? It could be something that will help us coordinate efforts among the Yoga Site team members. Let's find it out.

In this chapter, we will take a look at our options for setting up a Team Collaboration CMS. We will:

- *Understand the need for a collaboration CMS*
- *Manage documents and revisions with a CMS*
- *Set up an approval process*
- *Look at different systems we can deploy in our intranet*

Let's get started!

Why a collaboration CMS?

We normally use a content management system to develop a public web site. We publish different content or articles in a specific content hierarchy for our visitors. What can we accomplish by setting up an internal CMS? What can you put on a web site accessible only to your organization? Such a system may be hosted on the Internet or on an intranet. If it's on the Internet, we can even use it to collaborate with suppliers and partners. An intranet system may be open only to our employees and internal team members.

When you think about it, there are a lot of things that can be put on a collaboration CMS. We can use it to store HR policy documents and templates of commonly created documents, post company news, write articles, and post videos for continuous learning or even run an internal blog! You can certainly find something valuable for your organization.

Can we use any CMS on the intranet?

Technically, you can use any CMS, such as Joomla!, Drupal, WordPress, DotNetNuke, as an internal CMS. You can very well use them on your intranet. The value of an internal CMS will be determined by the content you add.

At the same time, there are a few enterprise CMSs that can elevate your team's productivity by making it easier to collaborate and communicate. A team collaboration CMS should make it easy to share documents and collaborate with other team members. It should manage content revisions, have some kind of workflow system, and provide additional tools for better system integration. Such features are generally not available in typical Web CMSs. That is the reason why we need to look specifically at team collaboration CMSs.

Another point to note is that CMSs that are branded as enterprise CMSs will have some of these team collaboration features. They may even have many more features. For the purpose of this chapter, we will focus only on team collaboration features.

Let's now evaluate one such CMS to learn how it can help us manage the "behind the scene" efforts of the Yoga Site team.

Alfresco—an enterprise CMS

Alfresco (`http://www.alfresco.com`) is an enterprise CMS. It allows document management, web content management, collaboration, records management, knowledge management, imaging, and much more.

Some of the organizations that use Alfresco include Electronic Arts, the American Stock Exchange, Fox Entertainment, Kaplan, and MIT. Most of them use it for their internal sites, but some also use it for their public sites.

Alfresco has different components. We will focus only on Alfresco Share, a client for team collaboration. Let's set up Alfresco and use it for team collaboration, and discuss the logo design for our Yoga Site.

Time for action-planning the Yoga Site with Alfresco

1. Download and install the open source version of Alfresco Labs. You may refer to the Alfresco Wiki for installation instructions (`http://wiki.alfresco.com/wiki/Installing_Labs_3`).
2. Start the Alfresco server.
3. Log in to the Alfresco Share web site. The URL will be something like `http://localhost:8080/share/`.
4. This brings you to the **Dashboard**. The first thing we want to do is create a new site for our team. Locate the **Create a site** link in the left column and click on it.

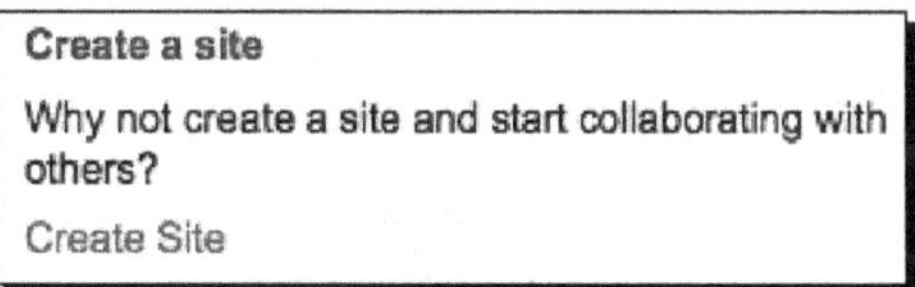

5. Enter a **Name**, **Short name** (without spaces), and **Description** for this site. Make it a **Collaboration Site** with public access.

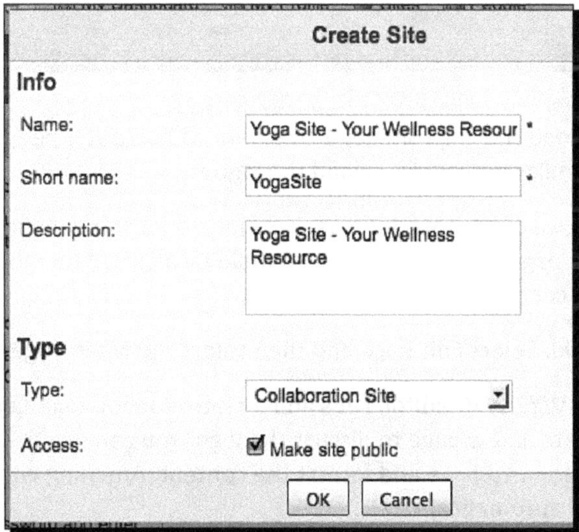

6. Once the site is created, select it to enter it.
7. You will see links for **Wiki**, **Blog**, **Document Library**, **Calendar**, and so on in the top bar. We want to discuss the Yoga Site logo, and the ideas our team has for the whole site. Let's start by adding a few image files.

8. Go to **Document Library**. Create a **New Folder** called **UI Assets**.

9. Navigate to the newly created folder. Click on the **upload** button.

10. This displays the file upload window. Here, we want to upload some photos of Surya Namaskara. We can shortlist them to put them on the web site later. **Browse** and select the files to upload. Alfresco uploads all the files. Click on **OK** to close the window.

11. Let's also upload the Yoga Site logo. We want to find out if people like the logo. Follow the similar process to upload the logo.

12. We want to give our team a little background about this collaborative system. Let's create a Wiki page for this. A Wiki is editable by all team members, so everyone can enhance the content.

13. Go to the **Wiki**. Select **Edit Page** and then select the **Main Page**.

14. This shows a WYSIWYG editor. Let's add an introduction text. Let's also add the logo and create a new page to discuss the logo. You can use the Wiki syntax to create a hyperlinked page and format the content. Anything within `[[` and `]]` will be linked automatically.

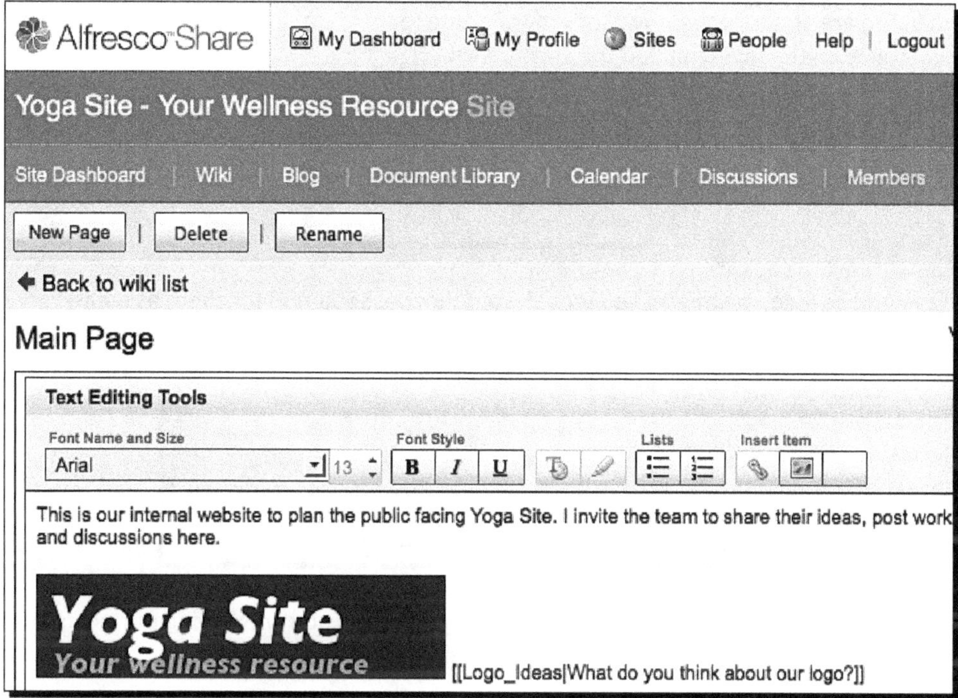

15. Go ahead and add a **Discussion**, a **Calendar** event, and a blog post. Once you are done, your **Site Activity** (on the **Dashboard**) will look like this.

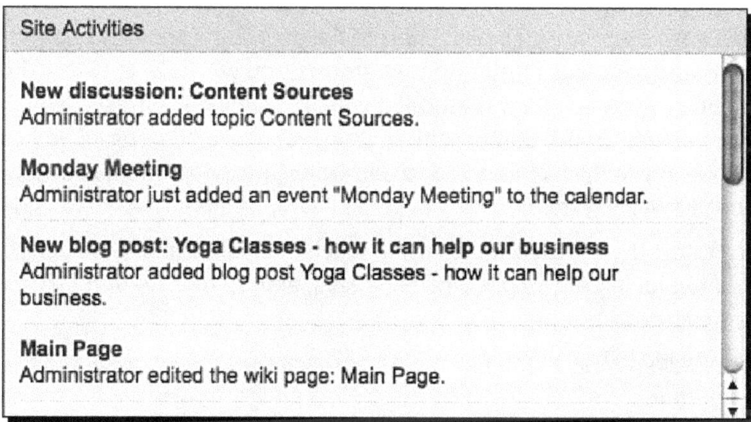

16. We are almost done now. Let's invite some team members to start the collaboration. Click on the **Invite** link on the **Dashboard**.

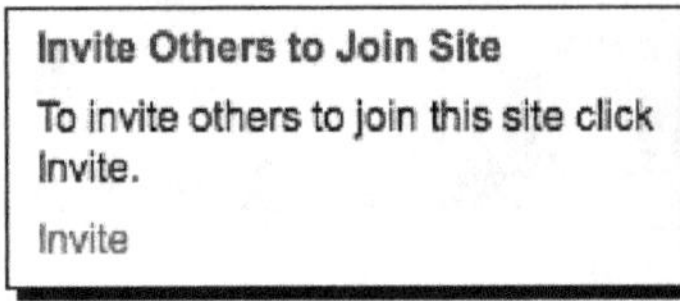

17. Add as many people as you would like to invite. Set a role for them as well—for example **Collaborator**.

18. We are done now! Our invitees can now join in and start reviewing our posts. They can also comment and start collaborating.

What just happened?

We created a new collaboration site with Alfresco Share, added some content to it, and invited users to join. Let's review a few key points of what we accomplished.

- Installing Alfresco: Alfresco has different flavors—Enterprise and Community (Labs) versions and packages for different platforms. You will have to select the package based on your deployment method. If you are trying out Alfresco, you can take the full package, which comes with built-in web server, database, and OpenOffice.org extensions (which allows you to add OpenOffice documents directly to Alfresco without converting them to HTML).
- You can start the Alfresco server using batch or shell scripts available in the installation folder. Alfresco is written in Java, and is huge. So don't worry if it takes time to start.
- We created a new site. You can create as many sites as you wish and manage their content.
- We could add multiple files easily. Adding files is a cumbersome one-after-another process in most CMSs. Alfresco makes it easy. It creates thumbnails automatically and detects a lot of metadata as well.
- A collaborative site comes ready with a Wiki, discussion board, blog, and other features. This made it very easy for us to focus on adding content.

Users may need training

One of the biggest bottlenecks in implementing a new system in an organization is the users' acceptance level. To make your collaborative site successful, you will have to train your team on how to use the new system. Do this by building relevant examples. Convey your expectations clearly—if you expect the team to use the Wiki for one type of content and discussions for another, communicate that upfront. Define the way in which you want people to use the system. (And don't forget, not everyone will be tech savvy. Don't expect people to know the Wiki syntax. You will have to train them.)

- Alfresco's interface is easy to understand, and the look and feel is nice. We didn't take much time in adding initial content.
- The **Site Dashboard** gives a comprehensive overview of our site. We can also customize the items that show up there.
- That we can invite users to collaborate was a nice feature. Rather than just adding them in, we invited them.

Alfresco Explorer

We used the Alfresco Share site to create and manage our content. Alternatively, we can use Alfresco Explorer client. This web client is powerful, but very simplistic. It can be difficult for novices. I suggest using the Share site as much as possible. You can try out the Explorer web client via `http://localhost:8080/alfresco/`.

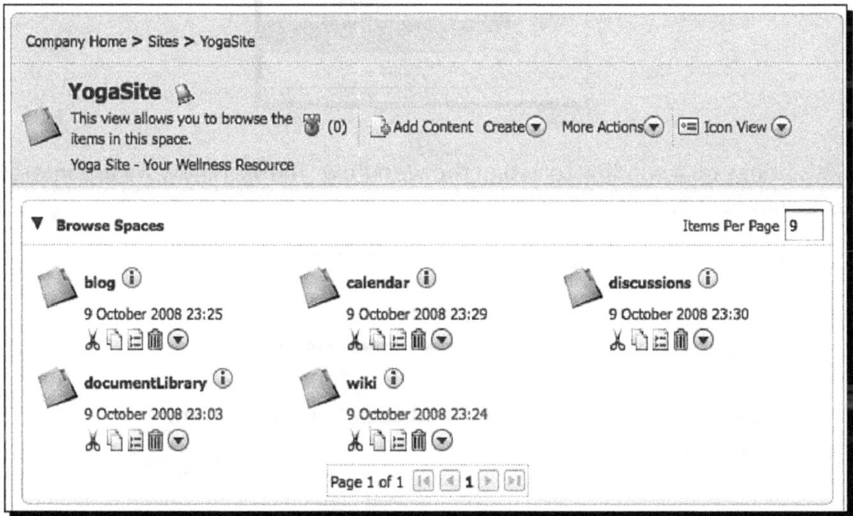

Now that we are getting the hang of the system, let's get some more work done.

Have a go hero-add a space and some users

Apart from sites, you can also create **spaces** in Alfresco. Spaces are like a collaboration place for people working on similar ideas. Use the Alfresco Explorer web client to create a new space within our Yoga Site. Go ahead and add some users too.

With more users in the system, we can collaborate better. A typical scenario in any organization is to get approval on a document from a superior or subject expert. Let's see how we can achieve this with Alfresco.

Time for action-creating workflows and revisions with Alfresco

1. Log in to Alfresco Share (`http://localhost:8080/share/`). Go to the site you created and navigate to the **Document Library | UI Assets** folder.
2. We want to get approval on the logo of Yoga Site. Locate the logo file.
3. When you move your mouse cursor over that item, you will see options on its right side. Click on **More...**, and select the **Assign workflow** option.

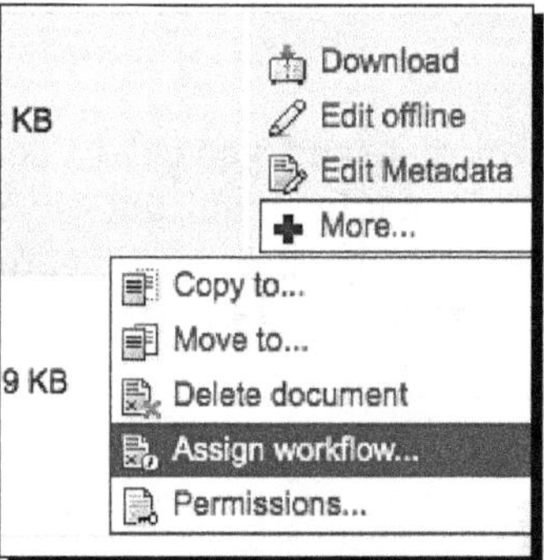

4. This brings up a window to assign the workflow. The workflow we are interested in is **Review & Approve**. Select it.

5. Assign this workflow to a user you want to get approval from, for example **Administrator**.

6. You can also set a due date and enter some comments.

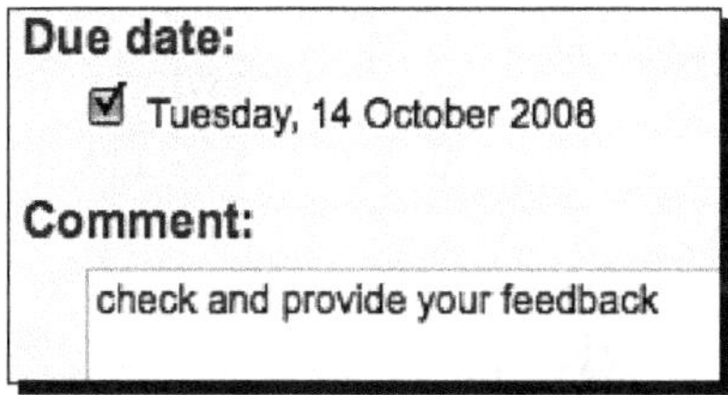

7. Complete the workflow creation by clicking on the **Assign Workflow** button at the bottom of the window.

8. Log out and log in as the user who's assigned the newly created workflow.

9. On the **Dashboard**, let's see if we have any pending tasks. Oh, the workflow is right there!

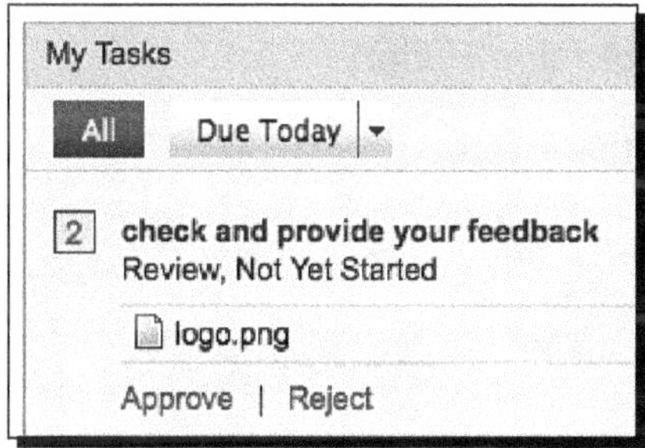

10. You can click on the name **logo.png** to view it.

11. We like the logo, but want to make small edits to it before approving it. To do this, we will need to check out the file for offline editing. Checking out a file is like taking a book from a library. You can keep it on your computer, review it, make changes, and check it back in. To check out **logo.png**, go to **Document Library** and locate its file.

12. Click on **Edit offline** from the options on the right side. This downloads a working copy of the file and puts it in the **Documents I'm Editing** list.

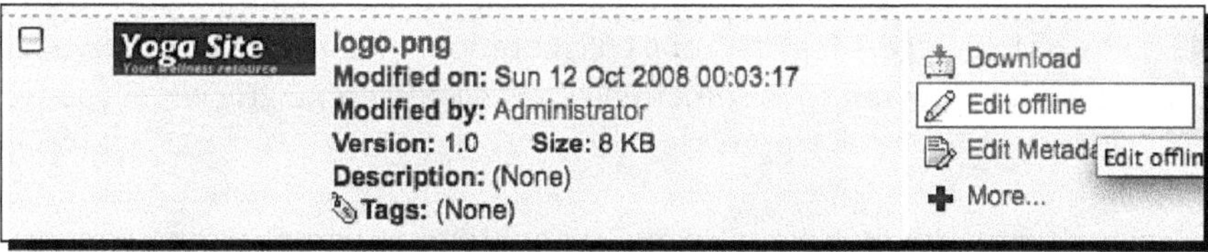

13. We have now made our changes to the logo. Go to the **Documents I'm Editing** list, and upload the latest version using the options on the right side of the page.

14. Once this is done, we can return to the task on the **Dashboard** and approve it.

15. That completes a loop. If you go to the document detail page (click on the file name in **Document Library**), you can see that our new version is in place.

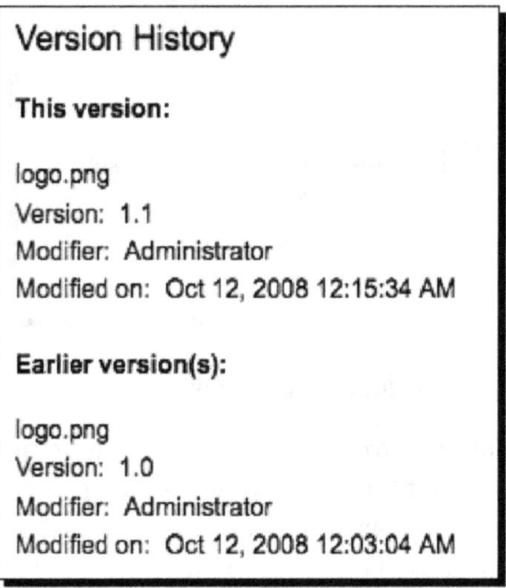

What just happened?

We created an approval process for a document. We also created a new version of a document. In the process, we got to experience the tasks system and the document detail page. This is one of the biggest features of a collaboration system. The ability to track versions and approval of workflow is something you will need regularly when you work in a team.

The workflow assignment was straightforward: select the workflow, select users, set a date, and get started. For the approver, all pending workflows show in **My Tasks**. He or she can review the document and approve or reject it.

In our case, we wanted to make minor corrections in a document. Rather than rejecting the document, we felt it would be easier to make corrections and then send it back. That would save us some time. To do this we downloaded a version for offline editing, made those edits, and uploaded it back. It created a new version of that document. This allows us to keep enhancing the content or document as it passes through the approval process.

We worked with the Yoga Site logo, but you can apply this to any document—a business plan, some HR policy, or an executive report. All documents can be tracked.

Document detail page

The document detail page shows preview, metadata, version information, available actions, and comments. It also has URLs to directly access this document. The comments provision keeps feedback in one place on a document. When someone sees this document later on, he or she can easily understand its evolution by looking at comments.

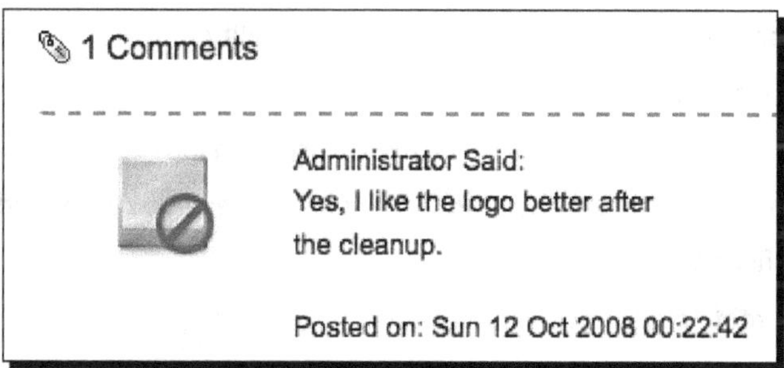

Editing metadata allows adding tags for each document. Tags are keywords and can help us locate this document easily later on.

Have a go hero-workflows with multiple users

A workflow can be assigned to multiple users. What will happen when one person approves, but another rejects? What happens if two users want to edit a document offline? Time to have some action. Go ahead, figure it out!

Alfresco can do much more

What we covered so far is only a fraction of what Alfresco can do. You can customize the look and feel and can use extensions available form **Alfresco Forge** (`http://forge.alfresco.com/`).

One feature that puts Alfresco in the enterprise category is its WebDAV or CIFS support. You can access sites and documents created in Alfresco natively from your computer, from Windows Explorer or OS X Finder. This means people can work without a web interface. A designer can save a logo revision in the Alfresco folder that shows up on his or her computer, and it will become available via the web site as well. This is really powerful. Such seamless integration is only available in a select few CMSs. For example, the Alfresco documents can be accessed from your desktop.

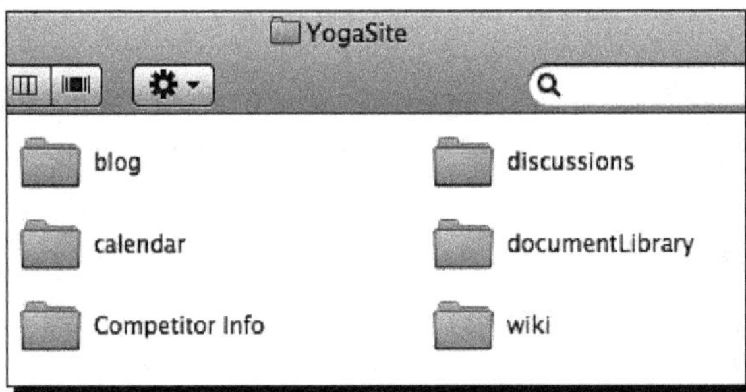

Some other notable features are:

- Support for industry standards, including the ability to run other portlets
- A fast AJAX-driven interface
- Collection of templates and forms to get started easily
- Support for Office documents and rich media—preview, zoom, and more
- Email notifications
- Ability to create custom workflow rules
- Publish a site to multiple servers
- Records management and image management

Alfresco Labs comes with no support:

Supplied free of charge with no support, no certification, no maintenance, no warranty and no indemnity by Alfresco or its Certified Partners. Click here for support. Alfresco Software Inc. © 2005-2008 All rights reserved.

The footer of the Alfresco installation says that it's supplied free of charge with no support, no certification, no maintenance, no warranty, and so on. Though this is true for all other CMSs we have discussed, an explicit mention is made to request you to buy the enterprise edition. Please consider buying the enterprise edition. That money lets the community edition grow as well. But if you want to stick to the community edition, don't worry. There is enough help available in forums and on Internet.

There is much more to Alfresco. You can learn about all of Alfresco's features from its web site. Alfresco looks very good, but are there any alternatives to it?

Finding alternatives to Alfresco

There are a couple of good alternatives to Alfresco.

Liferay (`http://www.liferay.com/`) is an enterprise portal system with very good content management and collaboration systems. It shines in community and collaboration aspects and has extensive features.

Jahia (`http://www.jahia.com/`) is another enterprise CMS and a good option to consider for your intranet.

Alfresco, Liferay, and Jahia are all Java-based. If you are looking for a non-Java solution, you may have to pick up some other CMS, add extensions, and customize it to your needs.

Mix and match

As I said, we can use just about any CMS on the intranet. Document management, versioning, and other features can be achieved by extensions or custom development. You will have to evaluate your needs and build a solution accordingly.

Here are some other things you may want on your internal site. These may not sound like typical CMS needs, but each could be an important organizational content storage system.

- Knowledge Management System
- Project Management System
- Groupware—calendar, files, tasks, and so on
- Customer Relationship Management System
- Issue tracking or Ticketing System

The requirements of an organization's collaboration system are specific to that particular organization. Some features may be critical, while some could be time wasters. Exercise your judgment when you build your team's collaboration CMS.

Summary

We extensively evaluated Alfresco in this chapter. Alfresco has exposed us to a lot of enterprise CMS features and the things that we can use on our internal sites.

In this chapter, we specifically looked at:

- Creating a site and adding content to the Wiki and Document Library
- Checking out a document for offline editing, checking in, and maintaining versions
- Collaborative features—workflow, comments, and so on
- Accessing Alfresco documents from the desktop
- Alternatives to Alfresco and building your own team collaboration CMS

The bottom line is that we can use any CMS. However, using a CMS such as Alfresco provides advanced enterprise-grade features. These features can raise the productivity of our team.

We have now looked at a lot of different CMSs. But there still many we have not seen—CMSs that couldn't be grouped as Web CMS, e-commerce CMS, Collaboration CMS, or Blog CMSs. In the next chapter we will look at some specialized CMSs, which serve a specific niche and do it very well.

12
Specialized CMSs

We have come a long way in evaluating CMSs. So far we have reviewed various CMSs by their kind—web, e-commerce, blogs, and collaboration. Many of the CMSs that we saw can meet the requirements of our Yoga Site. But what if we want something more? Or what if we want something different?

In this chapter we will try out some specialized CMSs, that is, CMSs created to address specific needs. We will cover some common specialized CMSs, and then list a few super-niche CMSs. We will:

- *Evaluate Wikis, and see how they can help us to collaborate*
- *Review discussion forums*
- *Host a photo gallery*
- *Check out an e-learning CMS and understand how we can use it*
- *Look at some other specialized CMSs*

There's a lot of interesting work ahead! Let's get started.

Wiki CMSs: The power of collective contribution

Wikipedia (`www.wikipedia.com`) is the most popular Wiki. Wikis turn consumers into contributors. They allow visitors to freely add and edit the site content. As more people use and contribute content, the authenticity improves. Wikis maintain a log of every change made to the content. If something goes wrong, you can quickly roll back to a previous version.

This ease of contribution makes Wikis special. We want to maintain an events listing on our Yoga Site. A Wiki will be an excellent solution here. Visitors can sign up for events in their locality directly. The collective contribution will filter out any questionable content and keep listings up to date.

Let's create an events listing section for our Yoga Site.

Time for action-creating events listing for the Yoga Site

1. Download and install MediaWiki (`http://www.mediawiki.org`). Wikipedia runs on MediaWiki. It's open source and written in PHP/MySQL.
2. Once you have it installed, open the installation URL. You should see a screen like the following.

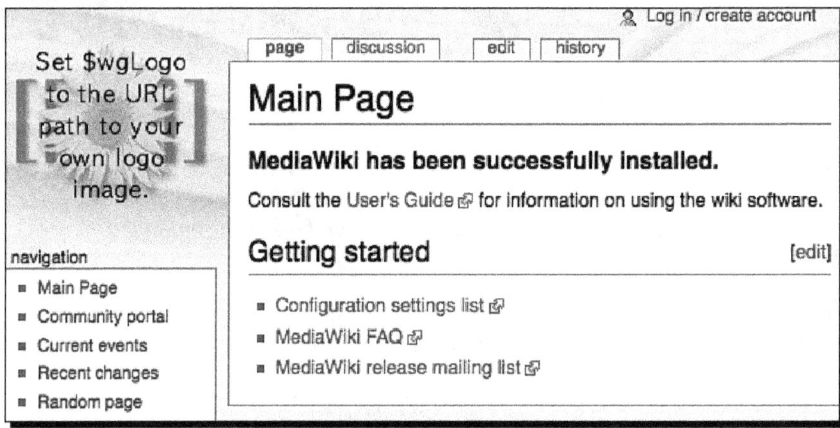

3. We want to add events listing, and it looks like MediaWiki already has a page for it. When we click on **Current events** in the left navigation bar, we see this.

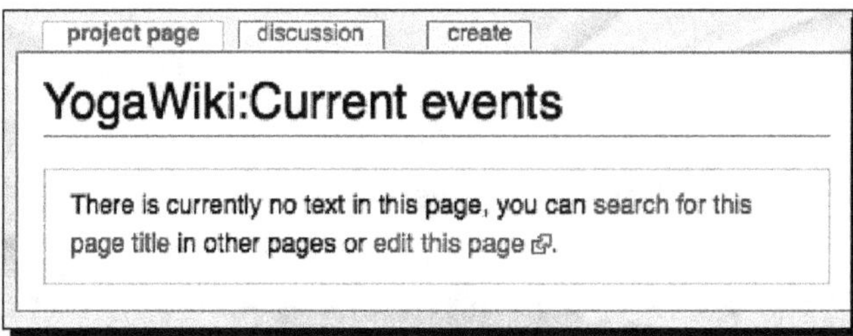

4. The page says that there is no text in it yet, but we can edit it. That's what we want. Click on **edit this page**.
5. We see an editor here. It's not like the WYSIWYG editors we have seen so far, but is similar. Let's write up an introduction for our events page.
6. The toolbar allows us to format content. The big **A** is for entering the headline text. Put a headline called **Yoga Events** after the introduction.

7. We want this page to link to location-specific event pages. The third button in the toolbar—with **Ab** on it—allows adding internal links. Click on that button. It inserts `[[Link title]]` in content. Anything we write within `[[` and `]]` becomes a link. Add a link for **San Jose**.

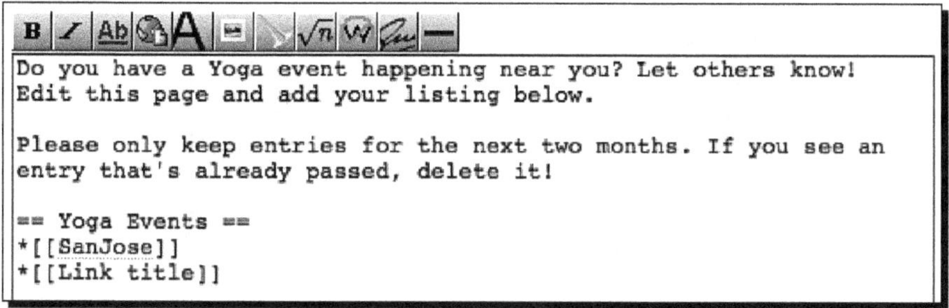

8. We can now add links for New York, Miami, and Seattle. The `*` will convert items into a bulleted list.

9. Once done, scroll down to the end of the text input area. Enter a short summary for the changes we made. Let's enter **First draft** for now.

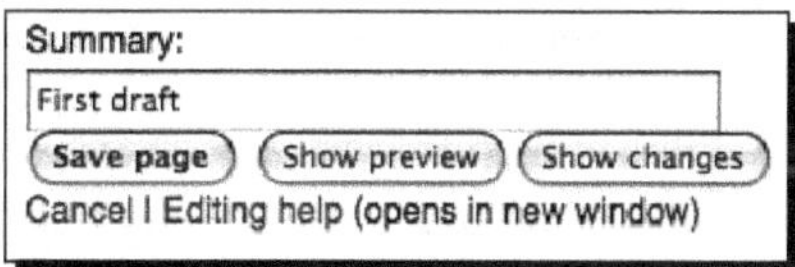

10. Click on **Save page**.

11. Wow! Our page is live! That was quick for adding a page to the site.

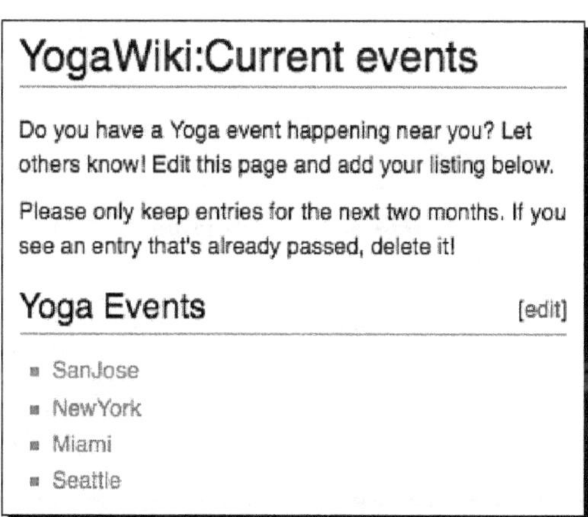

12. Links for locations are showing in bullets. They are red, which means they don't have any content yet. Click on **SanJose**.

13. That brings us straight to the editor. Add some content. We can add external links, bold text, and a short description for a yoga class happening in San Jose.

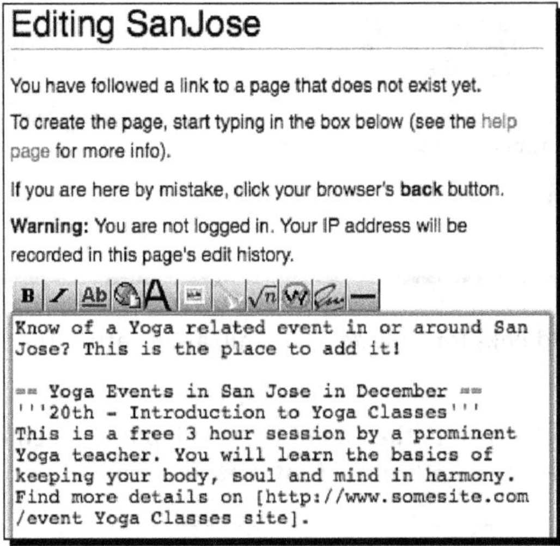

14. Review the messages above the editing region. They say that this page does not exist yet, and you can create it by typing in the box below. It also says that you are not logged in, but your IP address will be used in the history. Logging in is not mandatory to edit content. All these features remove barriers to contribution. People freely add content when it's so easy. In case you need to enforce logging in, you can turn it on from the administrator panel.

15. But that's sufficient for now. Here's how our final San Jose page looks like:

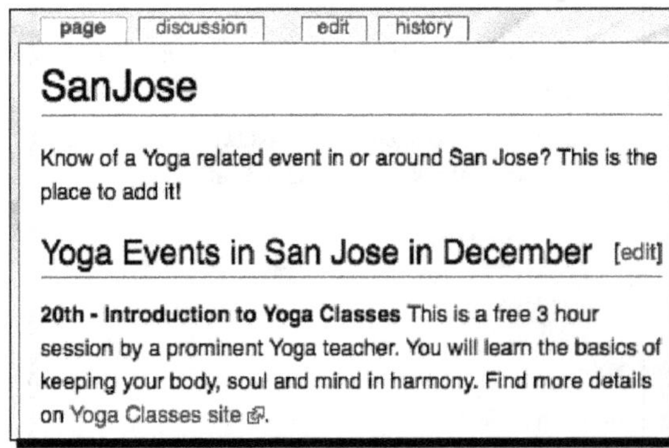

What just happened?

We added an events main page, created subpages for different locations, and added an event for one location. We accomplished all that without doing any code or complicated operations. All we had to do was to follow some simple rules of writing content. We put square brackets where we wanted links, equal-to signs for headlines, and single quotes for bold. An asterisk in front of the text made it a list item. MediaWiki took care of creating correct linking and formatting just based on the text we entered.

This is what makes Wikis powerful, and we experienced it firsthand. If you noticed, we can edit portions of content by clicking on the **[edit]** link at the right side of headlines. Non-existing pages (**discussion**) showed up as red text, but as soon as we added some content, their link (**page**) changed to blue color. External links showed up with an arrow. Such simple feedback makes it easier to understand and work with Wikis.

There is much more to Wikis. Why don't you try out something yourself?

Have a go hero-explore the power of Wikis

The following is a list of tasks that you can accomplish to understand the power (and limitations) of Wikis better.

- Add an image with an events listing.
- Create an account and make some changes to the events listings page with it.
- Click on the **history** tab at the top and review history, and roll back to the last version.
- Log in as an administrator, and explore configuration and administration options from **Special pages** in the left bar.

What makes Wikis special?

It's not only the ease of contribution that makes Wikis special. The following are some highlights:

- Effortlessly create links and content; create links even without content
- Full access control—users and pages
- Many Wikis don't even need a database backend, which makes them portable
- Revision control—review changes and roll back
- You can even categorize pages for better organization
- Top Wikis also have keyboard controls—for example, press *Ctrl+S* to save
- Automatic Table of Contents creation
- Extensive search capabilities

This is all good. But how do we know which Wiki software is right for us?

Other Wiki software

MediaWiki is popular, but many other Wikis are available for all platforms and needs. Here are some of the top choices:

- **Twiki** (`http://twiki.org/`): Powerful Web 2.0 Wiki, interesting plug-ins available
- **Xwiki** (`http://www.xwiki.org/`): An enterprise Wiki platform with an ability to run special applications on top
- **DokuWiki** (`http://www.dokuwiki.org/`): Aimed at documentation, and works without a database
- **PmWiki** (`http://www.pmwiki.org/`): Another popular Wiki
- **TikiWiki** (`http://tikiwiki.org/`): Wiki plus blogs, discussion forums, bug tracker, and so on; a full-featured CMS or Groupware

Additional resources

Want to know more? Here are some additional resources:

- A list and comparison of Wiki software on Wikipedia: `http://en.wikipedia.org/wiki/Comparison_of_wiki_software`
- **WikiMatrix**—another comparison site for Wikis: `http://www.wikimatrix.org/`
- Know more about Wiki: `http://en.wikipedia.org/wiki/Wiki`
- Ward Cunningham's original WikiWikiWeb site: `http://c2.com/cgi/wiki?WelcomeVisitors`

Note that different Wikis may have different formatting syntax. There are some common styles, but many variations. Review Wiki syntax and ensure that it's easy for your users.

Now it's time to change gears. Let's jump to the next specialized CMS.

Discussion forums: helping each other

Discussion Forums existed well before the age of blogs and Wikis. A discussion forum allows members to ask questions and respond to them. If you have a problem, you post a new discussion. Others respond and discuss till you get a solution. The discussion can be about anything. Discussion Forums (sometimes just called Forums or Bulletin Boards) are great for sharing knowledge.

We would like to have members discuss their Yoga-related experiences, questions, and suggestions on our Yoga Site. Another idea is to use forums for product reviews. This will get us real reviews of products. Let's go ahead and add a discussion forum.

Time for action-discussions on yoga products

1. Download and install **phpBB** (`http://www.phpbb.com/`).
2. Log in to the **Administration Control Panel**. You will see a screen like the following.

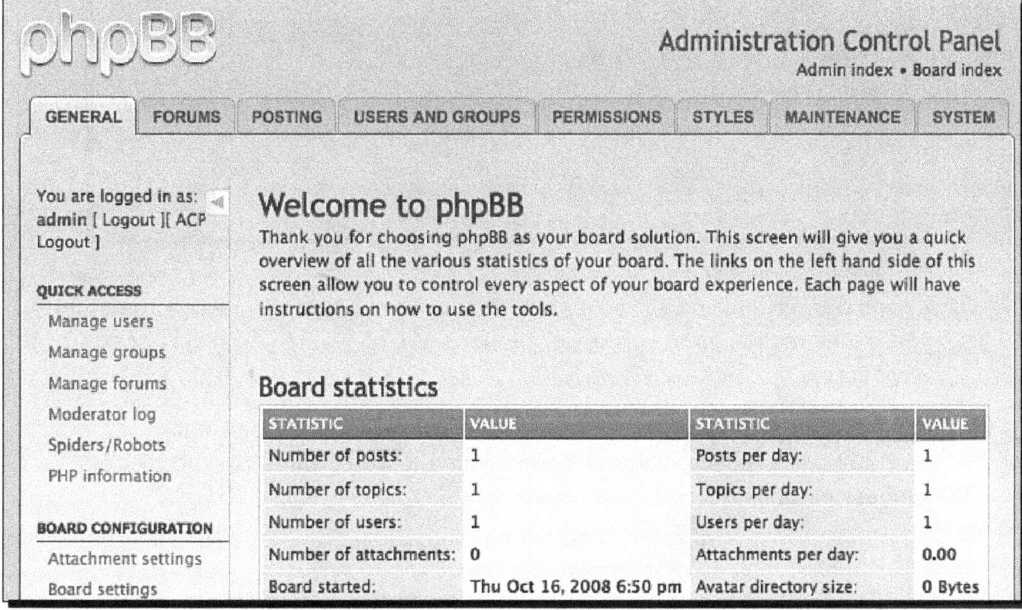

3. You can configure the forum from here, mainly with board configuration options on the left side. **Board settings** allow you to set up a name for the forum. Go ahead and set up a name.
4. Click on the **Forums** tab at the top of the page. You will find a text box to enter the name of a new forum on the right, below the list of current forums. Type **Yoga Products** and click on **Create new forum**.

5. This brings us to the **Forum settings** page. Keep this forum at the root by selecting **No parent**. Add a **Description** and set other options per your choice. The defaults are fine in most cases.

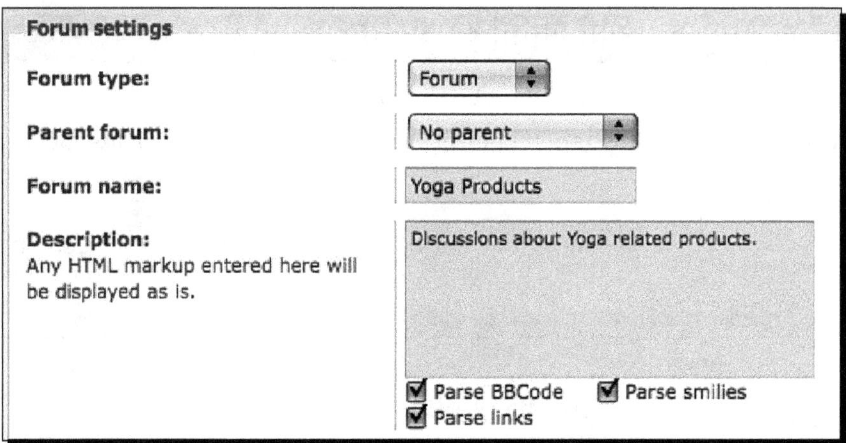

6. As you submit, a forum will be created. You will see a success message, and then you will be redirected to **Forum permissions**. We configure which user or group has what access on this forum from here.

7. We can work at group level. We want all registered users to read and post messages. Select **Registered users** from the **Add groups** list, and click on **Add permissions**.

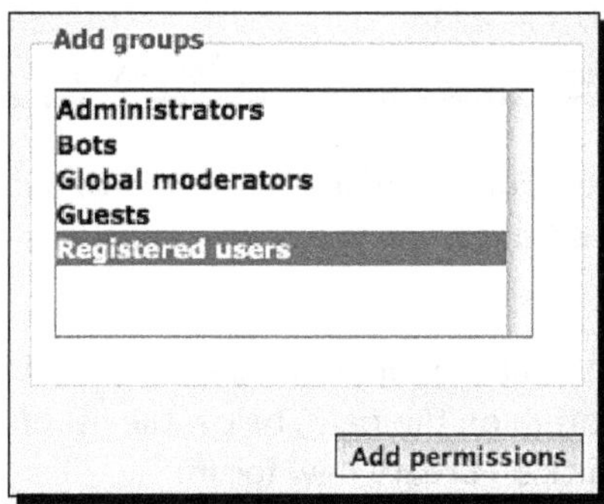

8. Select **Standard Access** as a role in the next screen. Click on **Apply all permissions**.

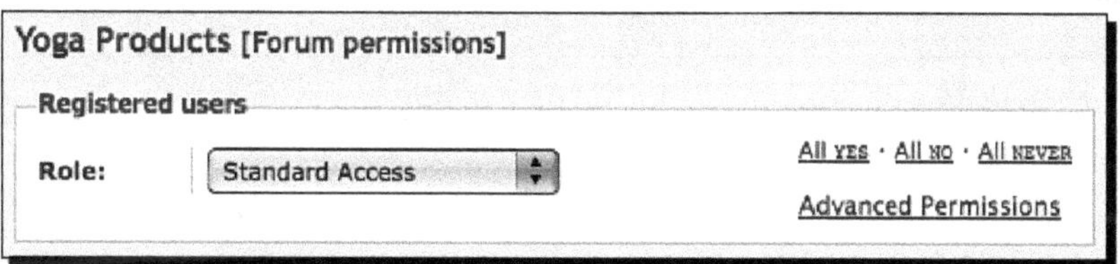

9. You will get a success message and a link to go back to the permissions page. Go back and configure **Read Only Access** for the **Guests** group.

10. We are now set up. Click on the **Board index** link at the top of the page. This brings us to the user-side view of our discussion forum. It looks like the following.

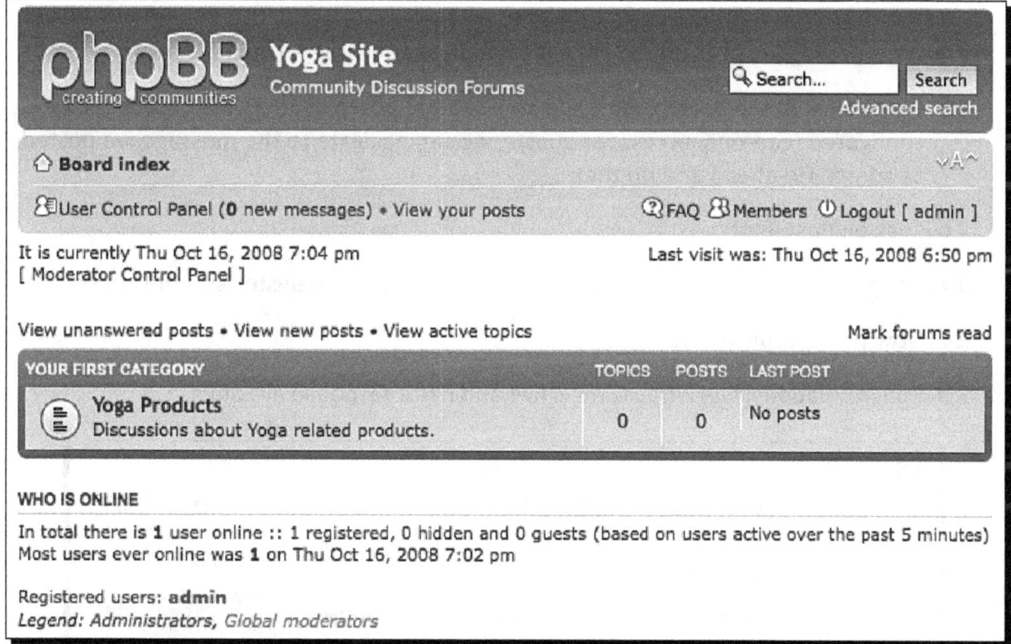

11. That's pretty neat, isn't it? Click on the forum name **Yoga Products** and to go into it. We can create a new topic now.

12. Click on the **New Topic** button.

13. Let's find people's opinion about our Yoga Mat product. Type a subject and message. Click on **Submit** to publish your message.

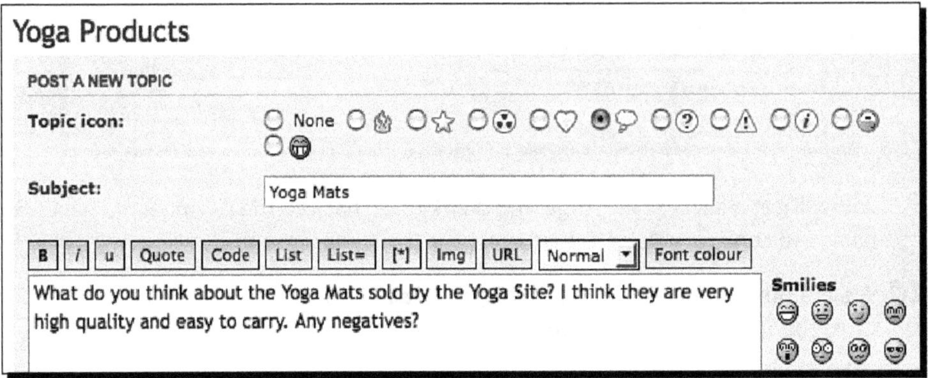

14. We were logged in as admin, so we could post a message. Log out now.

15. Come back to the board index. We now see the board in guest user mode. Since we configured read-only access for guests, we can navigate to the message we posted as admin. Go ahead and do that.

16. Click on **Post Reply**.

17. The next screen prompts us to either log in or register. Register as a new user.

18. Now post a reply to the topic.

19. Congratulations! Our discussion is live and has a response already.

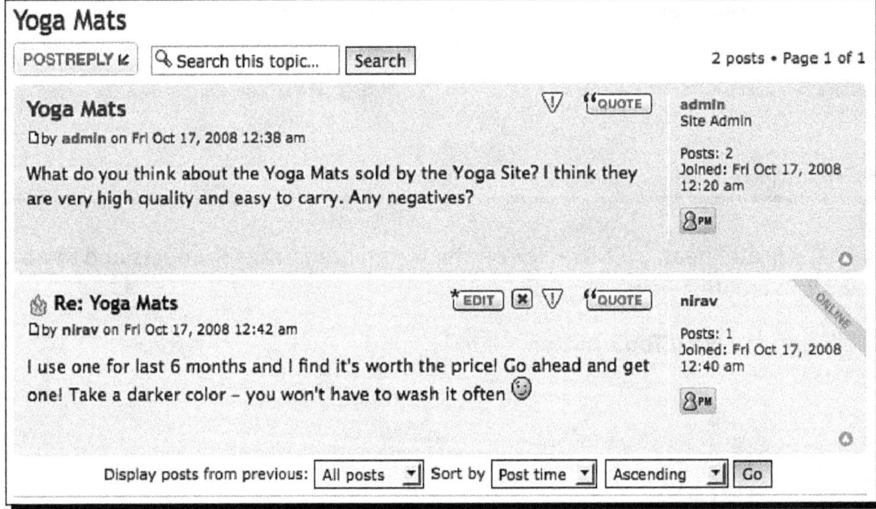

What just happened?

We created a discussion forum, posted a new topic, and replied to it. We even configured group access on the forum so that only registered users can post new topics, but everyone can read current topics.

Setting this up involved a lot of steps, but we learned many important concepts in the process. While doing this action, you learned how to:

- Configure board settings
- Create a hierarchy of forums
- Set up options for a forum
- Create different groups of users and assign different roles to them
- Use the Administration Panel, User Panel, and Guest view options
- Create new topics and replies, use smilies, post icons, and format a post
- Navigate to a topic
- Handle User registration, security, and automatic login

Of course, you can do a lot more things.

Have a go hero-trying out more with phpBB

- Create another user. Make him or her the moderator of the Yoga Products forum.
- Change the **Registered Users** role to be on the **Moderation Queue**.
- Post new topics. Learn how moderation works.
- Try private messaging and user panel features.
- Create a poll and evaluate the results.

What makes forums special?

As we saw, forums are great for sharing knowledge. Whether it is getting answers to your questions or voicing your opinion, forums provide a simple and effective solution. Forums are packed with features, some of which are as follows:

- Extensive access control and anti-spam features
- Hierarchy of discussion, highlighting important topics
- Discussion topics, quoting, word censors, attachments, saving drafts, and so on
- Solid search features, search engine friendliness
- User profile and basic networking, or community, features

- Off-loading administration workload by promoting users as moderators
- Increasing a site's stickiness—increasing page views and hits—as users keep coming back to interact with others, which also improves search engine rankings

There is no alternative to forums! If you want extensive user discussions on your site, discussion forums are the answer.

Other forum software

We looked at phpBB in our example—and it's one of the most popular. But there are many paid and open source alternatives.

- **Simple Machines Forum** (**SMF**, `http://www.simplemachines.org/`) is another popular choice, as it focuses on security and stability.
- **myBB** (`http://www.mybboard.net`) is compact on features, but good for small communities.
- **Jforum** (`http://www.jforum.net/`) is a powerful Java forum engine.

Additional resources

Want to find out more about forums? Want to know which one is right for you? Here are some resources that can help you out:

- Reviews, comparisons, and online demos: `http://www.forum-software.org/`
- Another comparison matrix site for forums: `http://www.forummatrix.org/`

It is time for another jump to something even more exciting—photo galleries!

Photo galleries: Sharing memories

You may have a lot of photographs and want to share them with your friends. You don't want to use a free photo-sharing service. You want a control over how the photos are published and who sees them. Your solution is a photo gallery: a CMS providing an option to categorize and publish options photos.

We want a photo gallery to publish team photos. Oprah takes her team on excursions, and there are lots of internal activities as well. She wants to put these photos online so that site visitors get a sense of her organization. Let's set up a gallery.

Time for action-posting team photos online

1. Download **Gallery** from `http://gallery.menalto.com/`.
2. Start the installation process.
3. The first step in installation is verifying that you actually own the domain you are installing Gallery on. This is a great security feature. Gallery asks you to upload a file on your server with a specific key. The installation continues only if Gallery can verify that file.

Authenticate

In order to proceed with the install, we have to verify that you are who you claim. The best way to be sure is to ask you to make a tiny change in the Gallery directory which will prove that you have the right permissions. So, we're going to ask that you create a new text file called **login.txt** in the `gallery` directory on your webserver (that's the same directory where main.php is located). It must contain the following randomly generated characters:

f8e3d868a7d74714d475f8c642c7c99d

As a convenience to you, we've prepared a correct version of login.txt for you. Download that and copy it into your `gallery` directory and you're all set.

Once you've uploaded the file, click below to continue.

Authenticate Me

4. Complete the remaining installation steps. It's straightforward from here on.
5. You will be taken to the Gallery home page as you complete the installation. Log in as the administrator.
6. You will see the administration options on the left side. Click on **Add Album**. We want to create an album for our team photos. Now, add photos to it.

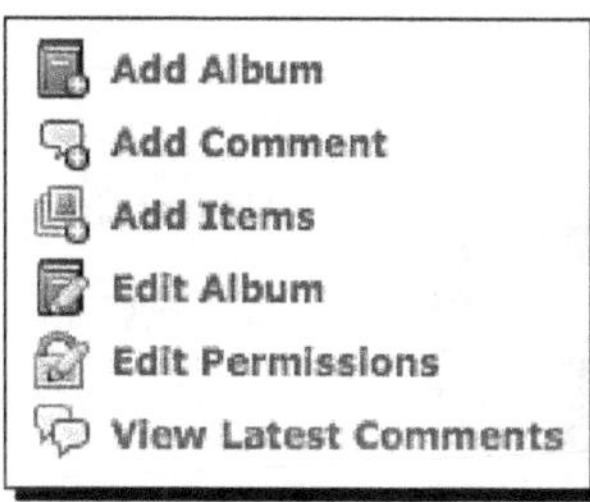

7. Fill in information for the new album. Enter name, title, summary, key words, and description. Click on the **Create** button to finish.

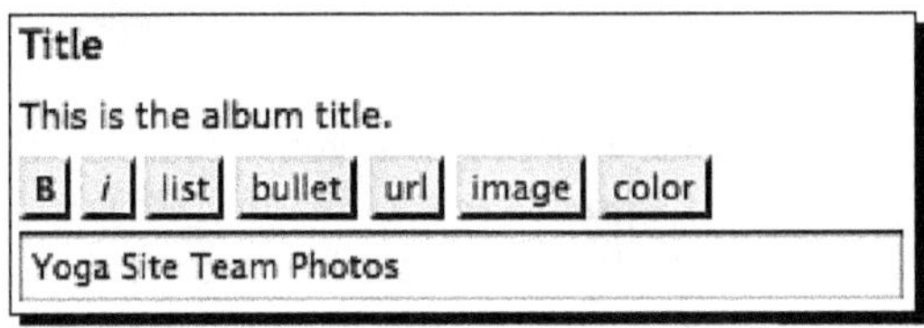

8. We can set up album options on the resulting page. We want to allow high-resolution images—not just up to 640 pixels. Change 640 to 1024 in the **Resized Images** option.

9. **Save** the options.

10. We are now ready to add photos. Click on **Add Items** on the lefthand side.

11. One by one, select each file and add a caption for it. Click on **More Upload Boxes** to get one more file upload box if you need.

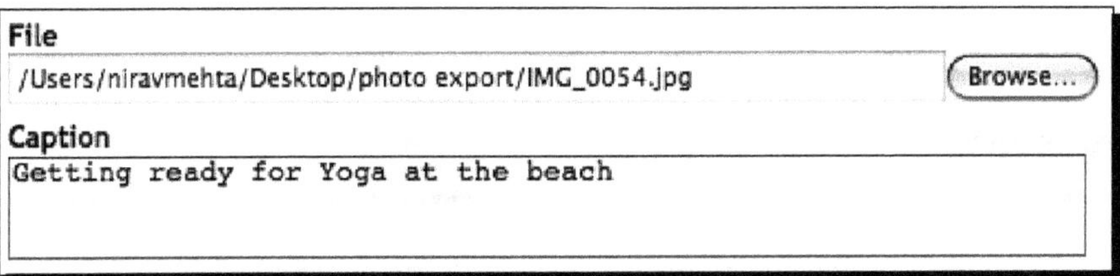

12. Once you have selected a few images, select an option for image titles. Making titles from captions is a good choice.

13. Click on **Add Items** to save.

14. Congratulations! Your photos are uploaded. Add more photos if you wish.

15. Click on **Gallery** at the top to see how your gallery looks. Navigate to our **Team Photos** album. Our photos are live!

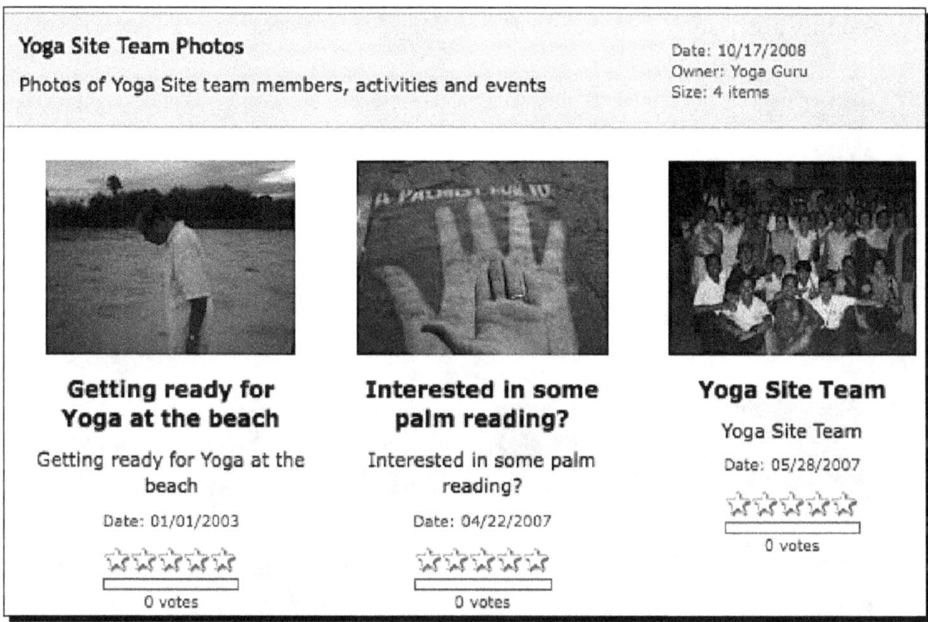

16. If you activated ratings, you will see rating stars below each image. Hover and click on a star to rate an image. The best images get 5 stars.

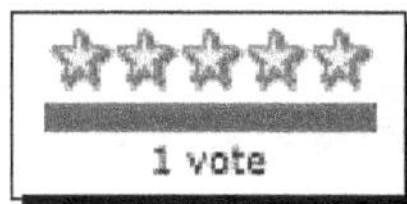

17. Visitors would like to see all the images in an album. Click on the **View Slideshow** link in the left bar. This shows the first album image and rotates through the other images automatically. You will also see an image caption and can manually go back and forward.

18. That's wonderful. Mission accomplished!

What just happened?

We created a photo gallery and added an album to it. Then we added some photos and captions for them. Visitors to our gallery could see the album, rate photos, and even see a nice slideshow. This was exactly what we wanted, and we could do it very quickly. Oprah will be happy.

In the process, we touched upon the following:

- Gallery installation procedure
- Album configuration—for example, sizing images
- Uploading images to an album and adding captions

- Viewing albums and photos
- Rating a photo
- Administration and user options in the left bar
- The slideshow view of our gallery
- Automatic thumbnail generation

This covers some basic operations in a photo gallery. What else can we do?

Have a go hero-digging into Gallery

Try out the following operations with Gallery:

- Password-protect an album.
- Allow visitors to comment on photos.
- Apply a new theme to Gallery.
- Upload videos to Gallery.

These are good features. Let's look at what makes photo galleries special.

What makes galleries special?

Photo galleries streamline the job of publishing photos. They automate tasks that you would otherwise have to do yourself. Here are some nice features of photo galleries:

- Auto resize, auto rotate, and auto naming of files
- Easy control of image quality and size
- Publish as many albums as you wish, and control access to them
- Beautiful display using themes
- Easy batch upload
- Embed gallery photos in other CMSs—for example, blogs
- Easy-to-remember URLs for albums and photos
- Slideshow

We have seen that Gallery is a feature-rich photo gallery CMS. But what are the other options?

Other photo gallery software

Gallery is one of the most popular photo gallery CMSs. But there are a few others as well. The top choices are as follows:

- **Coppermine** (`http://coppermine-gallery.net/`) has the most common features, plus some special features such as e-cards.
- **Piwigo** (`http://piwigo.org/`) is a powerful photo gallery software.

Additional resources

Want to know more? Here are some resources:

- Wikipedia's photo gallery comparison: `http://en.wikipedia.org/wiki/Photo_gallery_comparison`
- A number of desktop image-editing software applications allow publishing photo galleries in HTML.

Now that we have looked at photo galleries, it's time to shift gears again. This time we are taking on e-learning.

Online learning: facilitating learning

Online learning, or e-learning, has been a buzzword for many years. Education is important, and tools to facilitate learning have always been in demand. What if we wanted to create an online university for Yoga—a place where we teach Yoga, take exams (theoretical at least), and track students' progress?

Let's create a Yoga course and figure out the basics of the process.

Time for action-creating a yoga course

1. Download and install **Dokeos** (`http://www.dokeos.com/`).
2. Log in to the administration panel.
3. Before we create our Yoga course, we need to create a category for it. Go to **Portal Administration**. Under **Course**, locate **Categories of courses** and click on it.
4. You will see a default category list like the following.

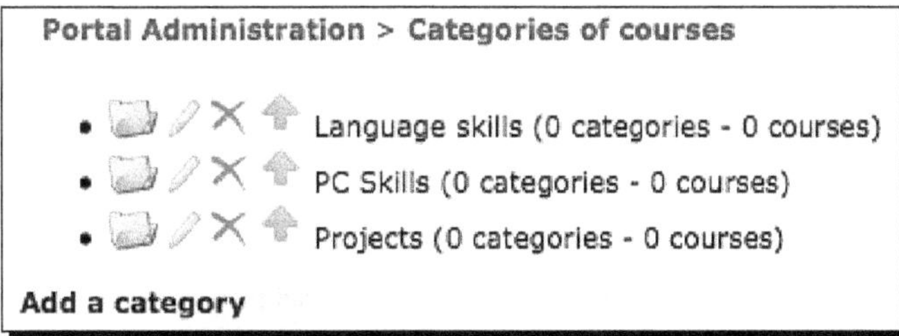

5. We don't need any of these categories. Delete all of them.

6. Click on **Add a category**. Enter a category code and name. Select **Yes** for allowing courses to be added to this category.

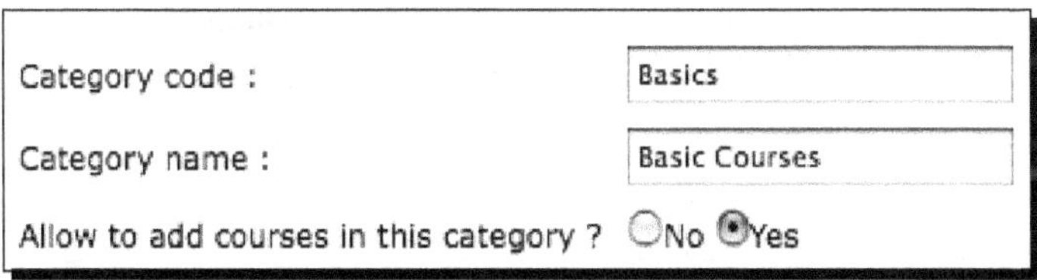

7. Once a category is created, go back to portal administration and click on **Create a course**.

8. What course do we want to create? Enter a course code, teachers, title, category, and other details. Allow people to subscribe to this course.

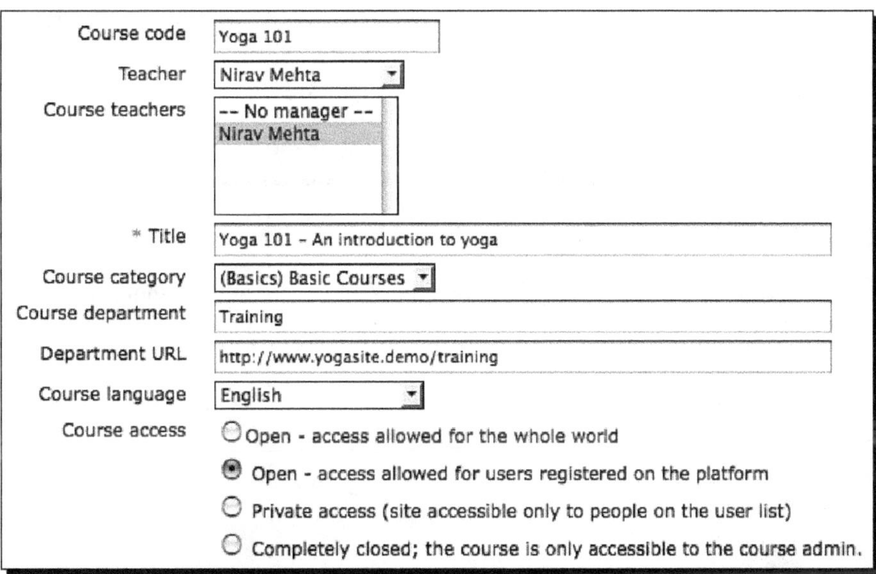

9. The course will be created and you will come to the **Course list** page.

10. Click on the home icon for our course. This is the course home page. It shows all course-related options.

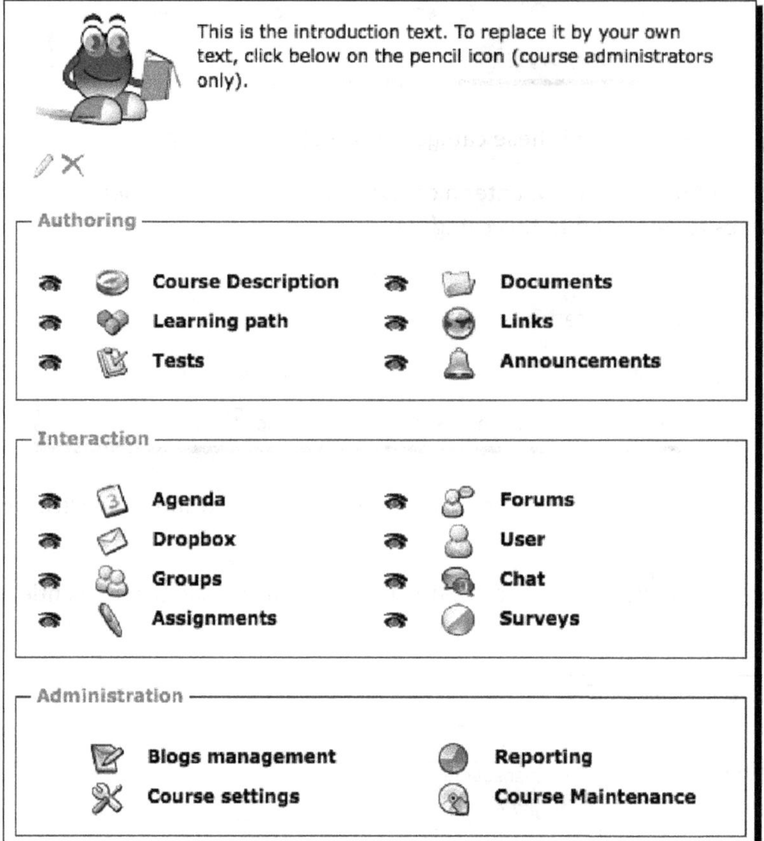

11. Click on **Course Description**.

12. Click on each icon and enter the course description details—**General Description**, **Objectives**, **Topics**, **Methodology**, **Course material**, and so on.

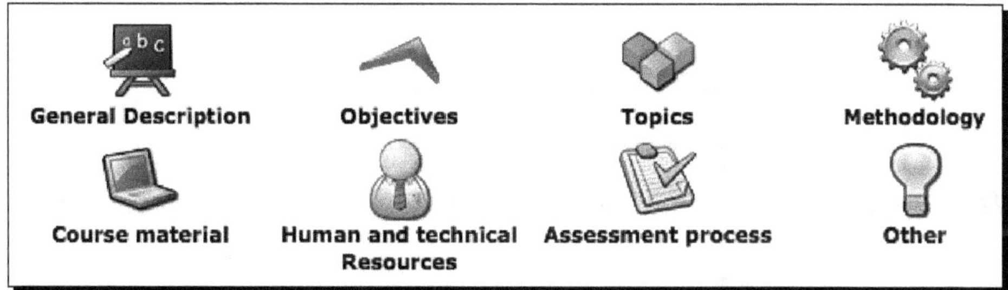

13. If you have a SCORM/AICC course contents package, you can import that to Dokeos. If you don't have one, you can download a sample from `http://www.dokeos.com/content/`.

What is SCORM/AICC?

SCORM is a standard for e-learning. It defines the standards for packaging course content and its media files. It also lays guidelines for user interaction and evaluations. Refer to `http://en.wikipedia.org/wiki/SCORM` for more information.

14. To import, click on **Learning Path** from the course home page, and then click on **SCORM and AICC import**. Upload your course file and it will be imported. If you don't want to work with a SCORM/AICC package, you can create the learning path manually.

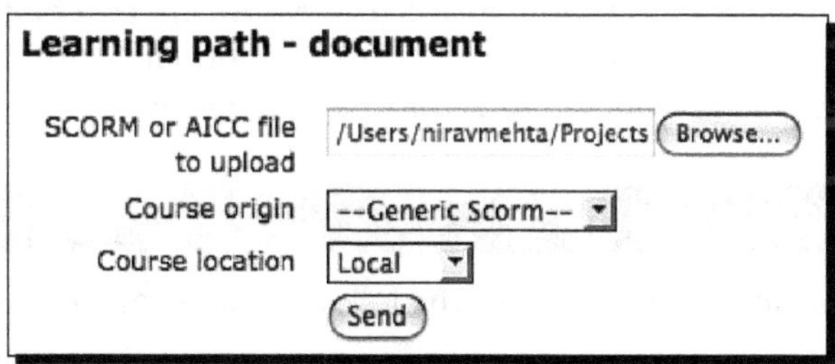

15. Log out from admin. Create a new user. Log in as that new user.

16. Browse and locate our newly created Yoga course.

17. Click on **Subscribe** to join this course.

Yoga 101 - An introduction to yoga
YOGA101 - Nirav Mehta Subscribe

18. You can now review the course contents, take exams, and participate as a student.

What just happened?

We created a new course category and a yoga course. We added learning activities to it by importing a SCORM package. Then we subscribed to that course as a student. Here are some important aspects of this process:

- Courses need to be in course categories.
- Every course has extensive options—from content, rules, exams, class agenda to forums, chat, documents, blog, and so on.
- Teachers can create assignments, tests, and announcements easily.
- Dokeos manages a range of aspects for online learning.
- Teachers can review progress and reports easily.

Setting up an online course looks daunting at first. But as you get a hang of it, you will feel at home with the Dokeos interface and its workflow.

Dokeos and other such e-learning systems are commonly referred to as **Learning Management Systems** (**LMS**). There is a content management part in e-learning—developing course contents. This is known as **Learning CMS** (**LCMS**). We are covering LMSs here to give an overview of these systems. Wikipedia has an informative article on this at `http://en.wikipedia.org/wiki/Learning_management_system`.

Have a go hero-take a test

We saw how to create and display courses. The following are some more things you can try out:

- Create assignments.
- Create a test and let the students take it.
- Review test results.
- Set a schedule for Yoga course.

Dokeos seems to cover most of our needs for online learning. Let's look at the highlights.

What makes e-learning special?

Top e-learning tools have an array of features. Here are some that make them special:

- Hierarchy of course categories and courses
- Access controls, tracking students' progress—surveys, tests, and reports
- Work with industry standards—SCORM, AICC, and so on
- Course-authoring templates
- Video conferencing, chat
- Ancillary tools—forums, blogs, announcements, file sharing, calendar, expense tracking, photo album, mailing lists, and so on

We can use a general-purpose CMS to put course contents online. But an LMS takes care not just of the course contents, but also of all the activities related to learning. This is what makes it special. If you want to carry out training online, go ahead and deploy an LMS.

Other e-learning software

We used Dokeos in our test drive. There are many top-graded e-learning CMSs available. Some of them are as follows:

- **Moodle** (`http://moodle.com/`) is comprehensive and well-known.
- **ATutor** (`http://www.atutor.ca/`) is easy to use and is feature-packed.
- **.LRN** (`http://www.dotlrn.org/`) is enterprise-grade e-learning software.
- **LAMS** (`http://lamsfoundation.org/`) is intuitive, and connects to other e-learning systems.
- **Sakai** (`http://www.sakaiproject.org/`) has collaboration and course management platform.

If you want to learn more, or find out other alternatives, here are some additional resources.

Additional resources

- TechWorld's 10 open source e-learning projects to watch: `http://www.techworld.com.au/article/223565/10_open_source_e-learning_projects_watch`
- e-learning center's list of CMSs (a bit old but contains most of the systems)—`http://www.e-learningcentre.co.uk/eclipse/vendors/opensource.htm`

We have covered the common special-purpose CMSs. Let's now list some specialized CMSs.

Other specialized CMSs

Sometimes you may have a special need that a general-purpose CMS can't serve. Here are some more CMSs, or software, that may interest you. Some of these may not typically be classified as CMSs, but they still manage content that is specific to their target use.

- **Elgg** (`http://elgg.org/`): General-purpose social networking
- **OpenX** (`http://www.openx.org/`): Manage advertisements
- **Open-Realty** (`http://www.open-realty.org/`): Realty listings management
- **PhpGedView** (`http://www.phpgedview.net/`): Manage family trees
- **OpenBiblio** (`http://obiblio.sourceforge.net/`) and **Evergreen** (`http://www.evergreen-ils.org/`): Library systems
- **JobberBase** (`http://www.jobberbase.com/`): Job board system
- **Andy's PHP KB** (`http://aphpkb.sourceforge.net/`): Knowledge base or FAQ system
- **Pligg** (`http://www.pligg.com/`): News-gathering in Digg style
- **Jackrabbit** (`http://jackrabbit.apache.org/`): Content repository system that can be used in CMS, Document Management Systems, and others

Of course, you can always do a Google search to find your match.

We covered more systems in this chapter than any other! Let's review what we learned.

Summary

We evaluated four different CMSs, all of which serve a specific need. We learned that specialized CMSs do a great job solving a particular problem—be it discussions or photo galleries. We also made a list of some other interesting specialized CMSs.

Specifically, we looked at how to:

- Set up a collaborative Wiki
- Create and edit pages with a Wiki, using Wiki syntax
- Configure a discussion forum with access privileges
- Create topics and respond to them

- Install photo gallery software
- Add albums and images, and showcase photos with Gallery
- Create and run an online course with the Dokeos e-learning system

And that completes our CMS reviews, yes! We have come to the end of this section. Over the last few chapters, we evaluated different kinds of CMSs and how they fit our needs. You are now ready to pick a CMS that's best for you. Go ahead and make a choice!

In the next section, we will look at tips and tricks for deploying and managing CMSs. This includes hosting your CMS, working with CMS communities and experts, and some more.

Section IV

Open source CMS tips

Hosting your CMS-Powered Site

Getting Involved in the Community

Working with a Specialist

Packt Open Source CMS Awards

13

Hosting your CMS-Powered Site

We cannot launch our CMS-powered web site without a place for it. That's what web hosting is all about. In this chapter we will look at the different aspects of hosting your CMS-powered site. We will:

- Evaluate hosting options—on your own machine or with a service provider
- Find an ISP that supports the CMS of your choice
- Understand the parameters of hosting
- *Perform common operations to launch and manage your site*

We will learn many important things in this chapter. Let's start by asking a fundamental question.

Do I need hosting?

Yes, you need to host your CMS somewhere because nobody can access your CMS without it being hosted. And if nobody can access it, there is no use of that CMS. In fact, even if you are using a CMS just on your computer, for your personal use, it is still hosted—albeit on your personal computer.

That's a technical interpretation of hosting. For all practical purposes, hosting would mean setting up your CMS on a server—on the Internet or on your intranet—such that your target audience can access it.

Wikipedia defines a **web hosting service** as following:

> *A web hosting service is a type of Internet hosting service that allows individuals and organizations to provide their own website accessible via the World Wide Web. Web hosts are companies that provide space on a server they own for use by their clients as well as providing Internet connectivity, typically in a data center. Web hosts can also provide data center space and connectivity to the Internet for servers they do not own to be located in their data center, called colocation.*

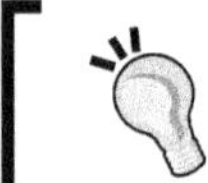

This Wikipedia article has useful information about hosting and related concepts. Check it out at `http://en.wikipedia.org/wiki/Web_hosting_service`.

If you want to deploy your CMS on your intranet, you don't need to scout for a good hosting provider. You can set it up on a good-quality machine in your local network. In any case, here are some key parameters to keep in mind while determining where to host.

Keep this in mind—hosting evaluation parameters

You will encounter jargon as you search for a good hosting provider. The following are some important things you should keep in mind:

- **Server Uptime**: How long the server is available. Most people will claim a 99% or 99.9% uptime. That's downtime of 3.65 days (1% of a year, that is, 5256 minutes) or 525 minutes (0.1%). If that looks small, consider that this would mean small downtimes of a few hours once a while. Most companies also mean by uptime when the server is powered on. They don't necessarily include network connectivity in their uptime guarantees.
- **Server Configuration and Load**: You may not need a high-end server unless you expect a lot of simultaneous visitors, and the application requires good CPU or disk resources (for logic or database). Most shared hosting companies host hundreds of sites on a single server. And this works well. Determine your needs before you get lured into higher configurations.
- **Backups**: You certainly need backups. Don't go without one. Take weekly backups, at least, and keep them on a separate server (or tape) if possible. Remember, there may be additional charges for this.
- **Support**: Email support comes by default. Phone support is very helpful during emergencies. But check the references before you decide. Quick and reliable support is the most important thing you will need after a web site launch.

- **Control Panel**: Many hosts come with some kind of web-based control panel. If you are not the "command-line geek" type, take a hosting account with a good control panel. Plesk, cPanel/WHM, and Helm are the most popular control panels.
- **Technologies Supported**: PHP is almost ubiquitous. Confirm that the host supports the technologies your CMS is using. Many hosts specialize in hosting a particular CMS. This is a good option if you are primarily going to use that CMS for your site.
- **Space & Bandwidth**: Hard drive space is cheap, and hosting options with gigabytes of space are common. Your CMS will not need this space. But if you are going to upload a lot of heavy files, you may need more space. One tip is to keep emptying log files, as they can eat up a big space. If your site is expecting high traffic, invest in getting enough bandwidth. Go for a host that does not cap per second bandwidth usage.
- **Security**: Restricted access control, physical security, disaster recovery options, and firewalls are some of the things you should check before finalizing.
- **Service Level Agreement (SLA)**: Service Level Agreements are minimum performance guarantees from the web host. Read them carefully. Even if you shy away from legalese, read them up. Put in refund or penalty clauses if you really need high performance.
- **Operating System**: Will Linux work for you? Most open source CMSs are designed to work on Linux, but will also work well on Windows. If you are on Windows, confirm that your CMS will work on your platform.
- **Shared, Dedicated, or Virtual?** A shared server has many web sites running on the same server. A dedicated server is where the entire server is yours, and you can configure and run it in any way you like. A Virtual Private Server is a combination of both. It gives you a full server, but a part of the physical resources—CPU, RAM, Disk, and so on.
- **Hosting Plans**: Most hosting plans are similar. Read the fine print for any setup charges (special monthly), support charges, and charges for the control panel.
- **Price/Free Hosting**: Price is not an indicator of quality. You may even find free hosting (Google for free hosting) to be sufficient for your needs. Compare prices with features and support levels. Get a friend's recommendation too.

That's a good list to start with. As you review your needs, it will be easier to compare hosts and select the best value for your money.

But before you set things up on the Internet, you will also need to set up a test environment. How do you go about that? Or if you are deploying an Intranet CMS, how do you set it up?

Hosting on your own machine

You can host a CMS-powered web site on your own machine. You can do this both for a test environment and a live system. If your CMS is PHP-based, the easiest way to do this is to take a bundle of Apache, MySQL, and PHP (AMP). For a list of AMP packages, check out `http://en.wikipedia.org/wiki/List_of_AMP_Packages`.

XAMPP (`http://www.apachefriends.org/`) is one of the most popular hosts, since it has cross platform versions and installs easily. XAMPP installation is faster and easier than installing individual applications separately. Here's a screenshot of the **XAMPP Control Panel** on Mac:

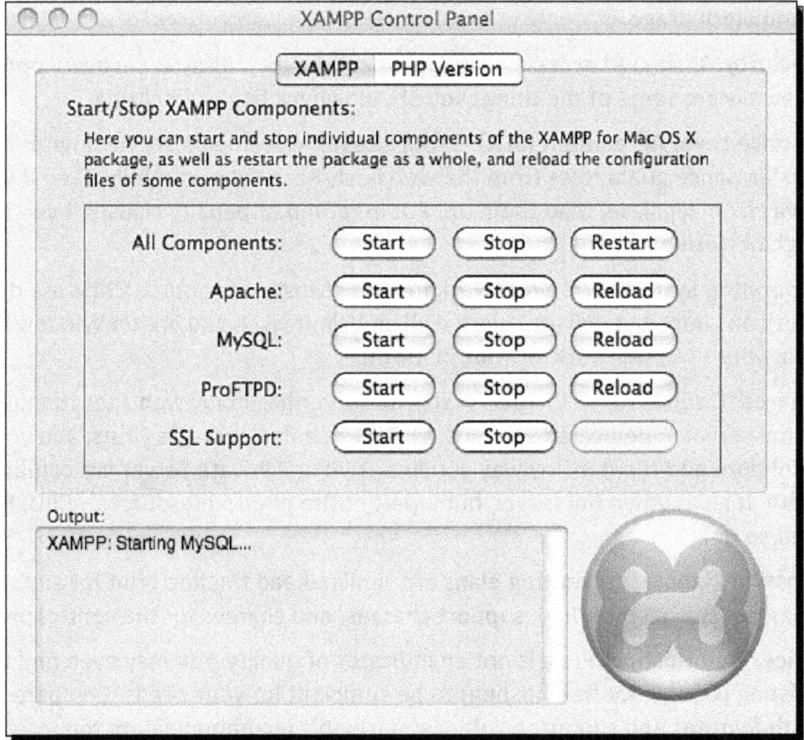

Once you have the core stack installed, you can go ahead and set up the CMS of your choice. In earlier chapters we have covered CMS installation and configuration. Refer to them as needed. We will cover some common hosting, or setup, tasks in this chapter.

If you are hosting on your own, make sure that you secure your server. Take expert help and ensure that your systems are set up correctly.

This was about hosting on your own, but if you wanted to find a good web host, how would you go about it?

Finding a good host

The best way to find a good host is to ask your friends. Referrals really work well because web hosting is a commodity business—everyone's trying to sell the same at the same price. The differentiator is service quality. So if a friend has experienced great support from a company, you can consider it positively.

Otherwise, here are some places to start looking from:

- **Hosting Directories**: There are sites that list and review hosting companies. This can give you a good starting list. Note that some such sites are fake, created only to promote certain companies. Google has a list of such directories at `http://www.google.com/Top/Computers/Internet/Web_Design_and_Development/Hosting/Directories/`.
- Other directories are `http://webhostingrating.com/`, `http://www.hostsearch.com/`, `http://www.hostindex.com/`, `http://www.hostreview.com/`, `http://www.findmyhost.com/`, and `http://www.webhostmagazine.com/`.
- **Free Hosting directories**: `http://www.absolutely-free-hosting.com/`, `http://www.freehostingdirectory.com/`, and `http://www.google.com/search?q=free+hosting+cpanel`.
- Go for a host your CMS recommends: Many open source CMSs recommend (or are supported by) some hosting companies. It's a good decision to evaluate them first.

WordPress Web Hosting

There are hundreds of thousands of web hosts out there, the vast majority of which meet the WordPress minimum requirements, and choosing one from the crowd can be a chore. Just like flowers need the right enviroment to grow, WordPress works best when it's in a rich hosting environment.

We've dealt with more hosts than you can imagine; in our opinion, the hosts below represent some of the best and brightest of the hosting world. If you do decide to go with one of the hosts below and click through from this page, some will donate a portion of your fee back—so you can have a great host and support WordPress at the same time.

- Ask a friend who knows: Someone who's experienced multiple hosting companies can give you a good recommendation.
- Review the articles at `http://www.tophosts.com/` and `http://webhosting.devshed.com/`. They have helpful material.

Fantastico and ready installations

Fantastico (`http://netenberg.com/`) is an autoinstaller for **cPanel** (`http://www.cpanel.net/`). It can easily install most popular open source CMSs. If you want to quickly try out something, this is fine. The Fantastico installations have had security issues and they are not very easy to upgrade. A custom installation is better if you want full control.

Now that we are getting closer to selecting a host, let's learn about the common tasks you have to perform in hosting your CMS-powered web site. Let's also cover some common problems.

Common tasks and problems in hosting

There are a few common tasks you have to perform to install and maintain a CMS on your hosting provider. We will quickly review them here so that you have a head start.

Making sense of the welcome email

When you register for a hosting account, you will get a welcome email from the host. This is an important email. Make sure you save it and mark it as important, or print it. You should look for the following information in it:

- Your FTP and control panel login and password
- SSH login information, if allowed
- **Domain Name Server** (**DNS**) information if you are going to use host's DNS
- Temporary URL to access your site (until DNS propagation makes your site accessible via your domain name)
- IP address of the server
- Instructions for FTP (file upload) and SMTP (mail sending)
- Any database-specific information (especially for Windows or MS SQL hosts)
- Backup information—how you can access or download it
- Support Ticket System—login and URLs; and support options—ticketing system, phone, email, and so on
- Billing account—your main billing account login details with the host

Time for action-create a database with cPanel

You will need to create a database to install a CMS. Here's how you can create a MySQL database using the cPanel web-based control panel.

1. Open cPanel for your site. It's mostly at `http://yourdomain.com/cpanel/`.
2. This will prompt you to enter your login and password.

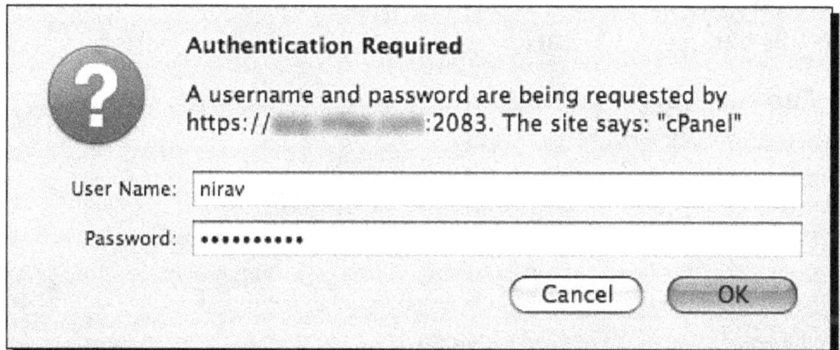

3. Once you are logged in, you will see a list of configuration options and useful server information.

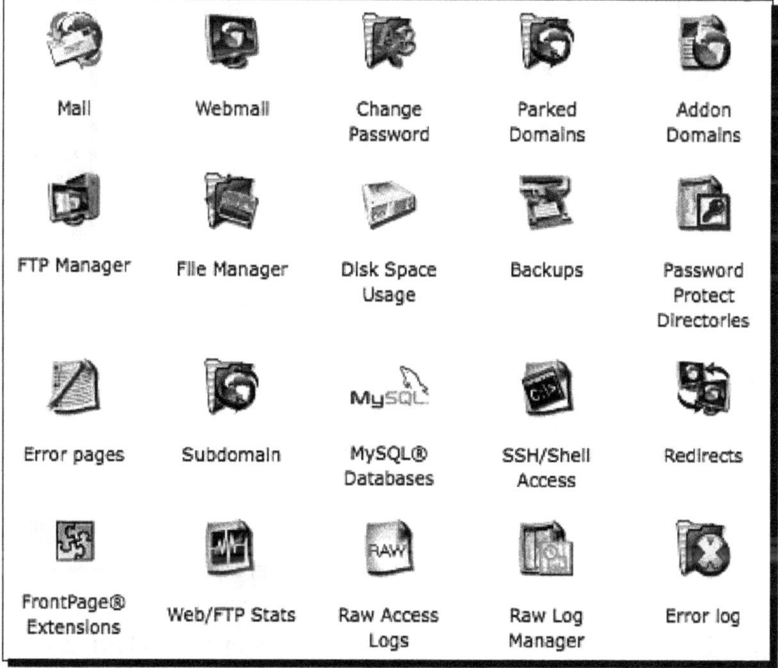

4. Click on **MySQL Databases**. You will see the options to create a database.
5. Enter a name for the database you want to create. Let's just call it **cms** for now. Click on **Create Database**.

6. Our database is created. But we still need to complete some work. We need to add a user to this database. Go **Back**.
7. Under **Current Users**, there is a form to create a new user. Enter a **Username** and **Password** and click on **Create User**.

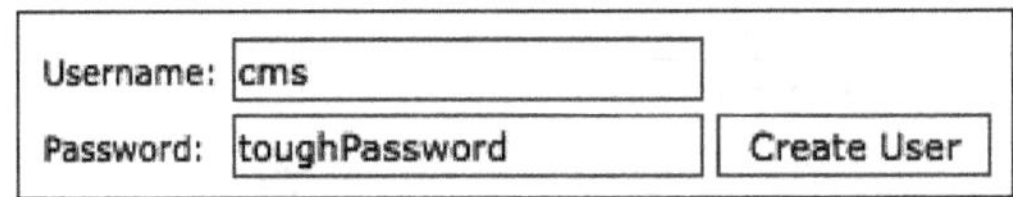

8. Once a user is created, we need to give the user access onto our database. Select the user and database from the dropdowns under **Add Users To Your Databases**. Keep **ALL** privileges selected and add the user to the database.

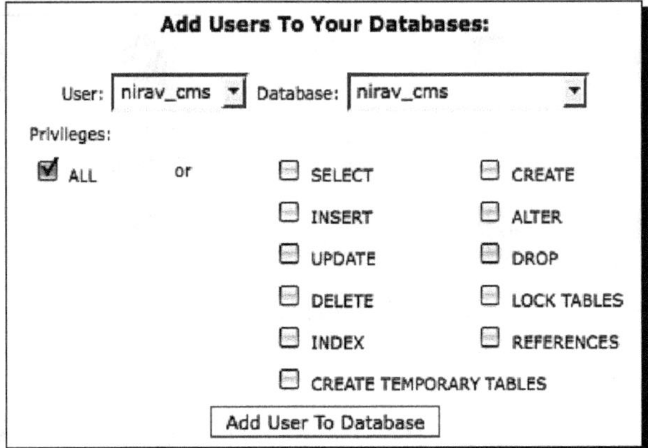

9. That completes the process. We can now use this information in our CMS configuration.
   - **Host**: `localhost`
   - **User**: `nirav_cms` (your cPanel username, underscore, and the database user you created)
   - **Password**: `toughPassword` (the password you created)
   - **Database**: `nirav_cms` (your cPanel username, underscore, and the database you created)

Make sure you choose a good password.

Don't use the Control Panel login/password for database

You don't have to create and add users to a database. Your cPanel login and password will work as database username and password as well. But this poses serious limitations. If you change your cPanel login/password, your database connectivity will break—until you update the new password in the database configuration files as well. Create a new user and assign it to the database—this is the best practice.

Using FTP to upload files

You would normally use File Transfer Protocol (FTP) to upload files from your test environment to your hosting server. The welcome email has the FTP login and password, along with the name and IP address of the server to connect to (which is usually your site's domain name).

You can use any FTP client software to upload and download files to and from the server. FileZilla (`http://filezilla-project.org/`) is popular and free. My personal choice is FireFTP (`http://fireftp.mozdev.org/`), a Firefox extension for FTP. FireFTP sits right in Firefox and works very well.

You may need to create an account in the FTP software (so that you don't have to enter login information every time). Then you connect to the server.

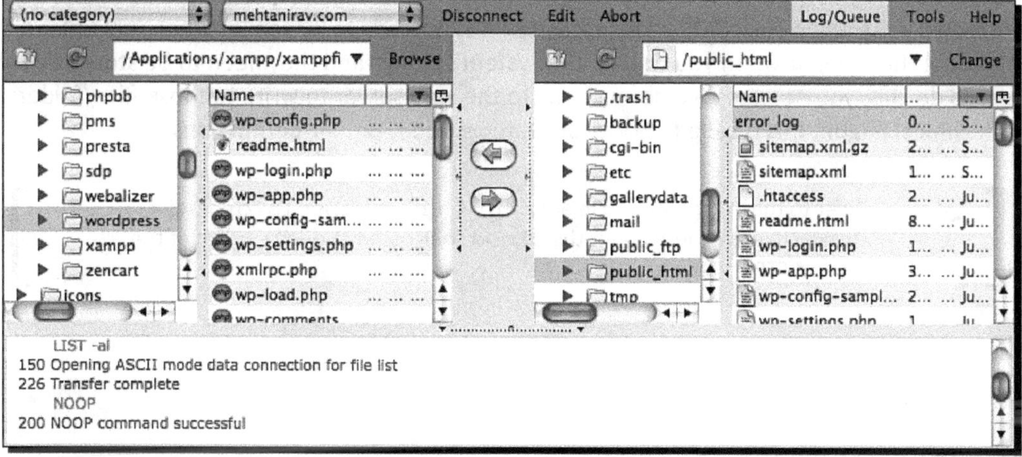

Once you are connected, you will see your local files on the left and server files on the right side. Navigate to the **www** or **public_html** folder on the server. This is typically the root folder of your web site—confirm with your welcome email/server support documentation otherwise.

Once you are in the web root folder, you can either drag and drop files, or select them and click a button to upload. The FTP software then takes care of queuing and uploading files. You can download files from your server (for backup or editing) in the same way.

SSH/Control Panel will be faster

If your server allows SSH access and you know basic system commands, SSH is a much better alternative to uploading a collection of files. You can upload a compressed archive (`.zip`, `.tar.gz`, and so on) and uncompress it on the server. Web-based control panels too have a feature to upload and extract ZIP files. Use this option if you have it available.

Changing permissions for files or folders

When you upload files to the server, they are uploaded under your name. Web servers must have tight security so that crackers are kept out. One security mechanism that web servers use is the permissions to read, write, and execute files and folders. For example, only you can delete a file that you uploaded. The permissions mechanism is slightly different on Windows and Linux/Unix.

Problems arise when your CMS wants to write files. It needs to write files when you upload a file using the CMS, or when you change the system settings and they need to be stored in a file. To do this, you need to give permissions to the web server to write to those files/folders. In technical jargon, this is called `chmod`, or `change mode`, or `777` permissions.

Refer to the Wikipedia article at `http://en.wikipedia.org/wiki/Chmod` to learn more about the `chmod` shell command—the origin of the `chmod` FTP command.

You can change permissions easily using your FTP client software. In FireFTP, you can right-click a file or folder to bring the **Properties** dialog box. From here, you can change read/write/execute permissions. If you want to recursively set a folder as writable, take the **Properties (incl. Contents)** option.

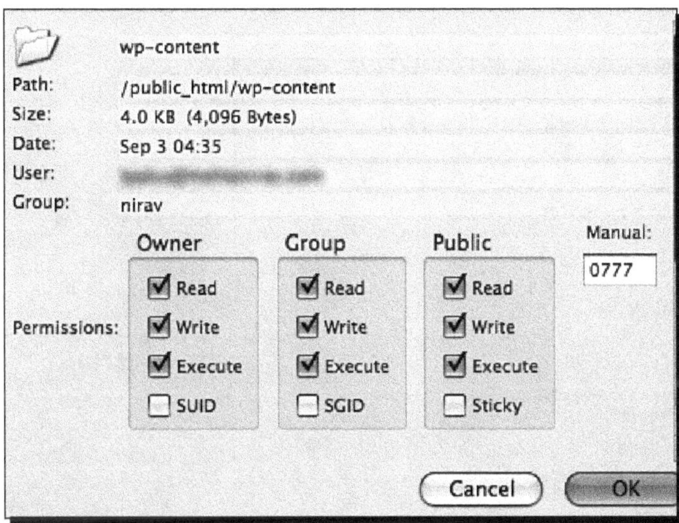

Checking **Read**, **Write**, and **Execute** for **Owner**, **Group**, and **Public** makes the folder (and its contents if you chose to) writable by the web server.

If this was a temporary change you made (for example, for the CMS to write configuration settings), turn the permissions back to 644 (the owner can read/write, others can only read) after the job is done.

Editing files with an online file manager

When you want to edit a file on your server, you can download it to your machine, make changes, and upload it back with the FTP client. But if you want to make a quick edit, editing it with the hosting control panel/SSH can be faster. File managers that come with hosting control panels are very powerful. They allow you to accomplish everything you can with an FTP client. Some have even better features such as uploading a ZIP file and extracting it on the server, or moving folders.

If you hosted your blog and wanted to quickly edit the WordPress configuration file, here's how you can do it.

Time for action-editing a file using cPanel File Manager

1. Log on to cPanel. Go to the **File Manager** option from the landing page. This shows you a directory listing of files on the left and options on the right. Click on the folder icon for **public_html** to navigate to it.

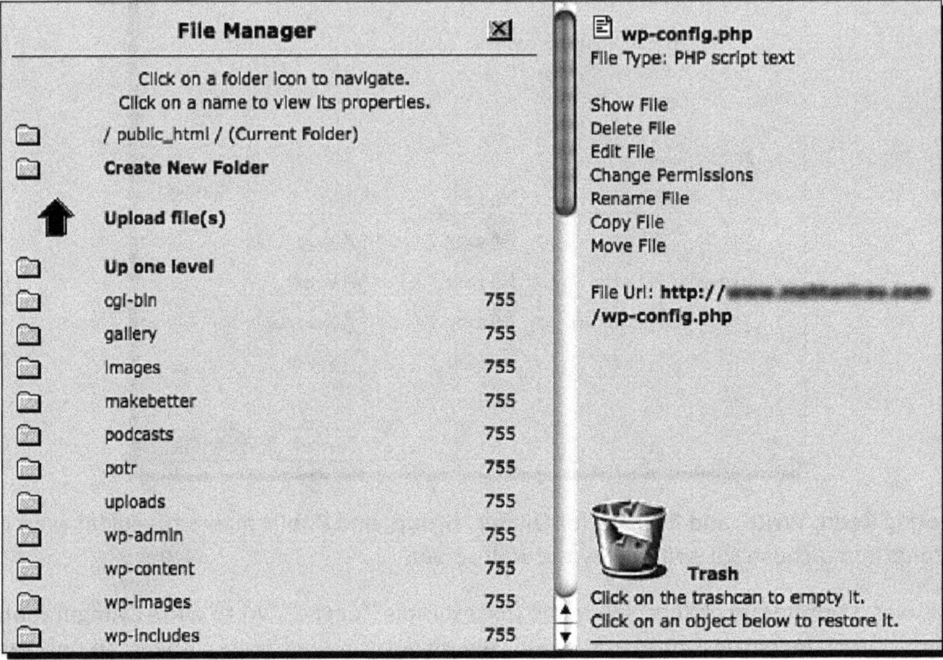

2. Locate the **wp_config.php** file and click on it. The file options show on the right.

3. Click on **Edit File** and you will see a text editor with file contents.

```
Editing /home/nirav/public_html/wp-config.php...

<?php
// ** MySQL settings ** //
define('DB_NAME', 'nirav_db');    // The name of the database
define('DB_USER', 'nirav_user');     // Your MySQL username
define('DB_PASSWORD', 'password'); // ...and password
define('DB_HOST', 'localhost');    // 99% chance you won't need to change

// Change the prefix if you want to have multiple blogs in a single database.
$table_prefix  = 'wp_';   // example: 'wp_' or 'b2' or 'mylogin_'
```

4. Edit it the way you like and save.

5. Job done!

Apache configuration with .htaccess

Apache allows configuring directory-level settings with a file named `.htaccess` (default name). CMSs use this file to create search-engine friendly URLs using Apache's `URL Rewrite` module. They may also use it to block spam or hacking attacks, or to prevent access to particular folders.

In most cases, you won't have to manually edit this file. The CMS will automatically write it, or give you full text for it. You can create a new text file with the name `.htaccess`, paste the contents into it, save it, and upload it to the server. That should mostly be what you have to do with this file.

If you have something wrong in your `.htaccess` file, you will start getting **500 Internal Server Error**. If you get this error, double-check your `.htaccess` file. Remove it and try again. Fix it and try again.

We can't cover the `.htaccess` file in detail here, but here are some resources that should suffice:

- Wikipedia on `.htaccess`: `http://en.wikipedia.org/wiki/Htaccess`
- htaccess cheat sheet: `http://www.thejackol.com/htaccess-cheatsheet/`
- A comprehensive guide to htaccess: `http://www.javascriptkit.com/howto/htaccess.shtml`
- htaccess tools: `http://www.htaccesstools.com/`
- Official documentation on htaccess: `http://httpd.apache.org/docs/1.3/howto/htaccess.html`

You may find this useful—some hints and tips

We have covered most of the common tasks. The following are some useful hints and tips:

- **DNS and propagation time**: Once you register the host's name servers with your domain, it may take time for them to propagate over the Internet. This means you site may not be accessible using its domain name, or may be accessible only from some places. Typically, it takes 24 to 48 hours for this.
- **Security**: Your web host may have tight security. You may not be allowed to execute system commands from your scripts, may not be able to access files outside your home folder, or it may not accept certain word combinations in data submitted by clients (especially to protect against SQL injection hacking attempts). Your server may also have SMTP authentication enabled. If so, a CMS that's trying to send out emails may not work out of the box.

- **Upgrading your CMS installation**: Many CMSs can automatically upgrade themselves. But if you want (or have) to do this manually, you can download the latest version on your machine, extract the files, and upload them to the server, overwriting old files. Of course, you will have to ensure that you are not overwriting the configuration files or any customizations you may have done. You can use SSH/ control panel to facilitate this as well.
- **Check the stats**: Keep looking at your server's access statistics. This will give you insights into where your visitors are coming from and what errors are they getting. Webalizer, AWStats, and Urchin are popular tools. Your server's control panel will mostly have them configured automatically. You may even want to try Google Analytics (`http://www.google.com/analytics/`) for comprehensive reports on your site visitors.

Alright, we are now well-armed to host our CMS. Go ahead and make it live!

Summary

In this chapter we evaluated hosting options, and went through solutions to some practical problems.

Specifically, we looked at:

- Different hosting options—own server, hosting service provider
- Parameters of evaluation for hosting—from bandwidth to technologies to SLAs
- Finding a good host—directories, reviews, and recommendations
- Making sense of the welcome email
- Creating a database with cPanel
- Using FTP to upload files
- Changing permissions for files or folders
- Editing files with an online file manager
- Apache configuration with `.htaccess`
- And some other tips

This chapter was full of practical advice, and the next one is similar. In the next chapter, we take a look at getting help. We will focus on working with CMS communities for support and contributions.

14
Getting Involved in the Community

As you work on your CMS, you will come up with questions. These questions could be about how to accomplish something with a particular CMS, or some technical snag you encountered. Getting correct answers to these questions is important. In this chapter we will learn how to get involved with your CMS's community. We will:

- *Explore different support mechanisms*
- *Look at finding answers using Google*
- *Learn how to ask questions on support forums*
- *Learn how we can contribute*

Asking correct questions is a pre-condition to getting correct answers. But we don't even need to ask a question if the answers are already available. Let's look at our options for getting support with typical open source CMSs.

Where to go for support

Most of the popular open source software applications have strong communities. They consist of users and contributors who are eager to help each other—after all, the whole open source concept is about sharing knowledge. As more people use software, the number of support requests for that software increases. Developers of open source software understand that users will need help. But they also want to focus their energy on development, rather than support.

Over the years, this has resulted in the evolution of support systems. Starting with mailing lists and discussion forums, support is now available through knowledge bases, frequently asked questions, and even blogs.

Open source does not guarantee community!

Not every open source project has a thriving community. Many open source projects die before making it big (just like any other venture). When you are evaluating a CMS, don't assume it will have strong community. Look around forums and mailing lists for activity levels. Also, understand the technical level of discussions. Some communities may be friendlier to new users than others. Pick up something that suits your needs.

When you have a question about a feature or problem, you may want to go to the CMS's web site to find answers. You may be overwhelmed with the options though. For example, the Magento web site (`http://www.magentocommerce.com`) has two sections that look promising: **Resources** and **Community**. Within them, there are even more options.

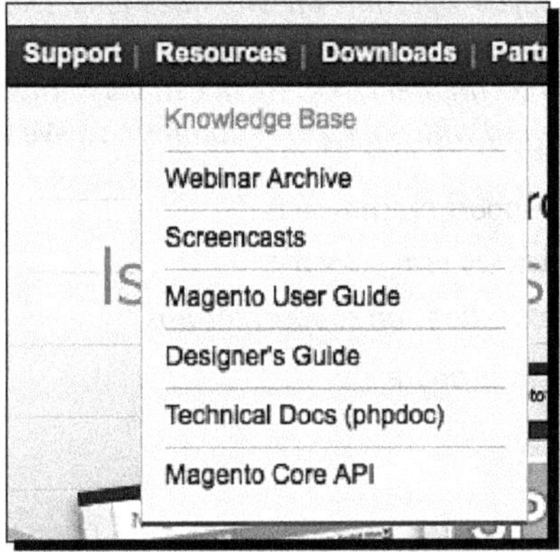

The **Resources** menu has seven items, from **Knowledge Base** to API details. The **Community** menu too has seven options, including **Forum**, **Wiki**, and **Bug Tracking**.

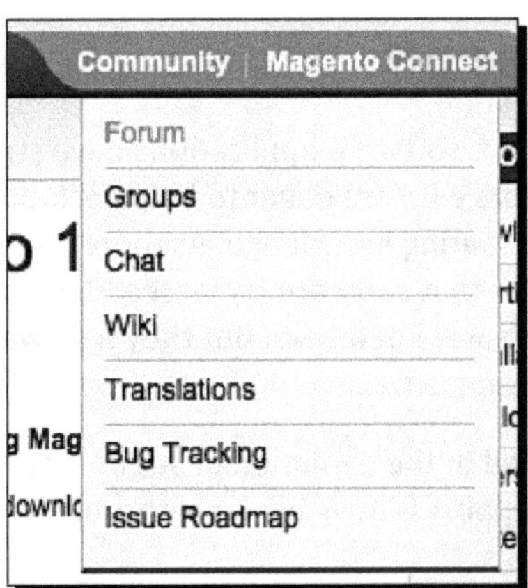

Where can you find the help you need? Let's start with a quick introduction to different support tools.

- **Knowledge Base**: This is a collection of frequently asked questions organized in categories. As it is searchable and has detailed instructions, it's a good place to start learning about a CMS.

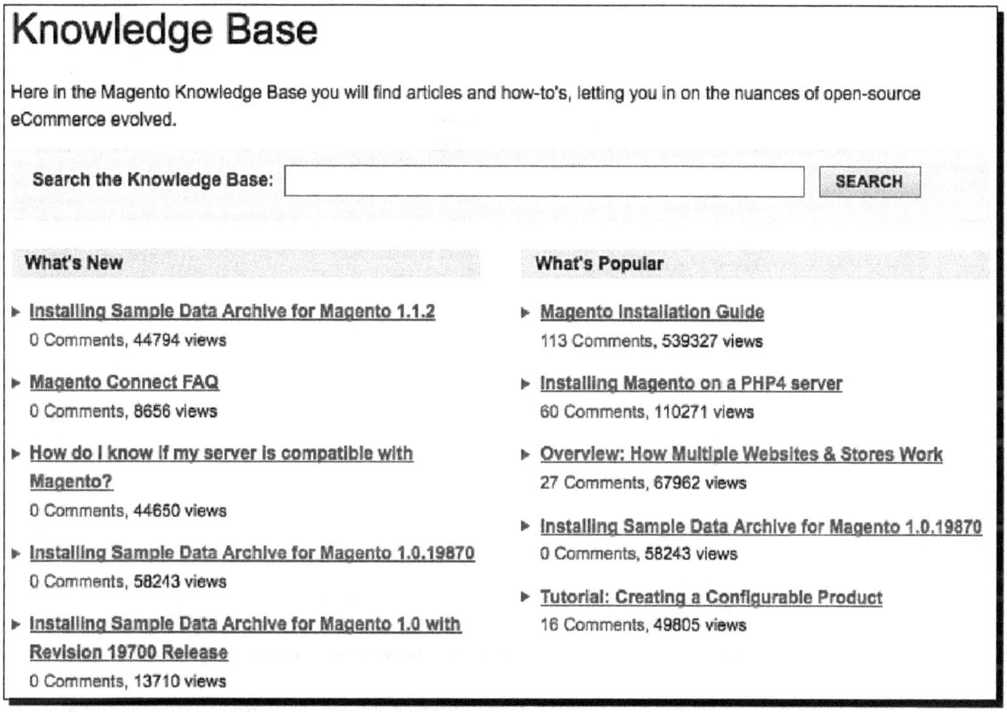

Knowledge Base

Here in the Magento Knowledge Base you will find articles and how-to's, letting you in on the nuances of open-source eCommerce evolved.

Search the Knowledge Base: SEARCH

What's New

- Installing Sample Data Archive for Magento 1.1.2
  0 Comments, 44794 views
- Magento Connect FAQ
  0 Comments, 8656 views
- How do I know if my server is compatible with Magento?
  0 Comments, 44650 views
- Installing Sample Data Archive for Magento 1.0.19870
  0 Comments, 58243 views
- Installing Sample Data Archive for Magento 1.0 with Revision 19700 Release
  0 Comments, 13710 views

What's Popular

- Magento Installation Guide
  113 Comments, 539327 views
- Installing Magento on a PHP4 server
  60 Comments, 110271 views
- Overview: How Multiple Websites & Stores Work
  27 Comments, 67962 views
- Installing Sample Data Archive for Magento 1.0.19870
  0 Comments, 58243 views
- Tutorial: Creating a Configurable Product
  16 Comments, 49805 views

- **Screencasts and Webinars**: These tools provides video tutorials on common features. "How-to" and introductions are common. They are great since they walk you through the whole process.
- **User Guides** or **Designer Guides** or **Developer Guides**: Focused on the needs of a particular type of user, Guides are almost like a small book.
- **Technical Documentation** or **Code Documentation**: This tool helps you with the inner workings of code, architecture, and code-level documentation. This is useful for developers who want to customize a CMS.
- **API Documentation**: Many CMSs come with a way for third-party integration. This is called an **Application Programming Interface** (**API**). API documentation tells you how you can integrate features provided by the CMS in your own third-party applications.

- **Forums**: This means community discussion forums. Forums are categorized in sections and are highly active. They can give answers to most of your queries.

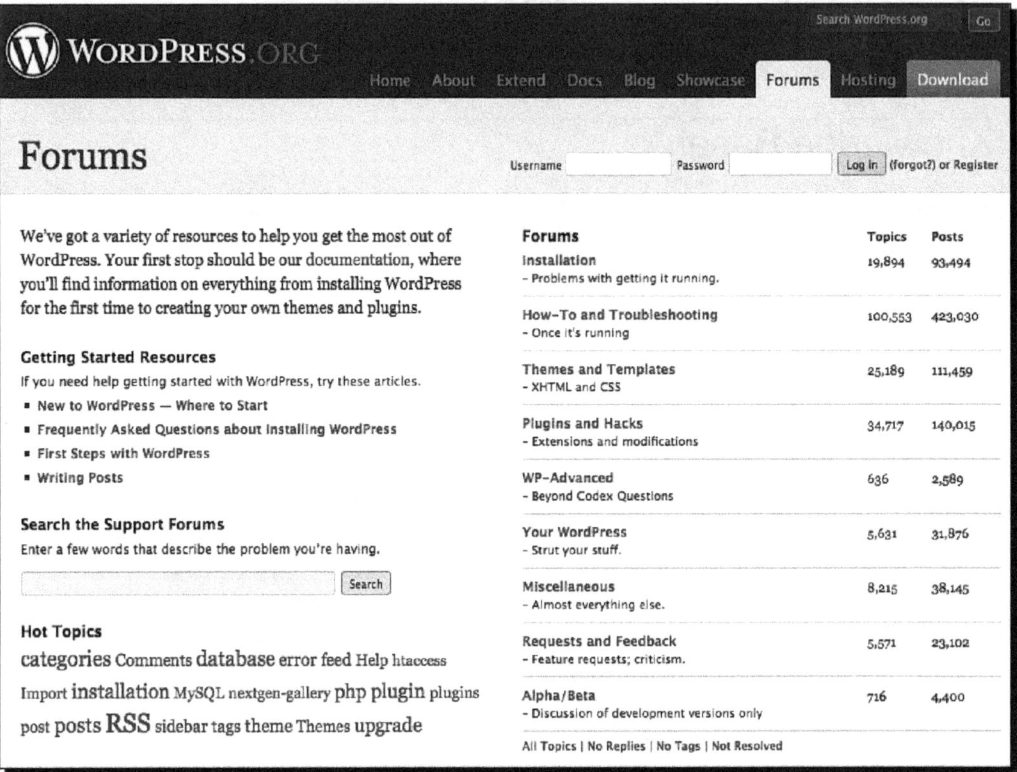

- **Groups** or **Mailing Lists**: These give email-based discussions and support for any software. They are archived and are also searchable via a web site. Mailing lists are interesting as they track the development and progress of a CMS in real time. Mailing lists are a good place for more technical discussions.
- **Wiki**: A Wiki consists of user-contributed documentation. It's easy to navigate through and easy to update. Wikis serve almost the same purpose as knowledge bases (since they are organized), but are directed towards user-submitted content.
- **Chat**: **Internet Relay Chat** (**IRC**) is still commonly used in many CMSs for discussions and support. You get answers almost instantly, but need to be tech-savvy to use this mode. I encourage you to start with forums and other resources before getting to IRC.
- **Bug Tracking**: If you suspect that something is wrong in the CMS, which can cause repetitive problematic behavior, post it as a bug. A bug tracking system records all problems and feature requests in software. It is mainly used by developers.

- **Project Roadmap**: This deals with the development blueprint for a project. Review it to understand the future plans—is the feature you want desperately already on the plans?
- **Blogs**: Blogs may be used by either developers or users. Blogs can provide answers to uncommon problems. You may land on a blog through a Google search too.

Among all these tools, **Knowledge Bases** and **Forums** are the most popular. Forums are more lively and active. They also allow asking questions.

Have a go hero-checkout the support systems of your favorite CMS

Go ahead and check out the support systems of your CMS. See what type of help content is available in different sections. Read an introductory article and a few forum posts.

Searching for an answer

If you have a specific question, you can Google it. Google is good at answering natural language questions. (**How do I change the template in Wordpress?** comes with close to two million matches!) It's always better to use key words (**change Wordpress template** comes with 3.4 million matches).

Google Guide (`http://www.googleguide.com/`) has useful articles and tips about searching effectively with Google.

Here are some tips on searching with Google:

- Use your CMS name in queries. For example, use **Wordpress plugin installation** instead of just **plugin installation**.
- The order of keywords is important. Think about how someone else would ask or answer your question, and use that order.
- If you get an error and are searching for possible causes, include as much error information as possible—but not URLs or paths specific to your installation. For example, instead of searching for **Fatal error: Allowed memory size of 8388608 bytes exhausted (tried to allocate 4608 bytes) in /home/john/public_html/wp-admin/admin-functions.php on line 2242**, search for **"Fatal error: Allowed memory size of" "bytes exhausted (tried to allocate " "bytes) in " "wp-admin/admin-functions.php on line 2242"**.
- Use the terminology of your CMS. For example, use **themes** instead of **templates**.
- Search with specific keywords or errors at the start, and then omit a few words if you need.

- Results from the CMS's web site or blogs can be more relevant. See them first.
- Search on your CMS's web site too as Google may not index everything. If you want to search the CMS site from Google, add `site:cmssitename.com` after your search keyword. That will restrict the matches to the `cmssitename.com` domain. Replace `cmssitename.com` with the domain name of your CMS.
- Ask a friend. A knowledgeable friend can easily get you a solution.

If you have searched everywhere but did not get an answer, it's time to ask. Let's learn how to ask questions.

Keep this in mind—asking good questions

Eric Raymond, a well-known open source spokesman, has written an excellent essay on How To Ask Questions The Smart Way (`http://www.catb.org/~esr/faqs/smart-questions.html`). This is a must-read for anyone asking questions online. He wrote:

> *"The first thing to understand is that hackers actually like hard problems and good, thought-provoking questions about them. If you give us an interesting question to chew on we'll be grateful to you; good questions are a stimulus and a gift. Good questions help us develop our understanding, and often reveal problems we might not have noticed or thought about otherwise. Among hackers, "Good question!" is a strong and sincere compliment.*
>
> *Despite this, hackers have a reputation for meeting simple questions with what looks like hostility or arrogance. It sometimes looks like we're reflexively rude to newbies and the ignorant."*

It's not entirely true that hackers and developers are rude to a newbie. If you put yourself in their shoes, you can understand their frustration with vague questions. They really want to help people, but for that people need to help them too.

With that cleared, here are some tips. You will improve your chances of getting an answer if you follow them.

- Search once again: Search once more about your question. Try different keywords. Nobody likes to answer questions that have been asked earlier!
- Look around other people's questions and the answers they got. Then form your question in a way you think will get you an answer. When you walk into a group of people, you wouldn't just jump with your questions. You will first listen to the conversation, and then pick up a thread as appropriate. The same rule applies to the Web.

- Ask a specific question: Use simple and clear language. Make sure you include as many details as you can because it gives people the background of your question. This will cut the back and forth of clarifications and you will get an answer quickly. For example, if file uploads are not working, give all details of when they don't work. Details may include whether the problem is reproducible, how to produce it, what's the scenario, any particular error messages you get, any configuration files you may think are appropriate to include.
- Use a descriptive title or subject: The title or subject of your message must make your question clear. *Urgent – Help! - File upload broken* is bad. *Uploading files bigger than 10MB gives 500 Internal Server Error, version 2.1* is better. When someone else is looking for the same problem, they will find it faster.
- Include code if necessary: If you have a code-related problem, copy and paste portions of your code (not the full code). This will help others understand your problem.
- Don't cross-post or post multiple times: Don't post your question in multiple sections of the same forum, or in multiple forums. Most people who answer read multiple sections and would be bugged to find your question across the board. Posting your question multiple times on the same board is a sure shot way of annoying everyone. If you did this by mistake, post a comment and point people to the latest message.
- Mention what you have already tried: Cut back and forth clarifications by mentioning what alternatives you have already tried. You may even want to include the results you got with those options.
- Be good: Use polite language and respect others. They are helping you out of their passion. Treat others as you would like to be treated.
- Answers may take time: Forums are typically active and you will get answers quickly. But this may not always happen. Be patient. Remember that you may be interacting with people across the globe.
- Not everyone will write perfect English: For many, English is their second, third, or even fourth language. Re-read if you don't understand, and then ask questions for clarification if you need to.
- Don't spam or advertise: Don't use support forums to spam or publicize your site—unless there is a "showcase" forum.

Many people don't know these basic rules and end up posting vague questions. And then they blame the CMS or the community. Take a look at the following screenshot from WordPress forums:

change login	1	tralala	2 hours
One blog on multiple servers	3	nemo-maritime	2 hours
Strange characters appeared after moving blog	4	Dave333	3 hours
embeding	1	Mickel	3 hours
redirect problem	1	rrsmith	3 hours
remove comments , archives and categories	1	meyya	3 hours
remove comments , archives and categories	1	meyya	3 hours
Browser issue, Sidebar appearing on bottom in i.e. 7.	11	samboll	3 hours
remove comments , archives and categories	1	meyya	3 hours
remove comments , archives and categories	1	meyya	3 hours
remove comments , archives and categories	1	meyya	4 hours
remove comments , archives and categories	1	meyya	4 hours

I highlighted the good questions, and as you can see they have replies. The **Sidebar** message has a long discussion with a total of **11** messages. A really bad case is **remove comments** question—posted 6 times, and without a reply so far.

Imagine you were an expert who came to the forum to answer others' questions. Which one would you answer first?

Recommended message structure

If you are posting a message on a support forum, here's a structure that Adobe recommends:

ISSUE DESCRIPTION

Summary:

Steps to reproduce:

1.
2.
3.

What went wrong?:

What should have happened?:

Product version:

- Product:
- Version:

Platform information:

- Hardware:
- OS Version:

As you can see, it's a good idea to include these details:

- A specific title
- A brief description about the question or the issue
- Steps to reproduce this issue or details of the problem
- Any error message you encountered or something that specifically went wrong—include a screenshot if necessary.
- What behavior were you expecting?
- The CMS, or software, or OS version details

Here are further guides to asking smart questions that get answered. Go ahead and read them.

Have a go hero-recommended reading

- How to ask a question on Microsoft Support: `http://support.microsoft.com/kb/555375`
- Adobe's forum posting guidelines: `http://www.adobe.com/support/forums/guidelines.html`
- Eric Raymond's How To Ask Questions The Smart Way: `http://www.catb.org/~esr/faqs/smart-questions.html`

How can you contribute?

As you gain experience with a CMS, you can answer others' questions. Contribution is what keeps an open source project going, and you don't need to know code to contribute. I strongly encourage you to contribute to all open source software you may be using. Here are some possible ways:

- Answer questions on forums, mailing lists, and IRC
- Provide code samples or examples of solutions you have found
- Write articles or how-tos, or blog posts about the CMS and how to use it
- Post bugs about problems in the software
- Make a theme or extension and give it out

You don't have to be an expert to contribute. You can start anywhere and work your way up. Remember that someone helped you when you were looking for an answer. You can pay for that favor by helping someone else.

This should give you a strong background on getting involved with CMS communities. If you have a question, go out and find out the answer.

Let's quickly summarize what we covered.

Summary

In this chapter we explored the different community support options for open source CMSs.

Specifically, we looked at:

- Types of support tools such as Knowledge Base, Forums, Screencasts, and so on; and what they mean
- Using Google to search for answers—tips and guidelines
- Asking questions on support forums—background and guidelines
- Additional recommended reading
- Ways to contribute and payback to a community

We have a good foundation in getting help now. But what if we wanted some customizations that were not readily available? What if there was no answer from the community? We would have to turn to professional help then. Let's cover that in the next chapter.

15
Working with a Specialist

You may need professional assistance while working on your CMS project. For example, you may want a professional graphic design of your site or some custom feature added to your CMS. Or you may want to outsource development and maintenance of your project. In this chapter, we will get ready for all of that. We will:

- *Understand the basics of software project management*
- *Learn how to find a specialist for your project*
- *Track progress and provide feedback*
- *Get insights into outsourcing*
- *Be prepared to handle conflicts and disputes*

Software Project Management is a vast subject. I can't go into details here, but this chapter covers the essence of my experience in managing software projects for over a decade.

Basics of Software Project Management

Software Project Management (**SPM**) is a tight rope balancing between feature requirements, time, cost, and performance. Similar to managing any other project, it is a lot about managing people. It is a vast subject, covering software development life cycle, estimation, control and monitoring, quality control and risk management, and so on.

Software projects traditionally follow a development style called the **waterfall method**. The following figure illustrates the steps in this process:

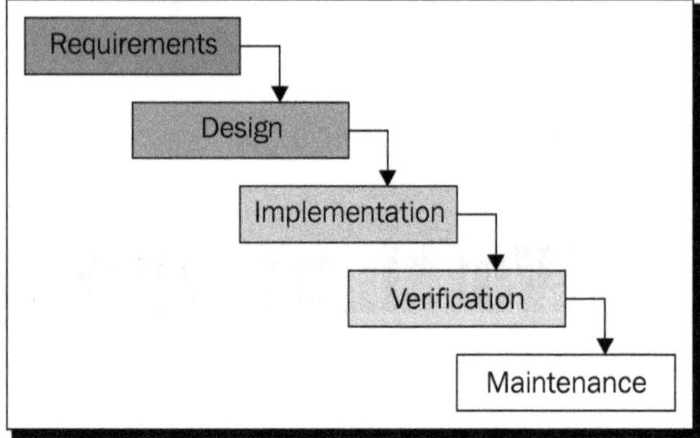

The waterfall or any method for that matter—will not fit all requirements. Agile and iterative software development methods are becoming more popular with web development, since they allow continuous improvements and better visibility. Choose a style that works for your needs.

Check out `http://en.wikipedia.org/wiki/Software_development_process` for an introduction to popular process models in software development.

Software development Stages

Depending on the development model you chose, your CMS project may go through these stages:

- Requirements definition—documents, flow, current process, limitations, desired outcomes, minimum performance required

Get as specific as you can in your requirements. It will save you a lot of trouble later on.

- Requirements—Approval or Validation
- Vendor Selection—Request for Proposals, Proposals, Evaluation, Negotiations, and Agreements

- Project Initiation—with vendor teams
- Software Design—Architecture, Platform, Technologies, and Database design
- Development—Graphic Design, Iterations, Testing, Quality Assurance
- Review, Feedback, and improvements on work done
- Deployment—on test server, live testing
- Handover—from vendor to you
- Maintenance and ongoing work

You may work with technical experts within your company or hire a vendor to carry out the project. In any case, it's important to learn how to manage each stage of a project.

There are numerous books and online resources available on software project management. Here are some of my favorites.

Recommended readings

Here are some great books and resources on software project management. They are especially relevant if you are involved with actual code or management of software projects.

- Two books by **Steve McConnell**—Rapid Development: Taming Wild Software Schedules and Code Complete
- Software Development Classic Mistakes 2008 at `http://www.construx.com/Page.aspx?hid=2537`
- **Jeff Atwood**'s excellent blog on software development at `http://www.codinghorror.com/`—Coding Horror
- The Mythical Man-Month by **Frederick P. Brooks**
- The Pragmatic Programmer by **Andrew Hunt** and **David Thomas**
- The Design of Everyday Things by **Donald Norman**
- Refactoring: Improving the Design of Existing Code by **Martin Fowler**
- **Joel Spolsky**'s blog at `http://www.joelonsoftware.com/`
- Getting Real by **37Signals** at `https://gettingreal.37signals.com/`
- If you want even more, check up Top 100 software development books at `http://knol.google.com/k/jurgen-appelo/top-100-best-software-engineering-books/`

When you start your CMS project, begin by defining your requirements. We discussed understanding your requirements in Chapter 3. Go back and review it if you wish to.

Once you have worked out your requirements, it's time to find an expert for your project.

Finding the right expert

Your team determines much of your success. Finding the right expert for your project is crucial. Even if you are working with an in-house team, try to get the best people. When you are working with external specialists, you need to go through a number of steps to find a suitable team. Here are some tips:

- Evaluate what services you need: Design, programming, hosting, or maintenance.
- Provide prospective partners with detailed requirements: Providing a document, some mockups or wireframes, and example sites is very useful.
- Decide on the budget and time you can afford: Are they non-negotiable? Make vendors aware of these things. That way neither of you will waste time.
- Ask for examples and references: Check the credibility and skills of a vendor.
- Check resource availability: Someone may have done excellent work earlier, but do they have the same level of resources available for your project?
- Company or individual: Determine this based on your needs.
- Personal interaction: If it's not required, you can outsource the project or give it to someone in another corner of the country.
- Project Coordinator: Who will coordinate from the vendor side? Are they competent enough? Do they understand your requirements? Do they have a lot of questions and suggestions?
- Keep in touch with your vendor. How much time can you spend? You will need to hand-hold the vendor! Be ready for it. You can't just leave it to them.
- Proposal: Is it a cookie-cutter response? Standard proposals that rephrase your RFP show lack of attention. Proposals that address your concerns (even if they are shorter) are better.
- Negotiate: The competition is heavy, and most people will negotiate on price. At the same time, make sure they make reasonable profits. They won't be interested in your project otherwise.

Finding experts online

How do you find someone who can do your project? There are various options. You can ask your friends and get their references. You can go to your CMS's site and see if they have a list of qualified developers or partners. You can also search online or in yellow pages to find someone. You can even check with the local chamber of commerce. But it's becoming increasingly common (and a lot easier) to find experts online. While classified sites such as CraigsList can be used for this purpose, you will find good success with `Elance.com`, `Guru.com`, `SoloGig.com` or `oDesk.com`. **Elance** is one of the oldest and most popular freelance sites.

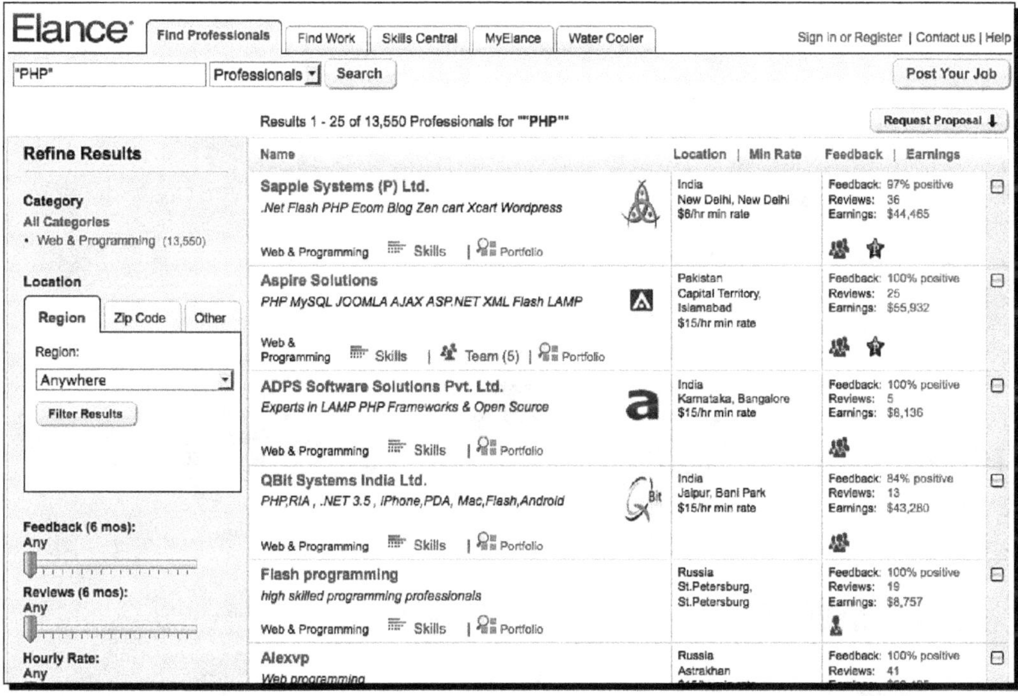

Here are some tips for hiring people from online marketplaces.

- Check their portfolio, feedback scores, earnings, the time from when they are on this network.
- Check their command of the English language and communication skills.
- Do they really understand your requirements? Double-check this.
- Ask their recommendations on the best way to do your project.
- Don't buy just on price, consider skills and communication too.

Online marketplaces are great to find experts for your project. Hiring someone for your project is like hiring someone for your company. You would take utmost care before recruiting someone. Use the same diligence and you will likely find a great service provider online.

Look for CMS experts

If you are working with a specific CMS, look for people who know that CMS well. You may find a listing of partners on the CMS's site itself. Prefer such service providers since they have a high commitment to that CMS. Someone who has contributed to an open source CMS is an even better bet.

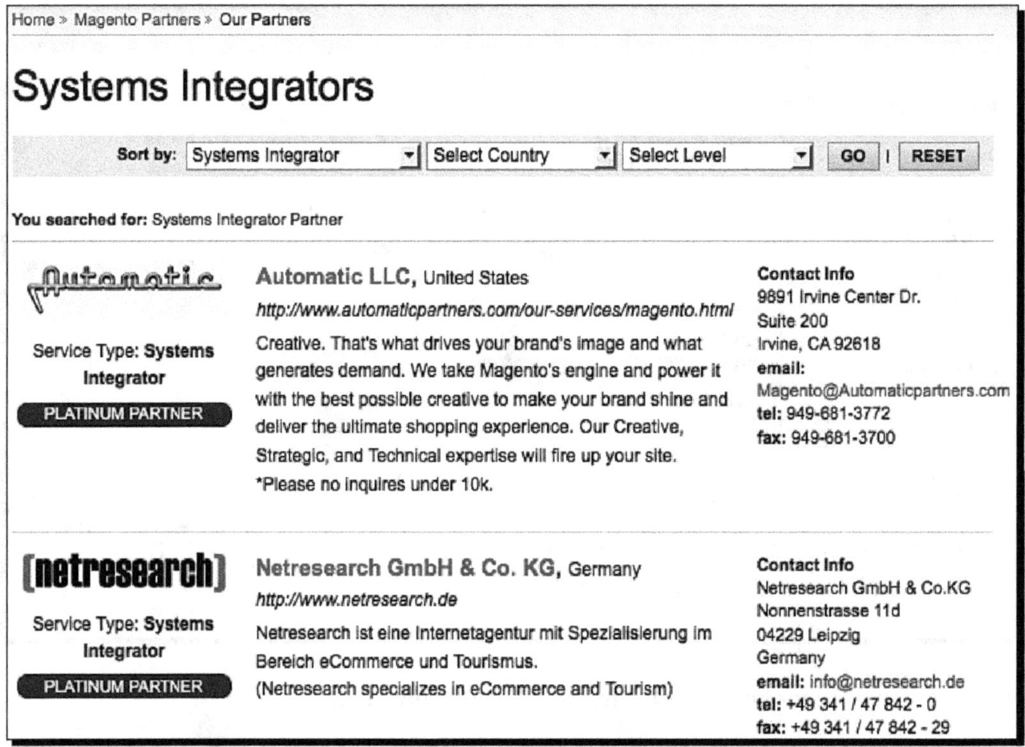

If someone has developed a plug-in for your CMS, there's even more a reason to hire them since they know the internals as well. Putting together a new theme or design for a CMS is much easier than developing a plug-in or an extension for it.

Outsourcing requires different thinking

You can find experts at a lower rate if you outsource offshore. Most online marketplaces we talked about earlier were designed to find cheaper yet qualified professionals from around the world. Outsourcing certainly has cost advantages, but managing an outsourced project requires different thinking and managing style. Outsourcing is not just handing away the job to someone. You too need to commit resources to make your project successful. Here are some tips you can follow:

- Find common working hours because communication is essential—and more so for an outsourced project.
- Talk—don't just rely on email or chats.
- Outsourcing is not a silver bullet. Matching requirements and vendor's skills is critical.
- A lower per-hour cost does not mean overall cost saving. Outsourcing adds in communication costs, and often the project moves slower due to inefficient communication.
- Ensure that you have specified your requirements in detail and they are well-understood. Do prototypes and mocks to ensure that everyone's on the same page.
- Find someone who uses your project management methods and tools. If you are an extreme programming follower and work with a waterfall guy, you will be stuck.
- Establish communication channels and frequencies—a weekly teleconference is a must.
- Remember that the company you outsource to is also a company. They probably do many projects together and have their own targets. Take full interest in your project, as you have more to lose if it fails.
- Be patient, understand the culture, and learn how to deal with your offshore partner.
- Don't expect too much for too little. Just because you are outsourcing does not mean everything can be done at throwaway prices. Be ready to pay a good price for good work.

There are lots of nuances to outsourcing. If you keep learning and fine-tuning your approaches, you surely can find big success in outsourcing. Here are some suggestions for further reading.

Further reading

- Top 10 Tips for Outsourcing Success on about.com—http://entrepreneurs.about.com/cs/beyondstartup/a/uc041003a.htm
- 5 tips for offshore outsourcing in Software Hacks—http://mashable.com/2008/08/19/offshore-outsourcing-tips/
- The http://freelanceswitch.com/ blog is a useful resource for people who provide freelance services. You can learn a lot about outsourcing there.

Once you have found a service provider of your choice—local or offshore—you need to focus on execution. Ensure that the project goes well and completes in time.

Tracking progress and controlling

You can't sleep peacefully even after finding a specialist. Once your project kicks off, you have to make sure that it is going on track. Weekly meetings and regular reviews of work done are very important. Here are some guidelines:

- Fix a time for weekly meetings with your service provider. Do as many extra phone calls, or Skype, or instant messaging sessions as required.
- Use an online project management tool. Track the project plan, regular communications, and issues or bugs.
- Set up frequent project deliveries on a staging server that you can access. This will allow you to see the work done so far and direct the team accordingly.
- If you are paying by the hour, make sure you get hour logs for all work done.
- Manage requirements—it's easy for requirements to balloon as time grows. Make sure you balance them. If you keep adding features, expect time and costs to go up. It's a better idea to remove features than add them.
- If you spot a problem, bring it to the attention of your project coordinator. If it is not sorted out, take it to the top authority at the service provider. Don't let problems grow.
- Celebrate success. Nothing motivates a developer more than appreciation for his or her work. Be generous with your praise of good work.
- Track bugs and prioritize them. Keep a time buffer for solving bugs, apart from developing new features.
- Testing and fine-tuning always takes a lot of time—sometimes much longer than development. Keep this in mind as you track timelines. If you don't allocate sufficient time for testing, you are making sure your project will be late or will fail.

- Read between the lines—especially when you and your service providers are far away. Get clues from the communication and work done. Sort out miscommunications or problems early on.

Using tools for tracking project progress is important. Here are some of my favorite tools.

Online project management tools

There are many free and paid online project management tools. The following is a list of some top-notch candidates:

- **Basecamp**: `http://basecamphq.com/`
- **activeCollab**: `http://www.activecollab.com/`
- **Trac**: `http://trac.edgewall.org/`

- **FogBugz**: `http://www.fogcreek.com/FogBugz/`
- **DevShop**: `http://www.devshop.com/`
- **Intervals**: `http://www.myintervals.com/`
- **GoPlan**: `http://goplan.info/`
- **Wrike**: `http://www.wrike.com/`

There are many more options available. To check them out, Google for web-based project management systems.

You may notice there is only one open source tool listed above (Trac). It's not that there are no open source project management solutions. I found most of them too complicated and insufficient. I believe it's worth the price to invest in a good project management tool.

If you are not using a full-blown project management tool, at least use an online bug tracking system. You can even track requirements using it. Don't keep bug tracking over email; it will not work. **Mantis** (`http://www.mantisbt.org/`) is a great open source bug tracking tool.

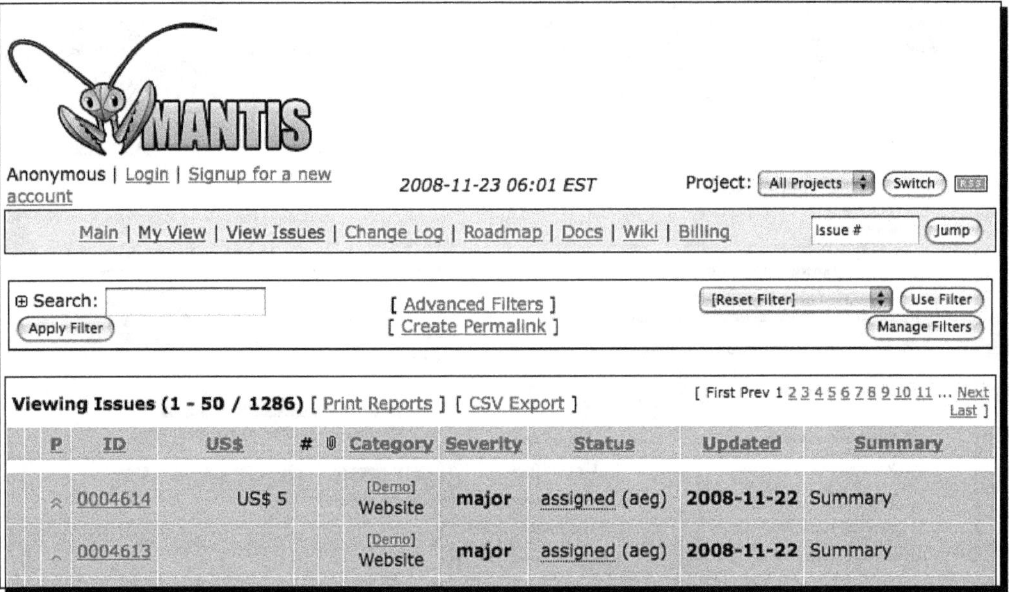

Bugzilla (`http://www.bugzilla.org/`) and **Flyspray** (`http://www.flyspray.org/`) are also very good bug, or issue, tracking software.

Some software companies would be using any of these tools to manage their projects. They may have their own online project management system. This is a signal of their maturity in project management. Give them a preference.

I hope your project goes smoothly. But you may have some conflicts with your service provider. What if they are too late? What if they can't be reached?

Handling risks and conflicts

Software project management has lot of risks. Anything can take your project off track. Delayed projects, software full of bugs, and abandoned efforts are all too common. Your service provider may refuse to accept a change you are suggesting, or may be unreachable. How do you handle all this?

Risk management

Knowing the risks you face is the first step in managing them. Make a list of the top risks on your CMS project. Keep revising it. This list should include both technology risks (for example, implementing a new feature in your CMS of which the team has no experience) and other risks. Here are some top risks:

- Scope creep: Features added to a project in its late development stage can take it off track.
- Doing too much—gold plating: Developers have their own notion of what's good and what's required. They sometimes do too much!
- Buggy software: If you don't check for quality, you may end up with perfectly buggy software on the schedule date—something that won't work at all.
- Unrealistic schedule: Let developers suggest dates for required features, or keep weekly iterations and push as much as possible. Unrealistic schedules give a sense of challenge at the start, but wash out enthusiasm as time progresses.
- Mismatched expectations: Failure in understanding requirements and mismatched vision about the project is a serious risk. Make sure the whole team is on the same page in terms of expectations. Keep expectations that everyone agrees to.
- Insufficient technical skills: If your service provider does not have enough skills, your project will either fail or take longer.
- Lack of tracking or control: If you are not tracking the project, it can go anywhere. Be on top of the situation.
- Estimation errors: This is bound to happen. When you or the developer estimates something to be done in eight hours, it rarely gets done in eight hours!
- Insufficient resources: Too occupied teams, employee turnover, or vacations can slow down your project.

Your project is unique and it will have its own set of risks. A good practice is to keep a list of risks and update it weekly.

Conflict resolution

Firstly, understand that there are less chances of your service provider having conflicts with you. You are a customer and everyone wants to please their customers. (You pay them.) Customers generally have an upper hand. If you and your service provider get into a conflict, look at your own mistakes first. It's easy to blame them, but consider that you gave them your requirements and direction. It's primarily your job to see that the project is successful. They are only people working for you to achieve your goals. If you see your vendor as a partner in success, most conflicts will go away. Communication is always the key.

Whenever you have a conflict, communicate. Try to understand the situation from a third person's perspective. If both parties are willing to accept their contribution to the problem, it's easy to move forward. Focus on what's next and move forward. At the same time, keep the lesson in mind and avoid the same mistakes in future.

You can meet some difficult service providers. They are the people who fail promises and are unwilling to take responsibility for their mistakes. How do you deal with that? Here are some tips:

- Put a proper contract in place at the start, and safeguard your interests.
- Get the source code of work done so far and terminate the project.
- You may need to pay to get the source code—settle for a reasonable fee.
- Ask the management at the service provider to change the team on the project if you think that will help.
- Get on the phone and talk to resolve.

Remember, very few people like fighting. Most people have better use for their time, and are ready to settle.

We have talked about a variety of things now—from finding a vendor to terminating one! But we are interested in your project's succeess. Here are my top recommendations for you.

Succeed with your project—recommendations

I have managed software projects for over a decade. My software development company has completed more than 200 CMSs. Over the years, I have learned simple rules for success. Here are my recommendations to you for your CMS project:

- **Communicate**: Make sure that developers or designers understand requirements, and demand a high level of communication. Software development can't happen in isolation.

- **Be clear on what you want**: If you know exactly what you want, you can get it faster. If you are not clear on your requirements, stop and get them clear first. Prototype if needed.
- **Give a business context**: Explain the purpose of your project—how you expect the CMS to solve it, and how the expert's work helps the business.
- **Asking questions is good**: If a prospective vendor asks you a lot of questions, take it as a good sign. You too should ask questions about the solution approach, its merits, and limitations.
- **Regular reviews are critical**: You won't know the project's status until you review it. Regularly (once a week?) review the work done and provide feedback.
- **Be open and understanding**: Developers appreciate clients who appreciate their work and understand that technical difficulties can spoil project timelines. They love clients who are willing to let go of features for better, or easier, solutions. Be open to new ideas and understand the other person—especially if you have outsourced the project.
- **Keep a good buffer**: Most developers won't complete a project on time or to the desired quality. The last mile of finishing a project is much longer than anticipated. Be ready for it. Follow an iterative development model and review the work regularly to keep on top of the estimated schedule versus the actual.
- **Be clear about your requirements**: If you are not clear, stop everything and document your requirements first. This is so important I have to mention it twice.
- **Partner with a vendor**: Software development is collaborative. If you treat your vendor team as your own extended team, you will see much higher morale and excellent results.
- **Focus on the users**: It's finally the end users who determine the value of your project. Make sure your project is usable and serves your end customers. Get end customers involved in the project early on. Take their feedback and improve as you go.
- **Keep learning**: Situations are dynamic and you will always find better ways of doing things.

This chapter was full of guidelines. I hope you got value. Let's quickly summarize what we covered.

Summary

In this chapter we explored the different aspects of working with specialists on your CMS project.

Specifically, we looked at:

- Software development processes, project management, and a list of recommended reading
- Finding a suitable vendor, using online marketplaces, and how to evaluate them
- Outsourcing your project
- Project tracking and control, using tools for success
- Managing risks and resolving conflicts with your service provider

We covered a lot about managing your project. You even have a good list of recommendations. Go ahead and try out some of them.

Once you are done, let's switch back to technology and review Packt's Open Source Award Winners next.

16

Packt Open Source CMS Awards

There are hundreds of open source content management systems available. How do you wade through them and find the best CMS? Packt Publishing—the publishers of this book—decided to sort things out and instituted the Packt Open Source CMS Awards in 2006. These awards have recognized the top open source CMSs from then and have a high degree of credibility. In this chapter, we will:

- *Understand the need for these awards*
- *Learn how winners are determined*
- *Look at the winners of the 2008 awards*

Let's get started!

Why an award?

When you started looking for a CMS, what was your reaction to the number of matches you got for your Google search? Most people feel overwhelmed looking at the number of CMSs available. The majority of us can't really figure out which will be the best CMS for us—almost all of them claim to be loaded with features and seem best for any needs.

So, there was a need to recognize the top CMSs. This is when the Packt Open Source CMS Awards (`http://www.packtpub.com/award`) were born. Packt is focused on community, and so the awards had to be community-driven. Packt did not stop at asking the community to vote for a CMS of their choice. It went ahead and set up cash rewards for the winners. The 2008 awards had $20,000 going to different CMS groups.

The awards serve two purposes: they help users to choose the best CMS, and reward people behind those CMSs for their hard work. Packt Awards have been very well received and recognized as the best evaluation of open source CMSs.

The reason for this credibility is also in the methodology used. Let's understand how the winners are determined.

Award methodology

It's not only the users' votes that determine winners. Here's an overview of the evaluation method:

1. Users nominate their choice of CMS in each category.
2. After the nominations are closed, voting begins in each category.
3. The top three choices in each category are voted by a panel of independent judges. The judges are experts and are well-known in the industry. Their vote is based on everything from performance and security to features.
4. Category winners are determined on a point-basis and are announced.
5. In case of a tie, additional judges take the decision.

The whole process is fairly transparent and regular updates are available from Packt's web site (`www.packtpub.com`).

It's now time to see the winners! Let's take a quick run through the 2008 award winners.

2008 award winners

The awards are given in different categories such as **Overall**, **Most Promising**, **Best PHP/ MySQL CMS**, and **Best Other CMS**. Here is a combined list of winners, followed by other finalists.

Drupal

Web site: `http://www.drupal.org/`

In this book: Chapter 9

Award status: First in the Overall Open Source CMS category, first in the Best Open Source PHP CMS category

Yes, Drupal won two awards!

Background

Back in 2000, permanent Internet connections were at a premium for the students of the University of Antwerp. So Dries Buytaert and Hans Snijder set up a wireless bridge between their student dorms to share Hans's ADSL modem connection among eight students. While this was an extremely luxurious situation at that time, something was missing—there was no means to discuss or share simple things.

This inspired Dries to work on a small news site with a built-in web board, allowing the group of friends to leave each other notes about the status of the network, to announce where they were having dinner, or to share some noteworthy news items.

Dries and his friends decided to put their internal site online after graduation so that they could be in touch. Dries settled for `drop.org` for the domain name, which was a typo for 'dorp.org'. Dorp is the Dutch word for village, which was considered an appropriate name for the small community.

Once established on the Web, `drop.org`'s audience changed as the members began talking about new web technologies such as moderation, syndication, rating, and distributed authentication. Drop.org slowly turned into a personal experimentation environment, driven by the discussions and flow of ideas. The discussions about these web technologies were tried out on drop.org itself as new additions to the software running the site.

It was only later—in January 2001—that Dries decided to release the software behind drop.org as **Drupal**. The motivating factor was to enable others to use and extend the experimentation platform so that more people could explore new paths for development. The name Drupal, pronounced "droo-puhl," is derived from the English pronunciation of the Dutch word druppel which stands for "drop."

Today, Drupal is an extremely popular and powerful content management system. So much that it won the Overall Open Source CMS award!

Joomla!

Web site: `http://www.joomla.org/`

In this book: Chapters 4, 5, 6, 7, and 9

Award status: Second in the Overall Open Source CMS category, second in the Best Open Source PHP CMS category

Background

Joomla! is a continuation of the work of the Development Team that unanimously resigned from the Mambo project in August 2005. The name was chosen from thousands of recommendations by the community, and even went through an arduous review session by branding and marketing professionals who also felt that Joomla! was the best choice of the lot. Joomla is a phonetic spelling for the Swahili word Jumla, which means all together or as a whole.

The Joomla! project has several Working Groups that have been created to utilize the wealth of knowledge its community provides. Each of these groups focuses on a specific aspect of Joomla! that is essential to the project's growth and development.

Joomla! has a thriving community and extensive support. It's easy to get started with Joomla! and even to customize it.

DotNetNuke

Web site: `http://www.dotnetnuke.com/`

In this book: Chapter 9

Award status: Third in the Overall Open Source CMS category, third in the Best Other Open Source CMS category

Background

In January 2002, Microsoft Corporation published **IBuySpy** (**IBS**) Portal. It was one of a handful of "Starter Kits" (sample applications) that provided full source code under a liberal EULA to demonstrate how to implement specific functionality on the new ASP.NET 1.0 platform. The kits were functional, but very simplistic, and were intended to aid programmers in developing projects of their own.

On December 24th, 2002, Shaun Walker released a modified version of the original IBS portal application. The new application was called the IBuySpy Workshop. It was released under an open source BSD license to allow for maximum freedom in both commercial and non-commercial environments. The release, which was posted as a link on the Microsoft ASP.NET Forums, included a variety of enhancements and innovations over the original IBS code. This included the ability to support multiple portals from a single installation, a feature that became very popular in the shared web hosting market.

After a number of rapid releases, the application was renamed **DotNetNuke** on February 28, 2003 (a name that was quickly abbreviated to **DNN** for simplicity).

Today, DotNetNuke continues to operate as the largest and the most successful open source project on the Microsoft platform. Passing the mark of 500,000 registered users and 5.0 million downloads in late 2007, the project is gaining rapid adoption across all business sectors, including mid-market and enterprise. With a dedicated management team, passionate developer community, and prosperous ecosystem of vendors providing add-on products and services, the DotNetNuke project continues to grow and create a wealth of opportunities.

SilverStripe

Web site: `http://www.silverstripe.com/`

In this book: Chapter 9

Award status: First in the Most Promising Open Source CMS category

Background

SilverStripe is a free software or an open source CMS for creating and managing rich web sites through an intuitive web interface.

SilverStripe 2.0 coding began in late 2005, with an initial public stable release in February 2007. It has received assistance through Google Summer of Code. SilverStripe is used to run blogs and online stores, larger business, and government web sites. It is designed for hundreds of hits per second. The CMS interface can also be easily repurposed for intranets, CRMs, or other web applications.

SilverStripe was made available as open source software in early 2007 after initially being developed as a commercial product. It received universal approval from the award judges for its features, and was praised as an excellent option for companies what want a powerful open source web site that is professionally created and well-supported. The judges were complimentary about SilverStripe's scalability, use of AJAX, its healthy community, and the impressive levels of input on the forums from its developers.

> *Receiving recognition in the Packt Awards means a lot to the core SilverStripe team, we are all extremely humbled. The award lets us both celebrate all the technical and design decisions we made, but also celebrate our reasoning to use an open source model.*
>
> *—Sigurd Magnusson, founder, SilverStripe*

What makes it most promising?

Despite its short lifetime, SilverStripe has many advanced features. These features include an MVC framework written in object-oriented PHP5, XHTML and accessibility compliance, multiple ways of organizing navigation through folksonomy, a flexible data object model, multiple templates per page, a separate "draft site" and "published site" through staging content, asset management, image resizing/cropping/rotating, versioning and rollback, friendly URLs with metadata, drag-and-drop sitemap reorganization, AJAX helpers, OpenID, a web-based form builder, and extensibility.

SilverStripe offers free themes, modules, widgets, and an area to showcase your work to its developer community. It is designed for UTF-8 support, including internationalization of character sets. A large translation community exists to provide interface translations. It also deploys content through RSS and full text search, and has numerous extensions to integrate with Flickr, YouTube, and other third-party systems.

CMS Made Simple

Web site: `http://www.cmsmadesimple.org/`

In this book: Chapter 9

Award status: Second in the Most Promising Open Source CMS category, second in the Best Open Source PHP CMS category

Background

CMS Made Simple provides a fast and easy way to create a web site and manage its contents. Use it to make a home page for your family or your multinational corporation. To get a site up with CMS Made Simple is just that—simple. For those with more advanced ambitions, there are plenty of add-ons to download. And there is an excellent community always at your service. Remember, no question is too stupid to be asked!

It's very easy to add content and add-ons wherever you want them to appear on the site. Design your web site in whatever way or style you want, and just load it into CMSMS to get it in the air. Easy as that!

Plone

Web site: `http://www.plone.org/`

In this book: Chapter 9

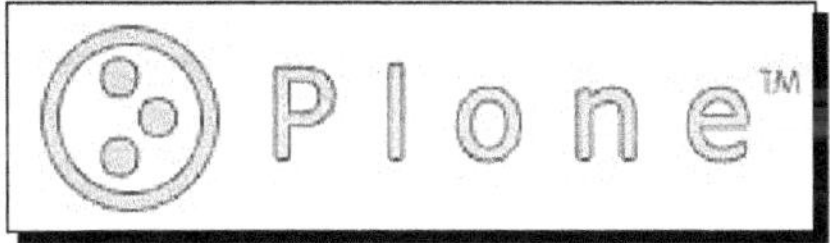

Award status: First in the Best Other Open Source CMS category

Background

The **Plone** project was started in 1999 by Alan Runyan, Alexander Limi, and Vidar Andersen. It has quickly grown into one of the most popular and powerful open source CMSs in the world. In 2004, the Plone Foundation was formed to handle development, marketing, and legal issues.

Plone is a content management framework that works hand-in-hand with and sits on top of Zope, a widely used open source web application server and development system. Plone is built from the ground up with focus on internationalization (over 35 translations are currently available) and accessibility for sight- and motor-impaired individuals.

By default, Plone stores its contents in Zope's built-in transactional object database, the ZODB. However, there are products and techniques to share information with other sources such as relational databases, LDAP, filesystem files, and so on if required.

Plone runs on Windows, Linux, BSD, Mac OS X, and many other platforms; "everything included" installers are available for Windows and Mac OS X. The RPM packages are available for Linux and the packaging systems of most Linux distributions.

dotCMS

Web site: `http://www.dotcms.org/`

In this book: Not covered

Award status: Second in the Best Other Open Source CMS category

Background

The **dotCMS** platform is an open source J2EE or a **Java Web Content Management System** (**wCMS**). Although it includes the features you would expect in a complete CMS—including true separation of content from design and ease of editing—dotCMS also includes many features you wouldn't expect such as AJAX calendar and events management, e-communications tools, personalization/CRM tools, eCommerce hooks, and more. The dotCMS platform provides a solid foundation to build world-class content-driven web sites and applications for current and future audiences.

ImpressCMS

Web site: `http://www.impresscms.org/`

In this book: Not covered

Award status: Third in the Most Promising Open Source CMS category

Background

ImpressCMS evolved from the award-winning XOOPS CMS. It makes managing web site content as easy as writing a Word document. ImpressCMS claims to be ideal for a wide range of users: from business to community users, and from large enterprises to people who want a simple and easy-to-use blogging tool.

Although the project is still in its early stages, it's highly scalable and powerful. You can use it to manage anything from a four-page brochure site to a vast online community. A good number of extensions make it easy to extend the core features.

MiaCMS

Web site: `http://www.miacms.org/`

In this book: Not covered

Award Status: Third in the Most Promising Open Source CMS category

Background

MiaCMS is Joomla!'s sibling. It too is a fork of the Mambo CMS. Al Warren, Chad Auld, Ozgur Cem Sen, and Richard Ong started the MiaCMS project because they were frustrated with the policies and procedures of the official Mambo Foundation. It's a recent fork and yet has some useful improvements over Mambo—the founding team believes it's already much better than Mambo.

Other finalists

The winners of the top three spots are not the only winners. Here are the finalists that did not make it to top, but are still superb:

CMS	URL	Category
TYPOlight	`http://www.typolight.org/`	Overall Open Source CMS Award
MemHT	`http://www.memht.com/`	Most Promising Open Source CMS
eZ Publish	`http://www.ez.no/`	Best PHP Open Source CMS
XOOPS	`http://www.xoops.org/`	Best PHP Open Source CMS
mojoPortal	`http://www.mojoportal.com/`	Best Other Open Source CMS
Umbraco	`http://www.umbraco.org/`	Best Other Open Source CMS

Behind each winner, there is a group of developers. This group consists of founders and community members who put in not only their time, but also their soul into the project. We must recognize them too.

Most valued professionals

Hundreds of developers give their time and dedication to their CMS. They become heroes of their community. Here are the Most Valued Professionals—a new recognition Packt started in 2008. Take a look at `http://www.packtpub.com/article/open-source-cms-most-valued-people-announced` for community comments for each of these heroes.

Content Management System	Most Valued Person
CMS Made Simple	Ted Kulp
DBHcms	Kai-Sven Bunk
DotNetNuke	Shaun Walker
Drupal	Earl Miles
Exponent CMS	Adam Kessler
ExpressionEngine	Michael Boyink
ImpressCMS	Marc-Andre Lanciault
Joomla!	Johan Janssens
Mambo	Lynne Pope
MemHT-Portal	Miltenovik Manojlo
MiaCMS	Chad Auld
mojoPortal	Joe Audette
PHP Fusion	Nick Jones
Plone	Martin Aspelli
Radiant	Sean Cribbs
SilverStripe	Sam Minnee
Tikiwiki	Marc Laporte
ToendaCMS	Jonathan Naumann
TYPO3	Dmitry Dulepov
Typolight	Leo Feyer
Umbraco	Doug Robar
WordPress	Matt Mullenweg
Xoops	Onokazu

Are you a developer? Do you think you can create the next killer CMS? There are many CMSs out there, yet there is strong need for innovation in usability. If you develop something that's easy to use, you might get into the Most Promising CMS category in the next Packt awards! Go for it!

Are you a user? Then evaluate the top CMSs and pick the one that suits you. Note that these awards are primarily for general-purpose CMSs. If your need is specific, march ahead with a specialized CMS. We have covered the top choices in detail in the earlier chapters.

To close, let's review what we've done.

Summary

In this chapter we learned about the Packt Open Source CMS Awards and the 2008 winners.

Specifically, we looked at:

- The need to recognize the best CMSs and reward them
- The community-driven methodology used to determine winners
- The various winners of 2008 awards

And with that, we come to the end of this book. We started with understanding our needs and covered a range of CMSs. We deployed them, customized them, and even added extensions. We covered general-purpose CMSs, blogs, forums and collaboration, e-commerce CMSs, and other specialized CMSs.

I hope this tour was useful for you in selecting a CMS for your needs. Oprah's Yoga Site surely got a lot of help. I hope your site becomes successful and you eventually contribute to an open source CMS.

Bye!

Index

Symbols

A

D

E

F

P

R

S

T

U

V

W

X

Y

Writing for Packt

We welcome all inquiries from people who are interested in authoring. Book proposals should be sent to `author@packtpub.com`. If your book idea is still at an early stage and you would like to discuss it first before writing a formal book proposal, contact us; one of our commissioning editors will get in touch with you.

We're not just looking for published authors; if you have strong technical skills but no writing experience, our experienced editors can help you develop a writing career, or simply get some additional reward for your expertise.

About Packt Publishing

Packt, pronounced 'packed', published its first book "Mastering phpMyAdmin for Effective MySQL Management" in April 2004 and subsequently continued to specialize in publishing highly focused books on specific technologies and solutions.

Our books and publications share the experiences of your fellow IT professionals in adapting and customizing today's systems, applications, and frameworks. Our solution-based books give you the knowledge and power to customize the software and technologies you're using to get the job done. Packt books are more specific and less general than the IT books you have seen in the past. Our unique business model allows us to bring you more focused information, giving you more of what you need to know, and less of what you don't.

Packt is a modern, yet unique publishing company, which focuses on producing quality, cutting-edge books for communities of developers, administrators, and newbies alike. For more information, please visit our website: `www.PacktPub.com`.

PHP 5 CMS Framework Development

ISBN: 978-1-847193-57-5 Paperback: 328 pages

Expert insight and practical guidance to creating an efficient, flexible, and robust framework for a PHP 5-based content management system

1. Learn how to design, build, and implement a complete CMS framework for your custom requirements
2. Implement a solid architecture with object orientation, MVC
3. Build an infrastructure for custom menus, modules, components, sessions, user tracking, and more
4. Written by a seasoned developer of CMS applications

Learning Drupal 6 Module Development

ISBN: 978-1-847194-44-2 Paperback: 310 pages

A practical tutorial for creating your first Drupal 6 modules with PHP

1. Specifically written for Drupal 6 development
2. Program your own Drupal modules
3. No experience of Drupal development required
4. Know Drupal 5? Learn what's new in Drupal 6
5. Integrate AJAX functionality with the jQuery library
6. Packt donates a percentage of every book sold to the Drupal foundation

Please check **www.PacktPub.com** for information on our titles

www.ingramcontent.com/pod-product-compliance
Lightning Source LLC
Chambersburg PA
CBHW062058050326
40690CB00016B/3133
* 9 7 8 1 8 4 7 1 9 6 2 2 4 *